To my wife, Holly and my daughters, Lauren and Maria - I would not have had the fire service career I have had or be writing this book without your continuous love and support over the past 36 years. You have always been the greatest joy and inspiration in my life. I love you, ladies! Thank you for all that you do for me!

First Copyright © Edition: August 2021

Validated Copyright © Edition and first printing: March 2022

MANAGING A FIRE COMPANY – John Brunacini with Tim W. Dietz
Library of Congress Copyright
ISBN # 978-0-578-33150-8
All rights reserved

Cover art by Maria Brunacini

Section and back cover art provided by Taylor's Tins @ www.taylorstins.com

Managing a Fire Company

John Brunacini

With Tim W. Dietz

This book is dedicated to Alan Brunacini (1937-2017)

America's Fire Chief

"Survive, Prevent Harm, Be Nice"

Managing a Fire Company

Validation Committee Members

John Brunacini
Captain (Ret.), Phoenix Fire Department, AZ

Tim W. Dietz
Captain (Ret.), Tualatin Valley Fire & Rescue, OR

Kyle Trumbly
Committee Sargent at Arms
Deputy Chief, Yukon Fire Department, OK

Renee Trumbly
Committee Secretary

Ralph A. Baena
Chief Fire Officer, Miami-Dade Fire Rescue, FL

Autry Cheatham
Battalion Chief, Surprise Fire Medical Department, AZ

Trish Connolly
Deputy Chief, Bend Fire & Rescue, OR

Joshua Jay Gehrke
Division Chief, Clackamas Fire, OR

Erick Gonzalez
Battalion Chief, Miami-Dade Fire Rescue, FL

Sean Kamai
Captain, Honolulu Fire Department, HI

Ocean Kaowili
Captain, Honolulu Fire Department, HI

Richard A. Kelley
Fire Chief, Oklahoma City Fire Department, OK

Steve Kraft
Platoon Chief, Mississauga Fire and Emergency Services, ON Canada

Kristan Maurer
Fire Chief, Clark County Fire District 6, WA

Jarett Metheny
Fire Chief, Ozark Fire Protection District, MO

Glen Powe
Sergeant (Ret.), Maricopa County Sheriff's Office, AZ

Trevor J. Stokes
Captain, TCESD#2 Pflugerville, TX

Chad Weaver
Deputy Fire Chief of Operations, Edmond Fire Department, OK

Lydia Woodman
Training Officer, Tualatin Valley Fire & Rescue, OR

Managing a Fire Company – Table of Contents

i - Acknowledgments

The biggest contributor and acknowledgment for *Managing a Fire Company* goes to my Father, Alan Vincent Brunacini (1937-2017). He has had the greatest influence on my life, as well as on my fire service career. I have been missing his wisdom and sense of humor every day since his passing.

My Father had also made a huge impact on the lives and careers of thousands of other Firefighters throughout his 50-year career to the point that he gained the moniker "America's Fire Chief." The more time that has gone by after my Father's passing, the more important it becomes to inform the youth coming into the fire service today about the tremendous impact and contributions he has made to all areas of our service that still affect us today (and will continue to do so far into the future). Here are just a few of his lifetime accomplishments and contributions to the fire service:

- Fire Chief of the Phoenix Fire Department from 1978 to 2006 (after serving in all ranks on the department)
- Several college degrees and fellowship programs that are highlighted with a Master's Degree in Public Administration (Arizona State University) and the Executive Management Fellowship Program at The Massachusetts Institute of Technology: MIT
- Chairman of NFPA 1500 (original standard) – Fire Service Health and Safety Standard (OSHA of the fire service). Over 65 NFPA Standards have come out of NFPA 1500.
- Chairman of NFPA 1710 (original standard) - Organization and Deployment of Fire Suppression Operations
- Chairman of the NFPA – Alan Brunacini was the only active Fire Chief appointed as the Chairman of the NFPA (two consecutive 2-year terms). During his 4-year tenure, he made several changes to the standard making processes that are still in place and are being used today.
- Author of:
    o Fire Command (1st and 2nd Editions)
    o Command Safety (with Nick Brunacini)
    o Essentials of Fire Department Customer Service
    o Anatomy and Physiology of Leadership (with Nick Brunacini)
    o Timeless Tactical Truths
- Pioneer of the labor management process known as "Relationships By Objectives"
- Public Official of the Year – Governing Magazine
- Over a dozen national fire service awards are named after Alan Brunacini.

This is a long list of major accomplishments, but my Father's greatest asset to our service was that he was a humanist. He cared about the people he interacted with and worked with more than any outcome he ever achieved. He was a lifelong learner, he had a very open mind, he actively listened to people, he acted upon what he heard, and he never took credit for anything he achieved, but gave it all to the people around him. America's Fire Chief, you will be forever missed!

Another large contributor to both my fire service career and to *Managing a Fire Company* is Gordon Graham. He and my Father were good friends. Dad introduced me to Gordon while I was studying for the Captain's test in 1992. His risk management and training philosophies that he has exposed me to since our first meeting have resonated throughout my career and this book.

Gordon, like Dad, is a true rockstar in his field and he also has a major list of lifelong accomplishments that includes a 33-year career on the California Highway Patrol. His education as a Risk Manager and experience as a practicing attorney, coupled with his extensive background in law enforcement have made him a leading professional speaker in both private and public sector organizations with multiple areas of expertise. In 2002, along with Bruce Praet, Gordon became a founder of Lexipol, a company originally designed to standardize policy, procedure, and training for local Law Enforcement agencies (on a national level) that has now branched into several other public safety fields, including the fire service. All of Gordon's efforts have greatly improved the safety and welfare of public safety personnel and his influence on our service will continue to help keep responders safe and effective well into the future.

A huge influence and contributing author of this book is Tim W. Dietz. I first met Tim at a Blue Card Command conference at the University of Notre Dame in 2013 when he was one of the keynote presenters speaking on Firefighter mental wellness and the treatment of Post-Traumatic Stress for people in public safety and the military. I was blown away by his presentation (along with all the other attendees, which made Tim the highest rated speaker at the conference). The whole time Tim was presenting, I was wishing I had heard his message 30 years prior when I was in the training academy first starting out my Firefighting career. If I had, it would have given me a whole different perspective on what Firefighters and our customers are going through during stressful incidents and the actions that need to be taken that reduce lifelong stress for everyone associated with the call.

Tim serves the fire service today from the unique perspective, as he has had a 30+ year career as a Firefighter Paramedic and Company Officer, has suffered through his own personal tragedies, and has educated himself to a Master's Degree level in Counseling, specializing in Post-Traumatic Stress counseling and therapies for Firefighters, Law Enforcement, and Military personnel. Tim's message becomes even more important as a career in the firefighting field is getting even more stressful. In two sections of this book, Tim provides keen insight to Company Officers on how to manage and assist not only their crew members dealing with stressful situations, but also on how to effectively interact with all the other people associated with a stressful incident scene. All of this information will help make these situations the best possible experience for everyone involved (for both the fire department members and the customers). There will be more information on Tim's background later and I hope his material helps all members get through their careers with healthy, well-functioning minds.

A big thank you needs to go to my good friends Kyle and Renee Trumbly. They have been excellent reviewers throughout the process of writing this book and have played vital roles in the management of the Validation Committee process. Additionally, a huge thanks also goes to all the validation committee members (previously listed). It was an absolute honor and pleasure to work with this exceptional group of professionals and I cannot thank them enough for all their valuable feedback and contributions to this book.

The other major contributors to my career and to the making of *Managing a Fire Company* are way too numerous to mention, but I must give kudos to the Phoenix Fire Department for hosting my 26-year career and the individual members of all the crews that I was permanently assigned to during my career, especially to the crew members of L-201 (a group of truly outstanding professionals).

All of these people have had an influence on *Managing a Fire Company,* my career, and my personal life. This book would not have happened without all of your help and support. Thank you all!

ii - Glossary of Acronyms

AHJ – Authority Having Jurisdiction

ALS - Advanced Life Support Unit staffed with Paramedics

API - Action Plan for Improvement

ARFF - Aircraft Rescue and Firefighting

AWR – Away Without Relief

BLS - Basic Life Support Unit staffed with Emergency Medical Technicians

CBA – Collective Bargaining Agreement

CDC – Center for Disease Control and Prevention

CE - Continuing Education

CISM - Critical Incident Stress Management

CPAT - Candidate Physical Ability Test

CQI - Continuing Quality Improvement

DNR – Do Not Resuscitate

DOB – Date of Birth

DOJ - Department of Justice

EAP - Employee Assistance Program

EEOC - Equal Employment Opportunity Commission

EMS - Emergency Medical Services

EMT - Emergency Medical Technician

ER - Emergency Room

ESS - Electronic Staffing Systems

FMS – Functional Movement Screenings

HIPPA - Health Insurance Portability and Accountability Act

HR - Human Resources

HRM – Human Resource Management

IAFF - International Association of Firefighters

IAP – Incident Action Plan

IDLH - Immediately Dangerous to Life and Health

ISO - Insurance Services Office

JPR - Job Performance Requirement

LODD - Line of Duty Death

LSD – Lost, stolen, or damaged

LT – Ladder Tender

MCS – Minimum Company Standards

MDC - Mobile Digital Computer

MDT - Mobile Data Terminal

MOU - Memorandum of Understanding

NIMS – National Incident Management System

NIOSH - National Institute for Occupational Safety and Health

NFPA - National Fire Protection Association

NREM – Non-rapid Eye Movement

OR - Operating Room

OSHA - Occupational Safety and Health Administration

PII – Pertinent Incident Information

PIO - Public Information Officer

PPE - Personal Protective Equipment

PPI – Pertinent Patient Information

PT - Physical Training

PTSD – Post Traumatic Street Disorder

PTSI - Post Traumatic Stress Injury

REM – Rapid Eye Movement

RMS - Record Management System

RP - Responsible Party

RSs - Revised Statutes

SCBA - Self Contained Breathing Apparatus

SIDS - Sudden Infant Death Syndrome

SME – Subject Matter Expect

SOGs - Standard Operating Guidelines

SOPs - Standard Operating Procedures

TIC - Thermal Imaging Camera

TRT - Technical Rescue Team

USAR – Urban Search and Rescue

SECTION 1
Up Front – General

Chapter 1

Company Officer Organizational Job Description

Let me start this book with a straightforward statement: **All activity on the company level needs to be directed toward the service that is delivered to the public.** This has to be the starting and ending point with everything a fire department does as an organization. Fire and EMS protection, along with all the other services we provide to our communities is not cheap. It costs the citizens of your community a lot of money to employ, house, and equip the fire department with the things needed to deliver this service.

Company Officers are the "working bosses" that directly manage the actual service that gets delivered to the customers. A fire department's agreement with the public is carried out on the company level. When a customer calls 911, they do not expect a dysfunctional crew to show up and make their problem worse. Customers expect their fire department to show up quickly and solve their problems while being nice. They expect to get what they paid for when they are having one of the worst days of their life. The **Company Officer** is the person most directly responsible for making this happen on every call a fire department responds to. Every call for service or interaction with a customer is an opportunity to make a positive impression and impact on the public we serve.

Crew members (the Company Officer's subordinates) also expect their bosses to prevent them from getting killed, getting hurt, getting sick, going nuts, getting fired, and looking/feeling stupid, dumb, or embarrassed.

A Company Officer's job description should be centered around managing their crew members delivering service to the public as safely as possible, as competently as possible, and as nicely as possible. Make that the focus. It is not about being in charge. It is all about your crew members and the service you deliver to the public.

This book is focused on managing the delivery of excellent customer and emergency services on the company level. Excellent customer service is the result of a well-trained and disciplined crew. Manage excellence, not problems.

Chapter 2

Company Officer Expectations

Most fire departments are connected to an overseeing, governing body. Our overseers collect taxes, decide on our budgets, and have a lot of rules (mostly good ones) that need to be followed to keep the overall order of things. I believe most of the agencies providing funding and oversight expect their fire department to show up quickly when called and competently solve the customers' problems while being nice. While delivering service, they also expect everyone to follow the rules of the overall organization and demonstrate its core values and mission. This is pretty simple, especially if your boss is right down the hallway reinforcing these concepts to the work force on a daily basis.

Company Officers do not really operate in this type of management system on a day-to-day basis. From a supervision level, a Company Officer could go several shifts without seeing their direct supervisor. Company Officers are basically on their own. This creates a very unique and dynamic workplace to manage and supervise (or be a part of). Think about it: there are not too many places that give their employees a "house" with bedrooms and vehicles that can violate traffic laws that are filled with tools that allow us to break into any structure in our community. So how does your organization expect you to manage all of this authority and responsibility?

Let's be honest: there could be page after page of material written down by your organization that outlines what they expect of their Company Officers- all good stuff, but all of it is inconsequential when it is put together with the above environment. To me, it all comes down to the individual personality traits and the overall **INTEGRITY** of the person who is filling the role of Company Officer.

For 26 years, I was part of a great organization that provided great training and support to all its members and I still witnessed both good and bad Company Officers (mostly good). On the other side of that, I have seen other departments that had terrible management and human relation issues and the ratio of good to bad company officers was the same (mostly good). It all comes down to the individuals running that specific company and how much they engaged with their crew members about doing the right set of things.

Background – I joined the Phoenix Fire Department in 1980. I was promoted to Engineer in 1987. I was promoted to Captain in 1994. I retired in 2006. As a Company Officer, I was assigned to Ladder 201 B-Shift from 1995 into 2004.

After being in the field for a few years as a Company Officer, people started asking me for help in preparing for an upcoming Captain promotional test (Phoenix does not use the Lieutenant rank). When someone would ask me for help in this process, I would try to cut through all of the nonsense and get right down to the capabilities of the individual who was asking for help.

The people asking for help had to have the personal qualities (or the capacity to develop them) that met the following expectations before I would be willing to help them through the promotional process. I was not going to waste any of my personal time helping a person who just wanted to be the cool one sitting in the right front seat. Filling the role of Company Officer is a serious job for serious people. It is not for the people who are incompetent or for those who are just seeking power, status/rank, or a bigger paycheck.

The Company Officer can easily be considered one of the most important positions in the fire service due to their direct ability to set the tone for both internal performance and external customer service delivery and they must emulate and fulfill the following expectations.

Expectations of a Company Officer:

1. Someone who respects and values their co-workers and the public they serve
2. Someone who creates a happy, harassment free working environment
3. Someone who will keep their entire crew's focus on delivering excellent customer service throughout the shift
4. Someone that the organization put into a position to understand, follow, and enforce all the department's SOPs, policies, rules, and regulations
5. Someone who acts as the overall safety manager of their crew that will not hesitate to stop unsafe or dumb acts
6. The overall training officer of their crew
7. A supervisor that addresses personnel and service delivery issues as soon as they occur, keeping them on the smallest scale possible
8. Someone who will manage being nice

The best Company Officers that I worked for and with throughout my career did all of the above. All of them usually did it with short and sweet sentences like "knock it off," "we don't do that here," and "get on the truck, it's time to drill." It was not a popularity contest with them. It was about competently doing a job that could kill you and going home to your family at the end of every shift. You always knew where you stood with these people. A serious job for a serious person. All of them were serious about doing what was expected of them, as well as doing the right thing.

The rest of this book will try to assist a Company Officer in performing/executing the above Company Officer expectations, also considered a Company Officer's job description.

Chapter 3

Organizational versus Personal Authority

A major subject discussed when writing and reviewing this chapter was: the differences between leading, managing, and supervising and where a Company Officer's role in managing a fire company fit into all of these different terms and definitions. Here are some definitions for the three separate terms:

Leadership – *the capacity to lead*. Not much help there. How about **Leader** - *a person who leads.* Another dead end. How about just **Lead** *–to direct the operations, activity, or performance of; to guide on a way especially by going in advance; and/or to bring to some conclusion or condition.* We get more information on the term "lead," but most of it sounds like higher end, chief stuff.

Manage - *to handle or direct with a degree of skill; to work upon or try to alter for a purpose; to succeed in accomplishing; to direct the professional career of; and/or to achieve one's purpose.* How about **Manager** *– a person who directs a team.* Here we have much more relevant terms that define a Company Officer's role than what we get with "lead" or "leader."

Supervise - *to be directly in charge of an activity*. Sounds like a lot of responsibility and a lot like the Company Officer's role.

I think the best term that describes the Company Officer's role is "manager." That is why this book is titled *Managing a Fire Company*, not *Leading a Fire Company.* Most organizations need a lot more administrators, managers, and supervisors than they need true leaders. Leadership is incredibly important and there are times when Company Officers will need to step up and "lead" their crew in certain situations. However, because one of the main expectations of a Company Officer is to follow and enforce standard operating procedures, it puts a Company Officer in much more of a management/supervisory position than in a leadership position. This does not mean that there are not true leaders and role models sprinkled in at all the ranks and positions of an organization, **but what a Company Officer needs to be is: a manager all the time and a direct supervisor whenever necessary.**

Authority

As a Company Officer, your organization has given you the **Authority** to carry out certain job actions in accordance with your department's policies and procedures without the need to consult others. This authority gives a Company Officer a certain amount of **Power**. What is the difference between authority and power? Of the two terms, authority must be defined first in order to define power:

1. Authority - *the right to do work*
2. Power - *the exercise of authority*

Understanding the difference between authority and power is very important and can greatly assist a Company Officer's personal interactions when dealing with their co-workers, management, the public, and representatives from other agencies.

The two types of **Authority** a Company Officer can use to manage are:

1. Organizational authority – *the ability of a person to influence the behavior of others using the authority conferred upon him/her by the organization pursuant to the individual's position or rank in the organization*
2. Personal authority - *the ability of a person to influence the behavior of others by means other than using the authority given to them by the organization*

Organizational authority is vital in establishing the legitimacy of the Company Officer's role because it is expressly sanctioned by the organization. The organizational authority given to a company officer allows them to:

- Manage and supervise the personnel of their company
- Bend the traffic laws (legally) when making 911 responses
- Call for and direct other resources
- Render aid with legal immunity (minus gross neglect)
- Take control of public property and right of ways
- Enter into, restrict access to, and take control of private property

There is a great deal of organizational authority given to a Company Officer by their department that "gets them in the door" to deliver our core services (our right to do work). The rig, the lights, the sirens, and the official uniforms we wear all represent the organizational authority given to us by our fire departments and the public we serve. This organizational authority also gives us a certain amount of **Power** to act in order to control things (the exercise of authority). We use our **Power** to shut down streets, tell somebody to leave their property while we control a problem, and we can have people arrested who interfere with our authority to deliver service.

Our organizational authority basically stops there. Everything we do past "getting in the door" should all be based on our **Personal Authority**. The best summation of what personal authority is:

The standing you have with others based on your competencies, behaviors, values, treatment of others, and your personal integrity.

Personal authority is the most important thing a Company Officer can possess when managing a fire company.

Successful Company Officers must manage their crew with personal authority first and organizational authority second. When you manage your authority in this manner, your right to lead is instilled by those around you. This puts the officer in a position of **SERVING** those they lead (and their citizens) which gives them a huge amount of credibility. My father had a saying that re-enforced this: "the best bosses are validated by their subordinates, not by their superiors." The higher up you go in the chain of command, the more important this statement is.

Let's look at each of the separate, individual, descriptive words contained in the definition of **Personal Authority:**

1. Competencies
2. Behavior
3. Values
4. Treatment of Others
5. Integrity

1. Competencies - is a plural word that indicates many. A Company Officer must be competent in many different areas/fields. They cannot be really good on the fireground and be a tyrant at the fire station. It takes a whole package of competencies to run a fire company effectively. Here are the minimum professional competencies that should be required to be a Company Officer:

- Certified as: Firefighter 1 & 2, Hazmat Ops, an EMT or PM
- Time and competency in the Firefighter rank
- Enough experience and knowledge in EMS delivery so the Officer can competently direct and document patient care
- Time and competency in the Engineer rank (or at least hold the qualifications of an Engineer) so the Officer can competently direct and evaluate their performance
- Comprehensive knowledge of the department's operational and safety SOPs
- Certified Blue Card hazard zone IC
- Any other certifications or certificate of completion required by the AHJ
- Reading, understanding, and following the principles and guidelines in this book

Background – To test for Company Officer on the Phoenix Fire Department, you had to have all your certifications maintained, a minimum of 7 years on the job, and hold the rank of Engineer at the time of the test (or possess the same professional qualifications/certifications as an Engineer). A member could take the Engineer promotional test after having 3 years on the job.

Interpersonal competencies a Company Officer should/must possess:

- Emotional intelligence
- Self-confident and mature (be the designated adult)
- Good communication skills (listener)
- The ability to put yourself in other people's shoes (empathy)
- Performance and outcome driven versus emotionally driven
- The ability to coach and motivate (get the best out of their subordinates)
- The ability to address problems and conflict, keeping them on the smallest scale possible

People who are placed in managerial and supervisory roles who are not competent, either professionally or interpersonally, have the most potential to abuse the **Power** of their organizational authority.

Emotional Intelligence

Because it will be referred to throughout this book, I want to take more time to describe what emotional intelligence is and how to display these behaviors in the workplace. Emotional intelligence is the ability to manage your own emotions and to understand the emotions of the other people around you (empathy). Being emotional intelligent is a primary trait that every Company Officer needs to possess and it consists of:

- Self-awareness
- Self-management
- Social awareness
- Relationship management

When leading by example (discussed later in this book), Company Officers will exhibit emotional intelligence by:

- Being able to accept criticism and responsibility
- Being able to move on after making a mistake
- Being able to say no whenever it is necessary
- Being able to share your thoughts and feelings with others (effective communicator)
- Being able to solve problems and issues on the smallest scale possible while being fair in your treatment with all the people involved in the issue

2. Behavior – *the way in which one acts or conducts oneself, especially toward others.* Acceptable behaviors in the workplace are well defined in our society. I believe these well-defined workplace behaviors are black and white with very little grey in between. Black and white SOPs are the easiest to recognize and enforce. Company Officers must have the integrity of immediately STOPPING violations of black and white SOPs, especially those that concern our safety and the way we treat each other and/or our customers.

A further chapter will focus more on creating and maintaining a harassment free workplace. There, I will discuss in detail the acceptable and non-acceptable behaviors a Company Officer will have to manage.

3. Values – This is a slippery slope. Only a true saint can write anything credible on the subject of values or ethics. I am not a saint, so I will try to cover the very basics on values as they relate to managing a fire company.

The short definition of values is - *the fundamental beliefs of a person, group, or organization.* There are many different types of values that fall under this basic description, but the 3 that apply most to managing a fire company are:

1. The department's values

2. The Company Officer's values
3. The individual crew members' values

The biggest factor that concerns values while managing a fire company is that **all levels of the organization must ALIGN with the department's values in order for a fire company to be effective**.

All Company Officers must have their overall values aligned with their department's values. It is the responsibility of the Company Officer to use their personal authority, as well as their organizational authority, to make sure that their crew members' values are always aligned with the organization's. It would be very difficult for the Officer to align their crew members' values with the organizations' if they did not exhibit these same set of values (leading by example is discussed later in this book).

4. Treatment of Others – Expectations of a Company Officer #1: Someone who respects and values their co-workers and the public they serve.

The way we treat each other starts out with respect. When a Company Officer projects respect towards their crew members and the public, the effect of this is that they usually reflect that same respect back to the Officer. Funny how that works - that leading by example thing again. Here are some ways a Company Officer can project respectful behaviors to their supervisors, crew members, and to the public they serve:

- Use good manners (courtesy and politeness)
- Active listener
- Acknowledge people's frustrations
- Try to put yourself in the other person's shoes (have some empathy)
  - My father summed all this up in two words: "BE NICE"

One of the biggest performance targets for a Company Officer to hit when managing the treatment of others (your crew and the public) is to be consistent in your treatment of others and your personal behaviors all of the time - on a shift to shift basis.

Background – My favorite Company Officers during my career were not only the competent ones (of course), but they were also the most CONSISTENT ones. The same Officer showed up for work every shift. My least favorite Officers were the Dr. Jeckle and Mr. Hyde types. I (and most others) gravitated away from these Officers. I did not like working for a person when I did not know what personality they were going to walk through the door with every shift – Dr. Jeckle or Mr. Hyde? What is even worse with these types of people is when they show up as Dr. Jeckle (all nice) and then in the middle of the shift, they turn into Mr. Hyde. I would rather them just show up as Mr. Hyde, so I would know what to expect the whole shift.

I always took notes from these people on how NOT to behave in the future with my crew. One of my biggest, personal performance targets as a Company Officer was being as consistent with my crew as possible. I wanted to be the same, consistent Officer every shift.

5. Integrity - *the quality of being honest and having strong moral principles; moral uprightness.* The most admired quality in the fire service is integrity. Integrity occurs when you align your words with your actions. When you "walk the talk." INTEGRITY! Protect and value it! It is the most important personal quality a Company Officer can possess.

Integrity is not just about telling the truth. Rather, it is about acting out your truth. Members want to follow and work with Officers who show and maintain a high degree of integrity. Company Officers who demonstrate an ability to be honest and open with no hidden agendas have the best interactions with their crew members and the public they serve. Sincerity cannot be faked with the people you directly supervise.

Having an open mind and freely admitting your mistakes is also a key component of integrity. If you make a mistake, be ready to quickly identify or acknowledge the mistake. Once diagnosed, make a mental note and try not to let the same mistake happen again. This is called being a lifelong learner. Most adult learning occurs from making mistakes or failing at something. Live and learn from your mistakes. Fix them, move on, and then do not dwell on them.

Managing Personal Authority (Yours and Your Crew's)

As a Company Officer, the organization has already given you all the organizational authority necessary to manage a fire company. But as stated earlier in this chapter, even more important than the organizational authority given to a Company Officer is their personal authority. The Company Officer should have the most overall personal authority on the crew because it is much more powerful than their organizational authority.

The person on the crew with the most personal authority has the most influence on the other crew members.

All members of a crew have their own personal authority in one form or another. It can be used in good ways or in not so good ways. The Company Officer wants to avoid having one (or more) of the members of their crew having more personal authority than themselves. This is usually a bad thing.

Background – I will tell you 2 personal experiences I had in dealing with crew members who were using their personal authority in both good and bad ways. Let's start with the bad example:

Back in my day, right after you were promoted to the Captain rank on the Phoenix Fire Department, you were used as a "Rover" on your assigned shift (A, B, or C). Rovers filled in for other Captains who were on vacation, sick leave, industrial leave, etc. Roving could go on several years until you built up enough seniority in your rank to bid into a permanent spot. Sometimes while roving (but not very often,) I would feel like a babysitter waiting for the crew's parent to get back home.

On one particular babysitting job, there was an Engineer on the crew, Mr. Grumpy Pants, that used his personal authority in a very negative way. He did not take good care of his truck, he sniveled about the organization all day, he complained about going on calls, and he was negative to co-workers and the customers.

I did not take this very well. After personally being frustrated by some of the same issues early on in my career (going on stupid calls), I concluded that it is much easier being nice than being rude or mean to people on calls. Being nice took less time, you felt better after the call, and nothing bad about the call followed you back to the station. When crew members were mean to the customer on calls, I stopped it immediately.

On the very first call of this particular shift, Mr. Grumpy Pants decides to be mean to Mrs. Smith. Not good. To me, he was not just being mean to Mrs. Smith, but he was also telling me he was the informal leader of the crew, I was just here for the shift (babysitting), and this was how it was going to roll out for the next 24 hours. Well, Mr. Grumpy Pants should have taken the Captain test so he could run his own third-rate crew. But he did not, so the one big thing Mr. Grumpy Pants was lacking in all of this was any organizational authority. I had that, so I used my organizational authority and I told Mr. Grumpy Pants to shut up and to go sit on the truck (in no uncertain terms).

As soon as I did this, the other two crew members on the company looked at me and smiled. I think I had just used my organizational authority to gain a lot of personal authority with the other crew members.

After taking care of the call and apologizing to Mrs. Smith for Mr. Grumpy Pants' behavior, I followed up with Mr. Grumpy Pants back at the station. I told him I would not tolerate the same behavior on another call and if he could not be nice to our customers the rest of the shift, I was going to write him up and send him home. He responded that he would be nice the rest of the shift. He was nice to the customers the rest of the shift. I then told him to clean the rig while the rest of us cleaned the station. He cleaned the rig while we cleaned the station. I told him the rig looked nice while we were headed to the store to buy groceries. He politely said thank you.

Every time that I worked with Mr. Grumpy Pants after this shift, he towed the line, did his job, and was nice to the customers.

Now, here is the good example:

I got the permanent Company Officer spot on L-201 when I had almost two years of seniority as a Captain. Station 201 also housed a 4-person ALS Engine Company and a 2-person BLS Ambulance. All ladders on Phoenix have at least 4 people- 1 Captain, 2 Engineers, and 1 Firefighter. After being on L-201 for about 5 years, we got a 5th person assigned to our rig, which was another Firefighter spot. The last 5 years I worked at Station 201, there were 11 people on duty at the station during a 24-hour shift.

One of the Engineers on L-201 had 10 years of seniority on me and the other had 8 years of seniority on me. Both had Type A personalities and both were two of the most highly capable and competent people I have ever worked with (along with my Senior Firefighter). All of them used their immense personal authority in positive ways (mostly).

The focus of the positive use of personal authority of this story will be on the Engineer with 8 years of job seniority on me, Mr. Joker. Mr. Joker could fix anything that ran on gasoline, he could force entry into any building, he could cut up a car using hydraulic tools in his sleep, and he could drive large apparatus better than a New York City bus driver. Mr. Joker (as well as me) did not like difficult or lazy people showing up to work at our station. I would always deal with these people in a positive, corrective manner, but I was constrained by politeness, protocols, and our department SOPs. Mr. Joker was not. He could say things to other co-workers that I could not say, like "why don't you get off your ass and help everybody else clean the trucks?" I just could not phrase things like this when trying to motivate other people. Mr. Joker could.

He did not do it very often, but whenever he did help "manage" the other crew members using his personal authority, it was always appropriate and it always helped the cause. Mr. Joker cared about the performance and harmony of our crew just as much I did, so he used his personal authority to help make it happen. Thanks Mr. Joker. I would like to also throw out kudos to my entire crew on L-201, as they all did this for me in one form or another and it was an honor working with a group of people who told their fellow co-workers "this is the way we roll on L-201."

A Company Officer needs to be a manager all of the time, and a direct supervisor whenever necessary. Being an effective manager and supervisor means always properly balancing your organizational authority with your personal authority, while always remembering that the most powerful form of authority is your personal authority. People who are in a position of authority who think and act in this way will seldom abuse the power related to their position of authority.

Chapter 4

Leading by Example

"Setting an example is not the main means of influencing others, it is the only means."
- Albert Einstein

A person is the direct product of their environment. This starts out early in life with children trying to imitate and emulate the behaviors of their parents and other family members. As children grow older and start to interact with more people, they also try to replicate the examples shown to them by their other teachers, tutors, coaches, and the people in their own age group (their peers). This behavior adjustment mentality does not stop in adulthood. People will always continue to try to model or imitate the behavior of their supervisors and/or co-workers.

The fire service only hires adults who make a personal decision to become Firefighters. Most of these people want to serve their community and run into burning buildings. They want to be on the job, they worked hard to get there, and for the most part, they want to do the best job possible. They also want to be successful and they want the respect of their bosses and co-workers. The most successful path in fulfilling these desires and aspirations is to closely examine the behaviors and attitudes of the people in charge and then try to emulate these same behaviors in order to succeed. Some overly enthusiastic employees may even take the behaviors and examples of those in charge and intensify them in order to be noticed, to please their superiors, and/or to impress their co-workers.

This brings me to an old saying: "if you follow bad kids home, you will most likely find bad parents." I am going to put a twist on this old adage with: "if you follow a bad fire company home, you will most likely find a bad Company Officer."

As talked about throughout the first section of this book, the first set of actions in managing or supervising anything is to lead by example. No matter what your behavior and attitude are as a Company Officer, most people you supervise will try to imitate, emulate, and in some cases, intensify the behaviors and examples you set - good or bad.

Let me simplify this: **the way your crew behaves will be a DIRECT REFLECTION of the examples you set and the way you behave**. If you are mean, they will be mean. If you are nice, they will be nice. It is really very simple. If you are already a Company Officer reading this and you are not happy with your crew's behaviors, you should probably look no further than in a mirror to see where the real issue lies. Your crew members in most cases are behaving/acting just like you.

8 Common Sense Ways to Lead by Example

Here are 8 personal behaviors that will help you project a good "leading by example" image to display to your superiors, crew members, and the customers you serve. All of the following 8 behaviors are critical in setting an example.

1. Always treat people with dignity and respect.
2. Take responsibility for your company's actions and always be a shield for your crew.
3. Watch what you say!
4. Listen to your crew members with an open mind.
5. Share the workload with your crew (get your hands dirty).
6. Respect the chain of command.
7. Delegate often and then get out of the way.
8. Take care of yourself.

1. Always treat people with dignity and respect. Always give your crew members an "out" and let them save face (dignity) whenever things are going wrong. Never sacrifice a personal/work relationship with a subordinate for an outcome (respect). My Father had a saying that reinforces this: "The most toxic smoke in our service is the smoke that is produced from a burning bridge." Again, Company Officers must base all interactions with their crew members around being performance driven versus being emotionally driven. Always try to manage around maintaining positive relationships with the focus on positive behaviors and outcomes.

You will hear throughout this book that the way your crew members see you treat and manage subordinates, your bosses, and the public you serve will be the same, acceptable way for them to treat others, as well.

2. Take responsibility for your company's actions and always be a shield for your crew. Poor performance is almost always a direct result of poor management and supervision. A good supervisor does not throw their crew under the bus when something goes wrong. When something does not go well, a good supervisor will OWN it as their responsibility. Conducting yourself in this manner has one of the greatest impacts on an Officer's personal integrity.

Background: My Dad became a Battalion Chief in 1967. His department at the time was very rigid with a heavy focus on discipline. My father's approach to running a battalion of five stations was quite different, as he focused on safety and service delivery. He was not big on the current rules, but he was big on results while not hurting anyone. The companies that he was in charge of soon recognized this and quickly gravitated to his style of management.

About a year after he became a Battalion Chief, he was at a battalion meeting with all of his Officers and they stated passionately to him: "Bruno, we work hard for you because you always have our backs." He responded to this statement by saying: "Thank you, and I know in this organization, you just gave me the greatest compliment I could ever receive, but what I really want to have is your "FRONTS." Having your backs, which I will always have, means coming in after the event is over and defending your performance. I want to be in front of you guys, making sure none of this bad stuff happens in the first place."

When you own other people's performance and manage in this fashion, your members will always be high performers and they will always have their boss' front and back when their boss has theirs.

3. Watch what you say! I was recently watching a movie about Sitting Bull, the Native American war chief. He told someone in the movie that he finally became a man when he started to think about what he was going to say before he said it. I thought this statement was a good barometer for anyone who wondered what it meant to act like an adult. Always try to put your brain between your ears/eyes and your mouth. Here are a few pointers to help make this happen:

- Always think about what you are going to say and how you'll say it before you say it. To help accomplish this, always act like you are being videotaped whenever you are awake.
- Always tell the truth. Inaccurate representation effects everyone, especially a supervisor's integrity. Telling the truth is ALWAYS the best policy, even if things did not go well.
- Acknowledge your own mistakes and failures (not the other person's) when trying to make a point. This makes it okay for your crew to do the same thing (owning it) and it enforces that making mistakes is part of the process of becoming excellent.
- Avoid using the word "why" when dealing with issues. The word "why" automatically makes people raise their guard and become defensive. Use the words "how" and "what." Example: A Firefighter arrives to work almost 15 minutes late with no notification to the station advising that they will be late. When addressing the issue, avoid using the phrase "Why are you late?" Instead, phrase it like "What were the circumstances that led to you arrive 15 minutes late to work?"
- Make the focus of what you are saying on improving the situation instead of trying to place blame on what went wrong.
- Never complain about other crew members, the organization, or the current circumstances you are trying to manage/supervise. Keep the focus on behaviors, performance, and outcomes.

4. Listen to your crew members with an open mind. The best managers have the most sensitive and open ears. As supervisors, sometimes we get caught up with running an operation, giving orders or direction, and/or providing feedback in such a manner that we do not slow down to listen to our crew members. If you are hiring the right people, you should have a whole team of experts on your company to turn to for advice on how an evolution or process could be done better/safer. Good managers know that they do not know everything. Listening and getting feedback from your crew as much as possible will make them all know they are important, contributing members to both the successes and the failures of the team.

5. Share the workload with your crew (get your hands dirty). A Company Officer is a working boss, not a sitting boss. We had a saying on Ladder 201: "If one person is working, the whole crew better be working." A Company Officer who is sitting in a recliner watching the news at 8:30 in the morning while their crew members are all outside checking equipment and cleaning the trucks does not inspire much confidence.

On the other side of this, a Company Officer has their own workload and duties that they must perform and there will be times while crew members are performing their responsibilities that the Company Officer will be performing their own as well (but not sitting in a recliner).

Background: L-201 consisted of 2 pieces of apparatus: the big ladder (a glorious 87-foot American LaFrance mid-mount platform bucket ladder) and a 5-ton chassis Ladder Tender (LT). The LT was a five-person cab that had enough compartment and storage space to hold all the equipment the big ladder had on it, minus the aerial and the longer ground ladders. When a 911 call would come in, the Company Officer would pick what piece of apparatus the crew would respond in. We used the LT to respond to just about everything except commercial building fires. It was a great deployment concept that saved the citizens a lot of money.

The bad thing about having an LT was that the crew had 2 trucks and sets of equipment to clean and maintain instead of just 1. On apparatus day (1 day a week when everything was taken out, cleaned, and inventoried), each person on the rig had specific equipment and maintenance areas of the truck that they were responsible for. We all helped wash and wax the outside of the trucks (the painted stuff). After the outsides were cleaned, my job was to clean the interior cabs and windows of both trucks while the other crew members inventoried and maintained the tools, equipment, and drivetrains of both trucks.

I would always finish cleaning my designated areas before anyone else did, but my job on apparatus day was not finished there. Being the Officer of the truck, I also had the administrative duty of completing all of the inventory and LSD reports for both rigs. My job was to verify and document that L-201 and LT-201 had everything we needed to perform our jobs effectively. This activity usually took me over an hour to complete and it was a total pain (but more than worth it).

When I was not outside helping my crew with their part, they knew that I was inside performing my part. The crew would much rather clean all of the chain saws than to do the paperwork, so they were very happy with the division of labor and there were no secrets about where I was or what I was doing. The whole crew was working towards the same goal at the same time: Clean, well maintained, shiny red fire trucks!

6. Respect the chain of command. One of the fastest ways to produce an underperforming fire company is for the Officer of the company to continually complain about the department and/or the supervisors they work for. If the senior leader of the fire company does not respect the chain of command, why would anyone else on the company? It also gives permission to the rest of the company to complain, as well.

As stated earlier, a Company Officer can go several shifts without seeing their direct supervisor and Company Officers are on their own when managing a fire station. This creates a situation where the Company Officer is in charge of the environment they work in. Even if you work under terrible management, a Company Officer has the ability to shield the fire station from the evil upper levels of the organization in order to maintain a happy and positive workplace. This only occurs without complaining about what happens above them and focusing on being prepared for the next call and delivering excellent customer service. Always complain up and control down.

7. Delegate often and then get out of the way. When actually delivering service, the Company Officer should not say too much to their crew members while they are performing their job duties (unless they are going to hurt themselves or someone else). Most competent people do not like getting micromanaged, especially in the heat of things. The drill grounds and after incident reviews are where an Officer should comment on performance issues and implement any APIs. I will talk much more about delegation in the later sections of this book.

8. Take care of yourself. Wellness and fitness are both crucial to managing anything. Key words associated with wellness and fitness that are essential for a fire company to possess are: resilience, strength, endurance, toughness, etc. It is tough to act the part if you do not look the part. Overweight and/or out of shape supervisors do not inspire much confidence in their subordinates (or the public) they serve. There will be much more on this topic in the readiness section of this book.

Chapter 5

Standard Operating Procedures (SOPs)

After the Company Officer's job description and expectations have been outlined, we start with item #4 on the Company Officer's job description list: following and enforcing the SOPs. SOPs are one of the most important pieces of equipment that a fire department can possess (if they are up to date, best practice policies and procedures). I am going to shorten things up throughout the rest of this book by referring to all policies, procedures, guidelines, SOGs, city and state RSs, memos, bulletins, rules, regulations, etc., as SOPs.

SOPs are the foundation of our job descriptions, training measures, and standards for operations and they are vital to providing employee and organizational accountability. SOPs create a uniform and detailed set of instructions on how to achieve a specified goal during organizational operations. In short, SOPs define the how to's of our job. I love SOPs because I have seen the positive effect they have on organizations and training systems. It is simply amazing to see what happens when you give people a good play book to use.

My father came into an organization where the only things written down were the disciplinary rules. It was stuff like this: if you do this, you are in trouble and this is what is going to happen to you. There was nothing written down that helped any supervisor do their job consistently or effectively.

An unfortunate organizational side effect of not having any written SOPs is that the rules can change for the workers based on the mood of the person currently in charge. This leads to a frustrated work force that creates a "bunker type" mentality and the corresponding sets of behaviors that go with it. It sucks having a boss who changes the rules on every deployment. Some common clichés that you hear from departments who do not have good SOPs in place are: "put it out before the chief gets here" or "you're only welcome in the fire station on official business." This is not good.

My father's solution to fixing all of this was implementing the "Management Model." His philosophy was that anything you wanted to effectively manage should have a good set of SOPs that go with it. This is especially true concerning critical activities that could severely injure or kill the work force and/or the public they serve.

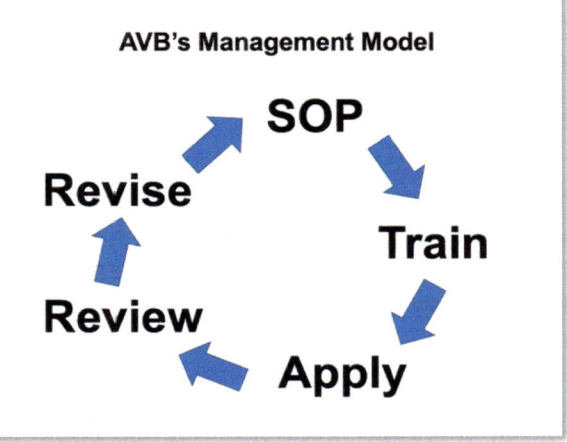

AVB's Management Model

SOP → Train → Apply → Review → Revise →

The Management Model starts out with developing (or adopting) an SOP. The people who develop/adopt the original SOP should be the group that are the most connected to the actual work being described in the procedure. I have noticed throughout my career that a lot of original SOPs are not written by the people most affected by them. While these might look and sound good on paper, they often do not work very well when applied. Additionally, most organizations that create or adopt an SOP do not do much with maintaining and updating the SOP past the point of initially adopting it.

All critical SOPs must become living documents. The management model takes care of this, as it aims to keep your SOPs current and always in a state of fixing themselves. If SOPs are well maintained using the management model, they become the backbone for the organization and its front-line supervisors. Well maintained SOPs provide accountability for an organization across the board, as they go both ways throughout the organization (up and down).

Background – The Phoenix Fire Department had very good strategic, operational SOPs, but did not have much guidance (or standardization) in the way of tactical guidelines. The tactics used on the fireground were driven by the individual Battalion Chiefs who acted as the Incident Commander for a particular incident. A competent Company Officer could not out-perform an incompetent boss with the SOPs set up this way. Based on who your boss was, the tactical "rules" could change on every deployment.

The last couple years I was in the field, my department started to implement a standardized command training and incident command certification program for all the Officers on the department. This caused the tactical level to become standardized through the implementation of new SOPs and through several revisions to our current SOPs. This coupled with standardized training, application, and constructive feedback into the SOPs lead to a level playing field for all the players involved.

It was amazing to see what happened when our organization gave their members a good set of tactical SOPs to do their jobs. Everybody knew what to do! Even the tactically challenged. Now, if the Company Officer's boss (BC) could not follow the new SOPs, their bosses could hold them accountable. No more changing the rules on every deployment! These changes raised the happiness meter of every Company Officer throughout the department. These SOP revisions also resulted in a sizable reduction in hazard zone injuries, fire loss, and sick leave use on the department.

I hope your particular organization has good SOPs because if you are a Company Officer (as Company Officer Expectation #4 states), you are "someone that the organization put into a position to follow and enforce all of the department's SOPs, policies, rules, and regulations." There is a lot of responsibility that comes with this job expectation. If you cannot do Company Officer Expectation #4, do not sign up for or take the test. If you are already a Company Officer and you are not doing Company Officer Expectation #4, demote yourself immediately or start enforcing the SOPs immediately. It is what your department promoted you to do in the first place.

Here is that phrase again: "lead by example." I know it is a cliché, but it is probably the three most important words to manage by. We are on the subject of SOPs, so if you are not following them, how can you credibly enforce them? Supervisors who do not follow the SOPs never enforce them. This leads to a crew culture in which nobody follows the SOPs because there is no accountability when the boss does not follow them.

Having a boss that does not follow or enforce the safety rules is a very bad, unsafe thing. One of my favorite timeless tactical truths from my father was: "You'd better be doing everything right when something goes wrong". Doing everything right equates to following all of the SOPs all of the time.

The following example details the upside of this tactical truth: A southern Great Lakes fire department is responding to a reported house fire. The particular unit we are focused on is the second due engine company to the alarm (they will be referred to as "E-2"). During E-2's emergency response, they come across an Opticom equipped traffic signal where the light changes green for their direction of travel at least 1,000 feet before they enter the intersection. As E-2 responds through the controlled green light intersection (3 MPH below the posted speed limit), a four-door sedan runs the red light at almost 100 MPH, striking E-2 directly on the rear duals on the driver's side of the truck. This impact causes E-2 to serpentine a couple times before rolling over and coming to rest on the driver's side of the truck. All 3 crew members exited the cab of the truck with no injuries. There were no other significant injuries to civilian drivers (E-2 bounced off two other vehicles before rolling over).

When something goes this extremely wrong, the only chance to survive the event is to be doing everything right when it occurs. Let's look at the SOPs the Company Officer was following and enforcing that ensured their crew members went home to their families at the end of their shift.

- ✓ All members were wearing their seat belts properly. This is an intelligence test. People who do not wear their seat belt (or have to be told to wear it) are not intelligent enough to work in public safety.
- ✓ All equipment inside the cab of the vehicle was properly secured.
- ✓ E-2 entered the intersection (with a green light) at or below the posted speed limit. Following this SOP ensured that E-2 could somewhat maintain control of their rig before flipping over. Going 10 MPH (or more) above the posted speed limit on impact could have caused E-2 to have been much more erratic after the impact, possibly leading to significant firefighter or civilian injuries.

I know a deep safety culture exists in E-2's fire department. But the moment of truth always comes down to the integrity of the Company Officer making sure the SOPs are always being followed. If the Company Officer on E-2 did not do their job on this run, people could have ended up in the morgue.

Now let's look at the unfortunate downside of this tactical truth: Another fire department in the northern Great Lakes region of the country is responding to a fire alarm from a multi-company station. E-2 is following E-1 on this emergency response. A mile into the response, E-2 is traveling too fast behind E-1 and to avoid rear-ending E-1 they have to do some extreme braking. The Company Officer of E-2 is not belted in and is ejected out of the front windshield of the truck. Before coming to a complete stop, E-2 runs over the Company Officer, instantly killing the Officer. E-2 did not rear-end E-1.

National Institute for Occupational Safety and Health (NIOSH)

"If it's predictable, it's preventable." – Gordon Graham

The Occupational Safety and Health Act of 1970 established NIOSH as a research agency focused on the study of worker safety and health and empowering employers and workers to create safe and healthy workplaces.

NIOSH is part of the U.S. Centers for Disease Control and Prevention in the U.S. Department of Health and Human Services. The NIOSH Firefighter Fatality Investigation and Prevention Program conducts independent investigations of Firefighter line-of-duty deaths.

NIOSH Firefighting Division Goals and Objectives:

- To learn from Firefighter fatalities and prevent similar events
- Better identify and define the characteristics of Firefighter line-of-duty deaths
- Recommend ways to prevent deaths and injuries
- Disseminate prevention strategies to the fire service

Through the Firefighter Fatality Investigation and Prevention Program, NIOSH conducts investigations of Firefighter line-of-duty deaths to formulate recommendations for preventing future deaths and injuries. The program does not seek to determine fault or place blame on fire departments or individual Firefighters, but rather seeks to learn from these tragic events and to prevent future similar events.

All Company Officers (and their fire departments) should be aware of, study, and conduct current operations in high risk areas based around current department SOPs that are all connected to NIOSH and OSHA recommendations. The more we learn from our past mistakes, the more preventable they are.

In almost **ALL** NIOSH LODD investigations (that concern an IDLH hazard zone, responding to, and/or returning from the scene) a leading contributing factor to the LODD was not following established SOPs or the lack of having best practice SOPs in place to follow. A tragedy! Tragedies that could have been prevented simply by following the SOPs. It is all fun and games until something goes wrong and if you are not doing everything right when it does, someone could get seriously injured or killed in the process.

Enforcing SOPs

Doing everything right requires an Officer who is not afraid to make sure it happens, every time. Some supervisors think that enforcing SOPs is difficult and politically unsettling. When in reality, it is really quite liberating. After a short while of SOP enforcement, the message is sent out to the workers that the boss follows and enforces the SOPs. Workers like to make their bosses happy, so if the boss wants the SOPs followed every time, it does not take the workers long to figure out that there is a lot less road rash in following the SOPs than in not following them. When a Company Officer is consistently enforcing the SOPs in this manner, it takes a very short time for a mini-safety culture to start to emerge within the crew. Following the SOPs every time soon becomes the new normal for the crew and it creates the desired "that's just the way we do it here" mentality.

I will talk more about the management style/traits a Company Officer should possess (or at least exhibit) later on in this book, but we need to briefly visit a couple of them now. When enforcing anything, it needs to be done in a positive, genuine, corrective way. I started this chapter with Company Officer Expectation #4: "someone that the organization put into a position to follow and enforce all of the department's SOPs, policies, rules, and regulations." However, while enforcing the SOPs, the Company Officer must always follow Company Officer Expectation #1: "A person who respects and values their co-workers and the public they serve."

A person who respects and values their co-workers does not micromanage them, they do not control or beat their crew in the head with a rule book, and they do not manage them with an "I'm in charge" mentality. They follow and enforce the SOPs in a positive and genuine way that projects to their crew members that they sincerely care about the way they do their jobs, their safety, and their overall welfare. When you manage the SOPs in this manner, most subordinates can sense that you truly care about their safety and job performance and they will happily follow and perform for a person who genuinely cares about them.

A company's attitude will usually reflect their Officer's attitude - good or bad. Company Officers who do not want to be burdened by following or enforcing the SOPs create an atmosphere which allows their crew to take on the same depressing attitude. Most subordinates expect their boss to act like a boss. When this does not happen, the workers will never be satisfied doing their jobs, they will never be part of a team that fits into the department model, their safety will always be in jeopardy, and most of their time at work will be spent wishing they could work with an Officer who actually did their job while caring about their crew's welfare.

Managing an SOP - Example

The sole purpose of this book is to help you manage and supervise your crew in a fashion that leads to safe and excellent service outcomes on all levels. This is not a book on how to manage a bunch of problems that happen in the aftermath of not understanding the task presenting itself. The focus of this book is to help Company Officers understand a set of SOPs or the required information for performing a set of routine activities and then preparing their crew to perform those sets of activities that are required to mitigate the standard situations presented to us while performing our jobs.

If you really want a lot of surprises in your daily life, along with a lot of problems to manage, then do not understand or follow what is contained in the SOPs, do not inform your crew or hold them accountable for what is contained in the SOPs, and then stand back and watch what happens when you deliver critical services that are SOP centered. Most people would call it a cluster. Clusters are bad (for everybody involved). Manage to prevent clusters and deliver safe and effective service. It all starts by knowing, following, and enforcing department SOPs.

Testing Fire Hydrants

I know this activity sounds fairly simple, but this case study will focus on understanding and following the SOP for testing and maintaining fire hydrants. The understanding of the SOP for this necessary function will go a long way in preventing problems while performing this activity, along with preventing any problems on the back end for not understanding and following this SOP.

Built in fire protection systems, including fire hydrants, play a vital role in the prosperity and overall longevity of a community - so much so that home and business owners' property insurance rates are primarily based on how close the nearest fire hydrant is located to the property being insured. If the fire hydrant is located more than 1,000 feet from the structure, that property owner will pay the highest insurance rates.

The Insurance Services Office (ISO), which is an independent, for-profit organization, scores fire departments on how they are staffed and equipped compared to its organization's standards to determine property insurance costs. A big factor in these ratings is how many fire hydrants are located in the community, along with how much water they will flow. The highest ISO rating a fire department can achieve is a Class-1 rating (out of 10).

The job of testing and maintaining fire hydrants usually falls on the local fire department. My former department had an ISO Class-1 rating. This came with fire hydrants spaced approximately every 300 feet throughout the entire city of Phoenix. This equals approximately 70,000 fire hydrants that had to be tested every year in the city. All of these hydrants were divided up to be tested based on all of the fire stations' first due areas (a first due area is the area within about a 2-3-mile radius around a fire station that they will arrive to "first" before any other fire stations' apparatus).

Once all of the hydrants in a station's first due area are identified, they are broken down to be tested between the 3 shifts. Each fire station's first due area has about 900 fire hydrants. This amounted to each shift having to test about 300 fire hydrants a year. If the station had another staffed piece of apparatus, usually a Ladder truck, the testing was divided up between the two rigs. The Engine had 150 hydrants to test and the Ladder had 150 hydrants to test.

When I was a Firefighter, testing fire hydrants was not one of my favorite activities. It takes about 5 minutes to test a fire hydrant properly, another minute or two to identify the next hydrant to test, and the amount of time needed to drive to it. A company could test about 10 hydrants an hour. A unit would typically test 10 to 15 hydrants per shift, taking at least a month or so to get through them all. For a Firefighter, this is a very boring activity.

As Company Officer, I loved testing hydrants. It gave our crew a chance to drive down every street, alley, and parking lot in our first due area. It also put us in the public eye doing something very productive, while also giving us a chance to smile and wave at people while doing our jobs (something that is very hard to do while working a full code).

Many people would think it was no big deal to test a fire hydrant - just remove the big steamer cap off the front and turn it on and once it flowed, turn it off, put the steamer cap back on it, and then go test the next fire hydrant. However, it is a bit more complicated than that. The biggest thing to avoid when testing a fire hydrant is creating a water hammer event.

Water hammer results from of a pressure surge, or high-pressure shockwave that propagates through a piping system when a fluid in motion is forced to change direction or **IS STOPPED ABRUPTLY.** Water hammer can cause serious damage to pipelines, pipe joint gaskets, and all other components of a water delivery system, such as flow meters and pressure gauges.

Water hammer events created by local fire departments cause millions of dollars of damage annually across the nation. Most of the fire departments' water hammer events are caused by improperly shutting down a fire hydrant.

With the knowledge of water hammer and all the damage it creates, a group of very smart scientists and hydraulic engineers from around the globe (NFPA) got together and they created a fire department standard on testing fire hydrants and the main objective was to properly test a fire hydrant **WITHOUT CAUSING ANY WATER HAMMER!** Most fire departments across the country have adopted this SOP in one form or another. Key points in this standard include:

- Always try to have a hose connected to any hydrant opening prior to opening the outlet
- Always avoid flowing water openly out of any hydrant opening (especially the steamer opening)
- Test the fire flow using one of the 2 ½ inch side outlets using a **DIFFUSER** that is at least 16 inches long
- Always open a fire hydrant slowly
- Always close a fire hydrant slowly

Here is an abbreviated version of the Phoenix SOP based on the standard:

- Remove all caps from the hydrant, apply a "break free" oil compound to the threads, then reconnect all caps firmly (except one of the 2 ½ inch outlets)
- Attach the 2 ½ inch diffuser to the open 2 ½ inch outlet
- With all other outlets closed, slowly and fully open the fire hydrant, inspect for an adequate water flow
- Flow water until all rust and other debris is flushed from the hydrant
- Slowly close the hydrant, remove the diffuser, and replace the 2 ½ inch cap firmly

Acting Out the SOP

Now let's look at the SOP in motion. It is that time of the year: fire hydrant testing time. **PRIOR** (a very important word here) to going out and performing this activity, the Company Officer should:

- Print a copy of the fire hydrant testing SOP and do a self-review of the SOP.
- Get the crew together at the dining room table and review the SOP with all members. Especially cover:
  - Avoid causing any water hammer by using the diffuser

- Where to stand when opening the hydrant
- The safety routine of driving from hydrant to hydrant
- Assemble all the equipment required to test fire hydrants. Usually, every station has a well-built box that contains: a diffuser, hydrant wrenches, spare hydrant caps and chains, an oil compound, pressure gauges, and work gloves.

Going over this SOP with your crew PRIOR to testing fire hydrants does the following:

- It puts the Company Officer in the position of knowing what is going on and being in charge of the activity.
- It provides the crew members with all the front-end knowledge and background to perform the activity properly, PRIOR to engaging in the activity.
- It establishes the safety routine that will be used and enforced during the activity.
- It ensures all the proper equipment will be ready and available for the activity.
- Most of all, it will prevent any WATER HAMMER events from occurring and the back-end problems that follow these type of events.

Background – As a probationary Firefighter, in 1 of my 3 probationary fire station rotations, I was assigned to a unit when testing fire hydrants was on the company activity calendar for the company for that quarter. We had over 300 fire hydrants to test and we would try to knock out about 15 of them a day. I need to start this out by saying that I was 19 years old at the time of this event. They taught none of us anything about testing fire hydrants in the academy. I had no idea at the time that the department had a fire hydrant testing SOP, no idea what water hammer or a diffuser was, and no idea what these words even meant.

The fire station I was assigned to was in a very nice part of Phoenix. My crew consisted entirely of old guys. The Captain, Engineer and Senior Firefighter were all in their 50's and based on their body language while testing hydrants, none of them liked the activity very much. This caused the whole company to have a "try to get it over with as soon as possible" attitude.

My Captain did not like testing hydrants that were on main, high traffic roads, so he wanted to get all of those tested first. Those were all completed in the first month of testing and then it was onto the residential streets and neighborhoods. Again, it was a very nice area of Phoenix where most of the houses in the residential areas were on big lots with big front and back yards.

We were into our sixth week of testing when at about 8:30 in the morning, the Battalion Chief pulled into the back of the station. About 5 minutes later, a nice 4-door sedan with "City of Phoenix Water Department" signs on the doors pulled into the back of the station. A gentleman got out of the car wearing a suit. Right after that, a Cadillac pulled into the back of the station and two more gentlemen got out of that car wearing suits. All of them wanted to speak to my Captain.

The meeting with my Captain and these 4 other people lasted about 20 minutes. All 4 people looked very upset when leaving the station. It took my Captain about 10 more minutes to exit his office after their departure. He came out looking like a ghost - he was as white as a newly bleached sheet. He told all of us to get on the truck and that we were driving to the neighborhood where we were testing hydrants last shift.

As we turned the corner to where we tested hydrants, all 3 of the cars that had parked behind the station earlier were now parked down one side of the road. They could not park on the other side of the road because about 50 yards of it was washed out, creating about a 10-foot deep hole in the ground that was about 50-60 feet wide. Along with that, 4 houses' front yards were completely destroyed because of more gigantic holes that were about 10 feet deep. One of the houses had about half of its foundation washed away and was tilting into one of the gigantic holes where its front yard had been just 3 days earlier.

Guess what? We did not use a diffuser to test the hydrants. WATER HAMMER! We opened the front steamer cap and let it flow. We shut it down as quickly as we could so we could get to the next hydrant faster. In the process, we blew up an 18-inch water main buried 10 feet underground that flowed over 4,000 gallons of water per minute. We tested the hydrant at 10 AM, they shut the water main down at 2 PM. It took the water department about a day to figure out what had happened.

The 4 other people involved were:

- *The Battalion Chief was there to write my Captain up for failing to follow an SOP. At the time (1981), our water hammer event caused more than $250,000 in damage to pipes, roads, yards, and houses. The only reason he was not given time off, demoted, or fired was because he had never been in any sort of other trouble during his entire career.*
- *The Water Department representative was there to coordinate the water main repairs with the street department and to also make sure he was in the meeting to witness my supervisor getting chewed out.*
- *One of the gentlemen who arrived in the Cadillac was the resident whose house was tilting into a gigantic hole, while the other person in the car was his lawyer. They also wanted to be there to witness the chewing out.*

I am sure all the neighborhood residents were not too happy with the fire department for the next several weeks, as they were inconvenienced by having only half a street in the neighborhood. I am also sure that the 4 homeowners who had significant damage caused to their "castles" never got over being mad at the fire department. A cluster! All of this bad stuff, for everyone involved, could have been avoided simply by the Company Officer understanding, following, and enforcing an SOP that already existed.

Because almost all the service delivered by the local fire department is done on the company level, Company Officers have the greatest responsibility and accountability for following and enforcing the department's SOPs. If those SOPs exist only as documents in department manuals and are not followed and enforced by the department's bosses, they are of no use to the organization. The Company Officer is the one person who can take immediate, direct action to make sure that their crew members are always operating in the best and safest manner (always following the SOPs). It is what your department promoted you to do. Do it!

Section 2
Managing Readiness

Chapter 6

Time Management and Administrative Documentation

"It is very hard to manage the daily schedule of a group of people who are so episodic."
- Alan Brunacini

The "episodes" my father was referring to come in the form of 911 emergency responses. This is when the lights come on, everybody drops whatever they are doing, they all get on the truck, and they respond to the call. Emergency service delivery will always come first on the daily schedule. This makes managing some of the readiness stuff (drilling, etc.) and the other administrative responsibilities of our jobs difficult to almost impossible to accomplish on a shift-to-shift basis.

A 5-Alarm fire that comes in at 8:30 AM and lasts a full 6 hours is definitely going to adjust the entire daily shift calendar- from the physical fitness routine to chow. Again, service delivery will always be the first priority. From there, it is about trying to fit in a "to-do" list of priorities.

Scheduling and Documentation Formats

In a previous **Background**, I stated that I was hired as a Firefighter in 1980. A lot of people who are reading this book were not even born then. Back in 1980, a fire department was driven mostly by paper because computers were not readily available until the mid 1980's. I date myself to make the following point: a Company Officer will probably use two different methods to document their daily shift and emergency service delivery activities. They are:

- A computerized, digital format
- Paper (still used for some things)

A Company Officer must connect to and be well versed in both of these systems on a shift-to-shift basis in order to be both punctual and administratively effective.

Digital

Most fire departments today use computerized, digital systems to plan department wide activities and to perform data entry for service delivery, maintenance tracking, and supply ordering.

Advantages of digital formats:

- Mostly secure and can be backed up (redundancy)
- Most fire service scheduling related data can be accessed by all field members with an internet connection (because most of the info/data is available to everybody in the digital age, it makes it hard for the employees to use the "I didn't know about it" excuse)
- Easy access to digital records on or off site

- Creates permanent, time stamped, legal records that are immediately available to the department or other connected agencies (a digital paper trail – no pun intended)
- Provides for permanent, legal documents
- All data going to a central point allows those in charge of the data to analyze the information to perform quality control, observe trends, fine-tune budgets, order the right amounts, adjust staffing levels, etc.
- All effective documentation and file management reduces the overall liability of the department

Disadvantages of digital formats:

- Security can be an issue with some applications
- Documenting inappropriate communications becomes a permanent, legal record for all to access (never send an email when you are angry)
- Difficult to interface with for the digitally challenged
- Complex interfaces require long learning curves
- Multiple digital formats within a department where none of them are compatible or can share information with one another
- Power outages, viruses, constant updates, etc.

Paper

Very little paper is used in the fire service today. Its only primarily uses are for a common station and unit activity calendar and for a Company Officer's personal log.

Advantages of paper:

- The best way to remember something is to write it down. Sometimes writing mental notes on paper is better and faster than typing mental notes digitally (you can always translate to a digital format later)
- Paper with time stamps will stand up in a court of law just as well as time stamped electronic data
- Paper is tangible and visible - a person does not need knowledge of computers to handle and work with paper-based documents (older generation)
- In poster or calendar format, paper can be viewed, added to, and edited by all who are connected to it, which provides a daily, constant reminder of scheduled activities or events
- All effective documentation and file management reduces the overall liability of the department

Disadvantages of paper:

- Once your dog eats your notebook, it is gone forever
- Requires lots of storage space
- Security issues
- Editing problems

- Limits communication and collaboration when on paper (good thing for HR issues)

Time Management and Documenting Your Shift's Activities

There are 4 major elements to managing the schedule and documenting the daily activities of a fire company. They include:

1. Department/Battalion/Training Academy wide activity calendar
2. Company activity calendar
3. Administrative documentation and data entry
4. Officer's personal log – to document non-standard events and behaviors

1. Department Wide Activity Calendar

Most fire departments use one of the several digital based systems available to schedule and broadcast the department's major daily activities. The department will electronically post a department wide activity calendar, which is usually done every month or every quarter.

The typical department wide events that are scheduled for the month/quarter/year include:

- MCS
- Special Operations training events (Hazmat, Technical Rescue, ARFF, etc.)
- EMS training
- Apparatus and facility maintenance
- Company Officer meetings
- Chief Officer meetings
- Inspections
- Furlough days (Kelly day schedule)

Scheduling Your Company for Department Wide Events

As opposed to other textbooks specifically written for Company Officers, this book will not get into the finer details of managing your "in and out boxes." This includes both the in and out boxes for your email and inter-department mail. I hope that all people who aspire to be a Company Officer have the brain power to know how to read and interpret an activity calendar in a manner where they know when and where to show up for "mandatory" department events.

All events listed in the department wide activity calendar that require your company (or an individual member of your company) to attend should be inserted into the company activity calendar (#2 on the list and described next) and planned well in advance of the event taking place.

Communications that address activities and events related to maintaining any member of the company's mandatory, in-class certifications should also be attended and it is the Company Officer's ultimate responsibility to help manage each member of their crew with their mandatory certifications (as well as their own).

Some department wide events will sometimes require just one member of the crew to attend. Examples of this are Company Officer meetings or in-class certification training sessions. In these cases, the Company Officer will also have to manage a vacancy on the apparatus. To remind yourself (and your crew members) of any shift vacancies, these should also be inserted into the company activity calendar and planned well in advance of the event taking place. Managing vacancies is covered in much more detail later in this book.

Scheduling Battalion Events

Battalion training and meeting events may or may not be included in the department wide activity calendar. Typically, smaller departments will have battalion events included in the department wide activity calendar and larger departments will leave the battalions to schedule their own activities around department wide activities. Most battalion level activities that end up in the company's activity schedule include:

- MCS drills and checkoffs
- Tactical drills
- Classroom sessions
- Employee annual grading schedule
- Battalion inspection and testing schedule

Again, as with all department wide events, all events listed in a battalion wide activity calendar that require your company (or an individual member of your company) to attend should be inserted into the company activity calendar and planned on well in advance of the event taking place.

Scheduling Training Academy Events

As with scheduling Battalion events, Training Academy events may or may not be included in the department wide activity calendar. Typically, smaller departments will have Training Academy events included in the department wide activity calendar and larger departments will leave the Training Academy to schedule their activities around department wide activities. Most Training Academy level events that end up in the company's activity schedule will include:

- Training academy multi-company drills
- Tactical drills
- Training academy in classroom training sessions
- In-rank/classification certification maintenance
- Annual MCS performance and checkoffs

Again, as with all department wide events, all events listed in a Training Academy activity calendar that require your company (or an individual member of your company) to attend should be inserted into the company activity calendar and planned on well in advance of the event taking place.

2. Company Activity Calendar

Every Company Officer should maintain their own company activity calendar for the unit they supervise. The details of managing your own company's activity calendar becomes the foundation of how you will manage your entire shift. The data you enter into the activity calendar today will become the activities you manage next shift, next week, next month, next quarter, etc.

Background: In my days out in the field, every quarter of the year the Operations Division of the department would send out a department-wide quarterly activity calendar. The calendar was sent out to each fire station as a paper copy about two weeks in advance of the next quarter. It was then put into a 3-ring binder and left on the main station desk for all station members to view.

Once delivered, I would take out all the B-Shift days of the quarter and I would make two xerox copies of them - one for myself and the other for the Engine Officer at the station. I would then reinsert the pages I just copied back into the main station calendar notebook.

I would take my copy of the activity calendar and insert it into a 3-ring binder that was dedicated for that year. My notebook had dividers for every quarter of the year. I kept this notebook in my locker. Once the year ended, I would place the notebook for that previous year under the new year's notebook, taking the notebook from two years ago home and filing it away.

The first thing I would do with the department wide calendar was highlight any and all department wide events that Station 201 – B-shift was scheduled for during the quarter. This included the Ladder, Engine, and Ambulance. From there, myself and the other members of the crew would document into the L-201 B-Shift company calendar the following:

- *Members' time off of any kind - this included both partial and full shifts off, the reason for the time off, and the type of leave being used*
- *Company, station, battalion, and department drills*
- *Certification maintenance (EMS, HAZMAT, Driver/Operator, etc.)*
- *Inspections*
- *Station tours*
- *Public appearances*
- *Ride alongs*
- *Employee annual and monthly evaluation schedule*
- *Any official department training or meeting that came down the pipeline that was not included in the department wide or battalion activity calendar (usually notified by email)*
- *Who would drive the front of the ladder and who would drive the back of the ladder*
- *Cooking days (a big deal at my station)*
- *Pay days*
- *Etc...*

Every morning, I would place the L-201 B-Shift activity calendar on the kitchen table for all crew members to not only refer to, but to also add any important information that concerned them being off or replaced. The calendar not only gave the entire crew the run-down for what was going on that shift, but it also gave everyone a run-down for what was going to happen next shift, next week, and so on. Using this format kept everyone informed on the scheduled company and member activities and it prevented any surprises from happening.

At the end of the shift, I would put our company's activity calendar back into my locker so that personnel on another shift could not insert any events into our calendar without our expressed permission (more on this later).

Let me end this background by saying that I felt that it was really no else's business in the department, except for my boss, what the daily calendar for Station 201 B-Shift included. There were several other digital formats that documented L-201's activity that everyone else could view, so the company activity calendar belonged to and could only be viewed by Station 201 B-Shift personnel. No other shift at the station or the rest of the department had permission to view, insert, or edit any details contained in our activity calendar except us (Station 201 B-Shift personnel).

Company Officers whose departments use digital based activity calendars could perform the same thing by printing the calendar from its digital format into a paper format and following the routine above.

Another paper-based scheduling tool that is quite common in a fire station is a very large, wall mounted calendar that is posted in the main office area of the station. While not as detailed as an 8 ½ x 11 piece of paper in a notebook for a single shift, it is mainly used to document training days and crew members' time off for that particular station. I was not a big fan of these calendars because they allowed the other shifts the ability to schedule activities for our truck and/or shift without our permission and this did not sit well with me (more on this later).

Scheduling Routine, Every Shift Readiness Activities

Having established that emergency responses will always come first, let's look at scheduling the other "to-dos" for the shift as they fit in between emergency responses. There is a certain set of "to-dos" that need to be scheduled and performed each and every shift, whenever possible. They include managing the following activities:

- Response readiness - (the trucks and allied equipment) because this activity is so important to safety and service delivery, it has a chapter dedicated to it
- PT - (the crew members) because one of the most important activities during the shift is maintaining the crew's overall health and wellness, it has a chapter dedicated to it
- Facility and equipment management - (the station) because this activity is also very important, it has its own chapter
- Chow (the crew members' stomachs) – because this is also a major shift activity, it has its own dedicated chapter
- Vacancies – Sometimes a Company Officer will have to manage members of the company (and themselves) taking time off throughout a shift. Because this activity is so important to safety and customer service, it has its own chapter

Scheduling Other Routine Station Activities

Other activities that do not occur on a shift-to-shift basis that need to be scheduled for an individual company include:

- Inspections
- Public events

Scheduling and Managing Inspections

Inspections can include the following:

- Fire code inspections
- Home safety inspections
- Fire preplanning inspections (walk throughs)
- Hydrant inspections and testing
- Hose inspections and testing
- Apparatus and station inspections
- PPE inspections

Some of the possible inspections listed above may or may not be included in the department wide or battalion activity calendars. Notification for the inspections that are not included in a department or battalion activity calendar usually come in the form of emails or a department's RMS sending out automatic notifications. To remind yourself and to plan around these and other events during the same shift, all inspection related events should be inserted into the company activity calendar.

Some inspections and other activities only occur during a particular quarter or month during the year, while other inspections occur throughout the entire year. While these events are to be done in the time frame publicized, often times the department allows the company to schedule the activity themselves in order to coordinate the completion of the activity, along with all the other stuff that needs to get done. Always schedule and complete these activities as soon as possible in the month/quarter. Putting them off until the last shift only leads to disaster and is a poor reflection of the Officer in charge.

Most of the different inspections listed will have local AHJ SOPs that will provide greater detail and specific department details to follow when performing the activity. All Officers will need to refer to and follow their local SOPs if they are in place on your department. This book will outline the basics of each of these events in order to give a Company Officer a good idea of the general activities that will need to be managed.

Inspection Event Scheduling and General Guidelines

Fire Code, Home Safety, and Fire Preplanning Inspections

- Performed while in service

- Usually not scheduled for a specific shift or time and they are left up to the Company Officer to fit into the company schedule. However, there is usually a due date for activity completion
- Once the occupancy is identified, always call the RP for the occupancy first – do not show up unannounced
- On the initial call:
    - Identify who you are
    - Give the purpose for the visit and how long it will take
    - Give the RP 2 or 3 dates to choose from, at least 1 shift in advance of showing up
    - Give the RP a 2-hour window to show up between
- If emergency activity causes a delay or cancellation, call the RP as soon as possible to reschedule
- Maintain professional behavior while on the premises at all times

Hydrant Inspections

- Performed while in service
- Usually not scheduled for a specific shift or time and they are left up to the Company Officer to fit into the company schedule. However, there is usually a due date for activity completion
- Divided equally between the shifts
- Probably best to perform in the morning
- Crew must be using all proper safety equipment (vest, gloves, goggles, etc.)
- Test high traffic areas during non-rush hours
- Use apparatus to block for and protect the crew
- Use the diffuser
- Aim the water in a manner that will not cause damage to any property (public or private)

Apparatus and Station Inspections

- Performed while in service
- Usually scheduled for certain days of the week/month
- Could be included in the department or battalion activity calendar
- More on this in an upcoming chapter

Hose Inspections and Testing

- Could be performed while in or out of service
- Usually scheduled during a consistent time of the year, but are not scheduled for a specific shift or time and they are left up to the Company Officer to fit into the company schedule. However, there is usually a due date for activity completion
- Divided equally between the shifts
- Usually done at the station
- Position all the hose that is going to be tested in a manner that does not block truck movements and can be quickly disconnected in case of an emergency response (some departments use a portable pump to test hose to keep the Engine available)

- Some departments use a 3rd party agency to test all of the hose and other equipment on an apparatus. When this is done, the unit is usually either taken out of service or they will use another response vehicle to remain in service

PPE Inspections

- Performed while in service
- Usually scheduled for certain days of the month/quarter
- Could be included in the department or battalion activity calendar
- PPE is high priority item. Any out of service PPE item must be replaced immediately

Scheduling Public Events

Again, most of the different public events listed will have local SOPs in place that will provide greater information and specific department details to follow when managing these types of events. All Company Officers will need to refer to and follow their local SOPs if they are in place on your department. This book will outline the basics of each of these events in order to give a Company Officer a good idea of the general activities that will need to be managed.

Public events include:

- Station tours and visits
- Ride alongs
- Public appearances (schools, churches, clubs, etc.)

These are all important activities that hopefully create and project good will and demonstrate our eagerness to serve and protect our local community.

Many departments will have a central scheduling system (or person) in place that will schedule all public events (department wide) for all shifts and apparatus. This is the best system to operate under because it prevents other Company Officers on other shifts from scheduling events for other shifts and/or units.

If the above system is not in place, here are a set of general guidelines that can help regulate and standardize these activities:

- Your boss or designated scheduling agent can schedule whatever they want on a company's schedule (within reason).
- An Officer of a company is only allowed to schedule an event for their company or shift.
- An Officer of a company is **NOT** allowed to schedule an event for another company or shift.
- Outside event requests that come directly to an Officer of a company that concern an event to be scheduled for another company or shift must be referred to that Company Officer or shift for scheduling. This could be as simple as giving the other Officers at your station a phone call (or talking to them at shift change).

One of the fastest ways to create hostility and friction between the different shifts at a fire station is to schedule an event for another company or shift without their permission. DO NOT DO IT!

Performing and Managing Public Events

Station Tours and Visits

These types of activities being permitted will vary between departments and the local AHJ's SOPs must be referenced on how to manage the event (this book was written during a pandemic when many of these activities were suspended). If permitted, some general rules to guide fire station personnel when the public is on fire station grounds include:

- All members are on their best behavior
- Appropriate uniform
- Station is always presentable
- Nothing imprudent or inappropriate on the walls or on TV (just turn it off and go clean something)
- No civilian person (non-fire department member) should be allowed to enter into a firefighter dormitory
- Truck movements in apparatus bays and station aprons cause the greatest physical risk to civilians at a fire station. As soon as they arrive at the station, civilians should be briefed on the safety routine used around the trucks and bays and any civilian that is present in these areas must be closely supervised and monitored (big deal!)
- No civilian should be allowed into an ambulance (infectious disease) or wear any firefighting garment (cancer)

Ride Alongs

The allowance of outside ride alongs (Riders) will vary greatly between departments and the local AHJ's SOPs must be referenced on how to manage these types of events. If permitted, some general rules to guide fire station personnel when hosting a Rider include:

- Riders should be contacted and given a brief rundown on the rider SOP PRIOR to their arrival to the station whenever possible
- All Riders are briefed on station, response, and scene safety guidelines
- Rider release form is signed
- Rider is appropriately dressed

Riders fall into two basic categories:

1. Civilians
2. People who are associated with public safety. This includes people performing vehicular rotations in EMS programs, hospital personnel, Firefighters from other fire departments, etc.

1. Civilian Rider emergency response guidelines

- Outside of the fire station, they must wear a safety vest identifying that they are with the fire department
- No photography or digital recordings of any kind
- Rider stays on the truck on all calls (HIPPA)

2. Public Safety Rider emergency response guidelines

- Outside of the fire station, they must wear a safety vest identifying that they are with the fire department
- No photography or digital recordings of any kind
- Can observe on EMS calls
- If credentialed and/or properly supervised, can assist with patient care on EMS calls
- EMS personnel on fire responses – stay on the truck (or stay at the station)
- Only authorized, credentialed personnel can operate inside of IDLH hot and warm zones

Public Safety Appearances

These types of events must always display the fire department in the best light. Some general guidelines when appearing in public for non-emergency events include:

- All members are on their best behavior
- Appropriate uniform
- Many departments have stickers, plastic mini-fire helmets, care bears, etc. that can be passed out to any children attending the event
- Adult centered safety brochures can also be distributed
- Many of these events are performed while in service. Always be prepared to make a prompt emergency response when performing any in-service activity outside of the fire station

3. Documentation and Administrative Data Entry

"If it is not documented, it did not happen." – unknown person, probably a judge

Documentation provides a written account of things as they happen or very soon after they happen. This is especially important regarding legal matters, audits, or disputes. As stated previously, the best way to remember something is to write it down. This is because a person's memory is not perfect and as more time passes, the more the fine details become less and less recallable. Documenting an account of any significant event, whether they are incidents, drills, HR interactions, etc., preserves the details of the event in a concrete manner that can be referenced at a later date, as needed.

Administrative Documentation and Data Entry

As stated throughout this chapter, there are several types of digital reporting and documentation systems available to the fire service. A Company Officer will have to effectively interact with whatever RMS systems their department is using to document the day-to-day activities of managing a fire company.

Administrative documentation RMS systems include:

- Fire code, home safety, and preplanning inspection reports
- Apparatus and allied equipment inspection, repair, replacement, and inventory reports
- Station and allied equipment inspection, repair, replacement, and inventory reports
- PPE inspection, maintenance, repair, replacement, and inventory reports
- Supply request reports
- LSD equipment replacement reports
- Hydrant maintenance service requests
- Etc.

4. Officer's Personal Log

"A person who documents, wins." – unknown person, probably another judge

Service Delivery and Personal Log Entries

The greatest service delivery risks of a Company Officer having to testify in a court of law for service-related activities include:

1. Fire incidents - most of these are "working fires" that represent less than 1% of a department's responses
2. EMS incidents
3. Driving or apparatus movements

The 3 categories listed represent the legal risks of our actual service delivery outside of the fire station. However, the biggest legal risk for a department, by far, is HR issues and lawsuits thereof. Documenting HR issues will be discussed in later in this book. The focus of documentation in this section will be documenting service delivery issues in a personal log for incidents or events in which civil or legal matters could be pursued in the future.

Using a personal log to document an incident or event in more detail than what is required by the department's RMS reporting systems can go a long way in reducing your company's liability, especially when all the SOPs were followed. In the event of a lawsuit, dispute, or disagreement, complete and thorough documentation goes a long way in protecting both the department's and the Company Officer's interests. Documentation into a Company Officer's personal log should -

- Include date, time, and location of the event
- Include a chronological and precise description of the actions and events as they occurred

- Be professional, neat, and organized
- Be easy to access and reference
- Be private and secure

Incidents or events that should end up in Company Officer's personal log include:

- Any working fire -
  - That is suspicious in nature
  - When the owner, occupant, or RP is acting funny or suspicious
  - When an investigator responds (pass the buck)
- Any EMS incident -
  - That involves law enforcement/when you treat a person in custody
  - That has two or more patients or people involved and one patient has a high probability of suing the other (auto accidents)
  - That involve any civil unrest
  - When any vehicle accident involves your apparatus. Make a detailed entry for any occurrence, despite any other official department reports that are filed
  - When you have a gut feeling the events that recently transpired need notes or more details to refer to later, just in case (memory joggers)

Personal Log Incident Entry Guidelines:

- Always time stamp your documentation by starting all entries with the date of occurrence
- Professional entries only
- Documentation on scraps of paper, envelopes, sticky notes, etc. can all be used in a court of law, but they reflect poorly on the documenter
- Avoid misspellings and/or poor grammar
- Write documentation that is objective, complete, and consistent
- Avoid opinions, name-calling, or making any assumptions you are not qualified to make
- Always get the facts straight (errors in documented events make the rest of the documentation suspect)

When keeping a personal log, KEEP IT NEAT! I say this because if you have to refer to it in an actual court case, your personal log will become a discoverable court document that the other side can view. If your log is sloppy, unreadable, misspelled, disorganized, etc. it will reflect poorly on you and could possibly make the situation worse, discrediting you as a "witness." I love paper, but keeping your personal log notes on a word processor will prevent all of these bad things I just mentioned from happening (bad writing, spelling, and/or grammar).

Special Event Reporting Systems

Some departments have electronic reporting systems in place to further document high liability responses. Many of the situations that require a higher level of documentation is specified by the department. These system will generally require an Officer to fill out many of the specific fields and checklists that have been covered previously. If available, a Company Officer must utilize these systems whenever they are required or whenever the Officer feels it is necessary to further reduce their liability.

Background – One of the gauges of a Company Officer's annual performance rating was if they had received any citizen complaints during the year. During my almost 10 years on L-201, we received just 1 complaint. It came on my 8th year and after a thorough investigation, it was dismissed as unfounded. The only reason it was dismissed was because I followed through with a gut feeling and the personal log that I kept at the station covered my back.

Here are the details: At about 5 PM, L-201 was dispatched to a car accident involving 2 vehicles with "minor injuries." When we arrived on the scene, both cars had pulled out of the street and were located in a parking lot. There were 2 people involved, John Doe had rear-ended Jane Doe at a traffic light at a very low speed. There was no visible damage to either vehicle. John Doe had no medical complaints and Jane Doe was complaining of neck pain.

A police officer showed up to investigate the accident. After 5 minutes, he told both parties that because there was no damage to either vehicle, he was not going to write a citation, both drivers needed to exchange insurance information, and in 7 days his report of the accident would be available from the city. After exchanging information, John Doe left the scene. As he left the scene, Ambulance-201 (A-201) was returning from another call and they pulled into the parking lot to say hey and assist.

We had taken all of Jane Doe's vitals, secured her neck with a cervical collar, and were interviewing her on how she wanted to proceed. She stated she did not want to go to the hospital in an ambulance. I told her one was on scene and available to take her, but she refused and said she would drive home and call her doctor. I finished my EMS paperwork and then I proceeded to have her sign a patient hospital transportation refusal form. She did not want to sign it. I told her that I had documented her medical complaints and by not going to the hospital in an ambulance was in no way an indication that she was NOT injured. She again stated that she did not want an ambulance and she reluctantly signed the refusal. My gut told me this call was not over...

Before leaving the scene, I added A-201 to the dispatch to document that they were on the scene and available to transport. I then took out a polaroid camera and took a picture of the back of Jane's car. Jane was in the picture wearing a C-collar and the ambulance was in the background. Once I was back at the station, I made a copy of the EMS report before dropping it in the mail bag. I put the copy of the report and the photo of the car in my personal log, along with a few more notes on the incident. A week later, I downloaded the police accident report.

About 2 weeks later, I got a call from my Battalion Chief (my boss) who was not a big fan of mine. "Ha ha ha Brunacini! Finally! I got a citizen's complaint on you and there will be hell to pay!" I knew what he was going to say before he said it. Jane Doe had just called and she informed my boss that she was in a terrible wreck, her neck was severely injured, and she had received no care or transportation from the fire department. My boss was the first person to field the call (complaint), so his first step in investigating the incident was to call me and relish in his new opportunity to bash me. I told him not to bother with pulling up any other information on the incident, as I had it all and would be at his office in 10 minutes.

Armed with my person log, I showed my boss the official 911 incident call activity printout with A-201 shown on the scene, the EMS report with her refusal signature, the police report that I had downloaded, and the nail in the coffin – the photo showing no damage to her car while she was standing next to an ambulance wearing a fire department C-collar. Although my boss did not want to believe his lying eyes, he quickly dismissed the complaint as "unfounded."

This is just one example from the many times that proper documentation of a company's daily activities reduced both the company's and the department's liability. It is a key element in being an effective Company Officer.

Chapter 7

Shift Change

One of the most important activities that a Company Officer will have to manage on a shift-to-shift basis is the shift change routine (most of the time, it is in the morning). Doing it the right way will set the entire company up for success for the rest of the shift. Let's start the chapter with the book's cliché phrase: "Lead by Example."

Getting to work early in order to ensure that the crew is ready for the start of the shift is the very FIRST example that a Company Officer can set during the shift. Managing people being on time and getting ready for the shift (a black and white activity - mostly) is tough to do unless you are actually there to see if your crew members show up on time and are getting ready for duty properly. The boss must be present to make sure all workers are present, as well.

As stated earlier, at a minimum, your crew members will at least emulate your behaviors, if not intensifying them to impress their bosses and/or co-workers. Being late to work is not an activity you want your crew members to emulate or intensify. They will. If you are a bell ringer, most people you supervise will become bell ringers, as well. Emulate the behaviors you want your crew members to emulate. To do this, you had better get to work BEFORE the time you expect your crew members to show up.

All On-Coming Members - READY for Duty at Shift Change

Most fire department shift changes occur at either 7 or 8 AM. This book will refer to an 8 AM start time.

Most professions do not "relieve" another counterpart. They show up to work anywhere from 15 minutes to 1 second before their start time and they start doing their jobs. Their workstations are exactly like they left them when they finished work the day before. However, for professions that do have to relieve a counterpart, it is essential that shift change relief happens in a standard manner so that the oncoming personnel are well aware of the circumstances they are inheriting.

Managing the relief process creates many challenges for a Company Officer. The most helpful thing to use when managing is an SOP. Let's look at an on-time station shift change unofficial SOP:

- All members for the oncoming shift should be READY for duty no later than 8:00 AM (shift start).
- Any member of the company who knows they will be vacant from work at shift change (not ready for duty by 8:00 AM) shall notify their Company Officer immediately once they are aware they will be vacant at shift change (this could be several shifts in advance).

Background: I am big on understanding the time it takes to do something safely and properly. I did not grade activities or people by a stopwatch, but we all need to know the realistic time frames required to perform the different elements of our job. One of the major elements of our job is showing up and getting ready to deliver service at shift change.

My former fire department had 3 shifts (A, B, and C) that worked 24-hours on, with 48 hours off (a 56-hour work week). The workday would "officially" start at 8 AM. As stated earlier, we had two Ladder trucks (L-201 & LT-201), which meant that we had to check two sets of equipment each morning. Each Engineer would do the morning maintenance checks for one truck, with each Firefighter doing all of the equipment checks for one truck. It would take at least 30 minutes for each member to relieve their counterpart and complete all the necessary morning checks if nothing was out of balance (missing equipment or if the previous shift just got back from a messy job). Out of balance equipment could add up to another 30 minutes to getting into a ready state. Based on this, the whole crew was always there to relieve our counterparts and to start checking our equipment before 7:30 AM in order to be "ready for duty" by 8 AM.

Based on this, it is not unreasonable to expect your crew to get to work early enough to perform a predictable set of activities that will ensure the company is in a "ready state" at the start of their work shift.

Legitimate Reasons for Being Vacant at Shift Change

With the invention of the cell phone, there is no reason for someone who knows they are going to be missing at the morning shift change to NOT call and notify their Company Officer as soon as they know they will be missing from work at the change of a shift.

Typically, when working with a permanently assigned crew, a crew member will know that they will be missing at shift change well in advance of the vacancy occurring. Some examples of predictable shift change vacancies are:

- Members are working back to back shifts at different fire stations and they will have to commute from one fire station to the next to make their second shift
- Planned vacation
- Education leave
- City business
- Some type of predicable family situation (working spouse with children who are of school age)
- Immediate family member with a medical condition
- Severe traffic conditions can cause a member to arrive late

All these examples should be coordinated with the Company Officer PRIOR to the occurrence happening whenever possible and all known company vacancies should be documented into the company activity calendar.

Managing a vacancy on the company will be covered later in this book.

Bell Ringing versus Actually Being Late

Bell ringer - *a person who gets to work anywhere from 15 minutes to 1 second before the start of their work shift.*

Bell ringers, in our profession, cause a lot of grief. An example of this is a Firefighter Paramedic riding on a 3-person Engine company. This person cannot vacate the truck at shift change until they are properly relieved from duty. At 7:55 AM on a Saturday morning, their relief is not yet at the station (for no known, legitimate reason) and the company is dispatched to a serious accident on the freeway that takes over 2 hours to mitigate and get back to the station. This caused several bad things to happen:

- The member could have had a long night and now could be working in a sleep-deprived state (not on their A-game when making decisions)
- The Paramedic also had to be paid by the fire department for the 2 hours of overtime they worked, at one and half times their normal payrate. This cost the city approximately $100 (plus) in pay, along with all the admin time that went into processing the overtime paperwork/data
- It caused the paramedic to miss their 4-year-old son riding a pony at his birthday party
- Not much love or respect is generated towards their bell ringing relief

There was much discussion on writing this section of the book. Can a supervisor hold someone accountable for showing up a half an hour early? I think they can create the "culture" of showing up early, while keeping in mind that an Officer cannot write someone up for showing up to work at 7:59 AM. So, let's call this the "etiquette" start time of shift change - the etiquette of everyone showing up for work at an informal start time so that everyone is ready to deliver service at the start of their shift. Managing this type of shift change culture also creates an environment in which everyone on all 3 shifts works just a 24-hour shift with no additional time being tacked on because of the bell ringers.

Managing People Who are Chronically Late

Most people who are vacant from work (especially at shift change) do not want to be missing from work and they have a good reason or set of circumstances for not being there. Typically, these events can be preplanned and coordinated so that everyone in the organization is on the same page and there is no interruption in service delivery or the morning routine.

Consistently being late for work without good explanations and/or abusing the leave system is usually a symptom of something else going on in a person's life that is leading them astray. Often times, there are other issues that a supervisor will also need to address when dealing with the chronically late. This book will cover these issues in much greater detail later on. The chronically late (and all the bell ringers) must be dealt with - safe and effective service cannot happen until your company members show up and are in a ready state.

The Shift Change Main Focus is Getting Ready

Until all members have performed all of their shift change responsibilities, their main focus needs to be on getting ready to deliver service for the shift. This includes the Company Officer setting the example while facilitating the morning readiness process.

Background: As a Firefighter, I thought I had the best job in the world. I looked forward to and loved coming to work every shift. Most of the people I worked with felt the same way. We could not wait to see our fellow co-workers in the morning to catch up on what happened on our 2 days off. We called this part of the morning "the time of fellowship." Fellowship is an important activity when it concerns a group of people whose lives basically depend on each other. Fellowship usually occurred around the dinner table, it involved the newspaper, lots of coffee and burritos, and it could last anywhere from 30 minutes to an hour.

I worked at stations where the Company Officer set the example for their crew of coming to work in street clothes (which is okay to do). As soon as they arrived to the station, they would get a big cup of coffee, they would sit down at the morning table, and they would begin fellowshipping before getting into a ready state. The example set by the Company Officer would, of course, allow their crew members to emulate this same behavior. This usually would work out okay. Fellowship would end and the crew would get busy on the morning routine. The rest of time, it would end up in what I would call a "3-Stooges fire drill." A 911 response would come in with the on-coming shift not being in a ready state because they were in the middle of fellowship. This fire drill fury would intensify if the response was for a working fire. There was lots of running involved, uniforms and turnout gear would go flying, and getting out of the station on the response would usually take at least twice as long. This type of unprepared response would:

- *Start a frenzied, out of control, hurry up mode*
- *Make riding positions unable to get their PPE on correctly, pieces of equipment would be lost when scrambling on the truck, and seat belt use would be sketchy at best while re-dressing on the way to the call*
- *Cause people to drive faster to "make up for lost time"*
- *Create a situation in which no one on the truck knew if they had any air in their SCBA bottles, if the EMS equipment was restocked, if any of the power tools had gas, etc.*

This type of response creates a very hazardous condition for the entire crew and should be avoided at all costs by getting into a ready state as soon as possible after arriving to work. Fellowship is a very important part of the morning routine, but it needs to occur AFTER the workforce is in a ready state.

Company Officer Morning Routine

Before focusing on the management of the crew getting into a ready sate, let's look at the routine a Company Officer should follow and set the example for at the start of every shift:

- The shift before leaving the station, review the company activity calendar for the next shift. Pay close attention to what is scheduled in the morning and any possible morning shift change vacancies occurring on the company.
- Get to work at least 30 minutes early. There might be an "early bird" assigned to your company. These people wake up and arrive to places at least 60 minutes earlier than

the rest of the general population. Do not worry about getting to work before these types of people. Worry about getting to work before the rest of the group.

- Get into the proper work uniform.
- Seek out the Officer you are relieving and perform a standard shift change briefing. This standard morning briefing must be conducted every shift change and it should include:
  o Start out with "how was your shift?"
  o Significant incident responses and equipment used during the previous shift
  o Any recently used equipment that still needs to be serviced or re-stocked
  o Any out of service equipment
  o Anything that has been added to your daily schedule (e.g., the light bar on the truck broke last night and you have a 10 AM appointment at the shop to get it fixed)
  o Any building or grounds issues that need to be addressed
  o Any information on something out of balance that effects anyone's safety
  o Any current vacancies with the off-going shift
  o Anything else I need to know
  o Inform your counterpart that "you got it"
- After the shift change briefing with your counterpart, check the company activity calendar and the electronic staffing system to see who is filling any vacancies in the department/battalion and any leave that is being taken at the station that you were not previously aware of (sick leave, emergency vacation, etc.).
- Go out to the truck and properly relieve your counterpart (covered more in detail later).
- Check all the equipment on the apparatus that your riding position is responsible for. This should include:
  o Company Officer's PPE
  o TIC
  o **All accountability hardware and data entry are current and up to date throughout the entire shift. This activity is crucial and it is also usually used in conjunction with a departments staffing system**
  o Cab radios are on the right channels and all portable radio batteries are fully charged
  o All computers, MDTs, and smart devises are fully charged and operating properly
  o All clip boards have the necessary paperwork in them (if you have poor eyesight, make sure your glasses on are the truck)
  o A quick check of all the sirens your responsible for operating
  o If you are on a 3-person company or are a PM, you may have other equipment on the apparatus to place in a ready state
- Check your department email once your riding position is in a ready state

After taking these steps, the Company Officer's position is ready for an emergency response and the example was set for the rest of the crew to also get into a ready state.

Crew Members in a Ready State

It is the Company Officer's responsibility to know the details of and to facilitate what it takes for the crew members to perform a standard set of activities to become response ready at the start of each shift. All of these activities should be completed before the actual start time of the shift, whenever possible. This includes:

1. Briefed by the off-going crew member they are replacing
2. Proper relief of the off-going crew member they are replacing
3. Morning equipment readiness checks for whatever areas and equipment their riding position is responsible for
4. Morning briefing on the company activity calendar and primary objectives for the shift
5. Making contact with the supervisor and/or the organization above you

Permanently Assigned Personnel

Permanently assigned crew members should basically be on autopilot during shift change. They should know who they are relieving and what equipment they are responsible for checking.

First Time Personnel

People who are working on your company for the first time will require a thorough morning briefing when first arriving at the station. This briefing should include:

- Their riding position and the person they are relieving
- Equipment on the trucks they are responsible for checking, maintaining, and operating
- Areas of the station they are responsible for checking, maintaining, and cleaning
- Company's activity calendar and routine for the shift
- PT routine at the station
- Chow routine for the day

There will be more on managing first time, new personnel at the station later on in this book.

1. **Off-Going Riding Position Briefings**

After arriving at the fire station and getting in the proper uniform, each riding position on the company should seek out and find the counterpart they are relieving and perform a standard shift change briefing. This briefing should include:

- Start out with "how was your shift?"
- Significant incident responses and equipment used during the previous shift
- Any recently used equipment that still needs to be serviced or re-stocked that your riding position is responsible for
- Any out of service equipment that your riding position is responsible for
- Anything that causes an activity to be placed on your company's activity schedule (e.g., the truck needs to be at the shop at 10 AM to have the front emergency lights replaced)
- Any information on something out of balance that effects anyone's safety
- Anything else I need to know
- Inform your counterpart that "you got it"

2. Proper Position Relief

Background: This was always a big deal to me because it involved someone else's PPE. Each individual member on the company's life depends on the proper use and performance of their PPE. To me, the way somebody treated their PPE was a direct reflection on how they treated all other aspects of the job (a serious job for serious people).

When a Firefighter was hired on my former department, they would be on probation their first year on the job. The first year of a probationary Firefighter's career consisted of an approximate 3-month fire academy, along with 3 – 3-month fire company rotations. One of the 3 probationary fire company rotations had to occur on a Ladder/Truck company. This created a situation where L-201 had a probationary Firefighter rotate on and off our company every 3 months.

On the first shift change of having a new probationary Firefighter, L-201 had a member that I will refer to as Mr. Enthusiastic (mostly a good thing). Mr. Enthusiastic got to work on his first shift very early, well before any other crew member (good start!) - so early that he not only relieved his counterpart, but he had also taken the liberty of taking all my PPE out of my equipment locker and he had placed it on the apron next to my riding position. I eventually found my PPE laying there after I had discovered that it was missing from my turnout locker.

This was not a good thing and it created a situation in which I needed to immediately and calmly describe the PPE respect routine in detail with Mr. Enthusiastic. I needed to do this without bursting his bubble on his first shift at the station. I started by thanking him for getting to work early and for his enthusiasm. I then asked him if this was a normal activity that he performed every shift and if the department was now teaching this activity in the academy. He told me they did not teach him this activity in the academy, but the Company Officer at his last station had directed him to lay out his PPE in the same manner.

After his response, I then covered the following PPE respect points with Mr. Enthusiastic:

- *Your life and my life depend on our PPE*
- *Each member is 100% responsible for their OWN PPE, this includes their SCBA*
- *The person who wears it has to manage it. Do not ever leave your personal safety equipment in anybody else's hands*
- *The only other members' PPE that you can touch is the person you are relieving*
- *Take great care and respect performing this activity while making sure that all of the off-going member's PPE (and any other of their personal gear on the truck) is properly stowed and secured*
- *Do not ever mess around with anyone else's PPE*
- *Do not let anyone else ever mess around with your PPE*
- *If it is ever proven to me that someone has messed with someone else's PPE, I will personally address it with very severe consequences. Never mess with someone else's PPE or their personal items ever!*

Mr. Enthusiastic nodded eagerly showing that he got my point. Other than the person he was responsible for relieving, he never messed with anyone else's PPE at the station while on his last probationary rotation. He did a great job while being assigned on the company - of course he did, he was Mr. Enthusiastic!

3. Equipment Checkoffs

Each company member is assigned a set of equipment that needs to be checked and placed in a ready state at the beginning of every shift. There is much more on this activity in a later chapter of this book.

Medic Unit – Drug Custody

If you are the Company Officer working on a Paramedic Engine company and/or you are also a Paramedic, you will either have to validate or actively participate in the checking off of all the controlled drugs carried on the apparatus, along with performing the proper transfer of custody of the drug box/bag to the oncoming shift. This activity usually takes 5 to 10 minutes to perform if everything is in order.

4. Morning Crew Briefing

During the course of everyone getting ready in the morning, the Company Officer should briefly cover what is on the agenda for the day. This usually happens in the apparatus bays while getting into a ready state. The finer details of performing the day's activities can be expanded upon during fellowship around the kitchen table. The morning readiness briefing should include:

- Ensuring that all crew members are okay, awake, alert, on their A-game, and they are ready to start delivering service
- Any vacancies on the company and the plan and personnel movements needed to maintain minimum staffing levels
- A basic rundown of the schedule for the day
- Remind everyone to get any personal PPE equipment to their off-going counterparts
- The Company Officer and crew member roles and functions to be performed on EMS and fire incidents with any new members working on the company for the first time

The morning briefing is important to get everyone on the same page and to set your crew up for success for the rest of the shift. Manage it the same way every shift.

5. Making Contact with the Supervisor and/or the Organization Above You

Many departments have a process in place in which all Company Officers will make contact with their Battalion Chief (and possibly other higher-ranking Brass) to get everyone in the battalion/department on the same page for the day's agenda. These meeting could be hosted via the phone or through video conferencing software. They usually happen during the morning readiness routine and they last around 15 minutes. More on attending these meetings in a future chapter.

Chapter 8

Vacancies

Another important item that a Company Officer will likely have to manage on a shift-to-shift basis are vacancies. Before getting into the details of managing this activity, we need to first look at the different types of response systems and the corresponding staffing levels that should be maintained throughout the shift.

Maintaining Minimum Staffing Levels

Most of the details of this book can be universally applied when managing a fire company throughout all fire departments. However, when it comes to staffing, there is wide gap of staffing levels and configurations across the US. Due to all of the different department types, this book will try to provide general scenarios for the major staffing routines used by most professional/paid fire departments, but a Company Officer must use and follow their AHJ's SOPs (and other agreements in place) whenever considering local staffing methods.

A Company Officer could be supervising a company in one the following systems:

- 100% professional/paid fire department with 4 (or more) people staffed on all Engine and Ladder companies
- 100% professional/paid fire department with 3 people staffed on all Engine and Ladder companies - this group represents over 90% of all professional fire departments in the US
- 100% professional/paid fire department that uses a combination of full-time Firefighters (permanent employees of the department) and part time Firefighters (not permanent employees of the department) - most of these systems also maintain 3 person staffing levels
- Combination department that uses a mix of full-time, part-time, and **volunteer** Firefighters - these types of departments have a mix of different staffing systems Examples:
    1. full-time/part-time staffing Monday-Friday from 8 am to 5 pm, volunteers staff the fire station all other times
    2. 1 or 2 officers are always on-duty 24/7 and the rest of the staffing is made up of volunteers - most of these types of departments have staffing levels from 1 to 3 people that will respond on an apparatus
- 100% volunteer fire departments - this group represents almost 70% of all fire departments in the US and they protect about 25% of the US population. Some of these departments may have a paid chief or administrator, but 100% of the Engine and Ladder responses are staffed with volunteers. Most of these types of departments have staffing levels of 0 to 2-3 people on an apparatus, all depending on the season of the year and the time of day.
    - ***Because volunteer fire departments do not have shift changes or any leave time to manage, the focus of this chapter will be on professional, paid fire departments.***

Most professional fire departments require a minimum number of personnel staffing the company at all times. The minimum number of personnel that is most often maintained is 3 people. This means there has to be at least 3 people staffed on a company at all times (24/7/365). Here are some minimum staffing scenarios for most career fire departments:

Departments with 4-person staffing:

- The minimum staffing level is usually 3 people (when down to 3 people, they will follow the 3-person staffing rules).
- Unlike a department with 3-person staffing, a department with 4-person staffing has more options to fill a short-term vacancy because it allows 1 person to be off the apparatus during a shift without having to fill the vacancy.
- There is usually a maximum amount of time that one position can be vacant before it must be backfilled/staffed with another qualified member. This could be anywhere from 30 minutes to 8 hours.
- If the staffing level falls to 2 people or less, the unit would usually be taken out of service
- Only a certain amount of people can be off at one time in a department or a battalion to maintain minimum staffing levels department wide.

Departments with 3-person staffing:

- The minimum staffing level is 3 people at all times. This means that any member who is going to be off during the shift has to have a qualified member in relief of their position for the entire duration of their absence.
- Usually, there is a maximum amount of time a person can be vacant from the apparatus. This could be anywhere from 30 minutes to 8 hours.
- If the staffing level falls to 2 people, the unit would usually be left in service, but the entire response system would be aware of the shortage. 911 calls requiring full staffing would have an additional unit dispatched to back up a unit running short with 2 people and the department would be working to staff the company back to 3 people as quickly as possible.

Background: My former fire department had 4-person staffing on all Engine and Ladder companies. The minimum number of staffing for a unit was 3 people. If the rig was staffed with less than 3 people, the unit was taken out of service (in most cases, this was NOT an option – the public is paying for a fire truck to be in service at all times). The longest a unit could run short with 3 people was 4 hours before the 4th spot had to be filled with overtime or a personnel shift/movement.

When I retired, Phoenix had about 60 fire stations, which were divided up into 8 battalions. Each battalion consisted of 7-8 stations. Each battalion only had 4 to 5 partial vacation slots available per 24-hour shift. This insured the battalion was adequately staffed throughout the shift, making it so only 1 or 2 units could have 1 member off at one time.

Partial vacation for a shift could be granted for up to 8 hours. After 8 hours, the member had to take the whole shift off. After 4 hours, the system had to pay overtime to constantly staff your spot, so partial vacation slots of over 4 to 8 hours were only granted to people who had a good reason to be off for that long during a shift (usually on city business of some sort).

Vacancy Considerations

"If you know you're going to be missing during a shift – NOTIFY!" – unknown

When a member of the crew will be vacant at shift change or will need time off during the shift, the Company Officer, along with the higher ups in the system, will need to determine:

- The length of time the person will be off
- The type of leave that will be used to account for the missing member
- The rank, position, and/or qualification(s) that are currently being vacated
- The minimum staffing levels required to keep the company in service
- The availability or willingness of a qualified off-going shift member at the station to hold over if needed or required
- If filling the vacancy with overtime personnel is required

How you respond to and manage riding positions that are vacant in order to maintain minimum staffing levels during a shift will greatly depend on how your station is staffed along with your minimum staffing level requirements and/or CBA.

Personnel Move-Ups (Acting-Up, Working-Up, Act in Capacity, etc.)

A "move-up" is defined as a member who holds a certain rank and is qualified to fill another position or rank above their current rank. This type of cross trained personnel can be temporarily moved up into higher ranking positions while the position is vacant. Some possible, basic move-up scenarios include:

- A Firefighter can be qualified to move up into the position of Engineer and/or Company Officer.
- An Engineer can be qualified to move up into the position of Company Officer.
- Members can hold the qualification as a TRT or Hazmat Technician while not being permanently assigned to a team, but they can move up (or over) from their current position to fill a vacancy on a TRT or Hazmat company.

Move-ups become a powerful tool in helping the department and their Company Officers maintain minimum staffing levels throughout a shift.

Managing Shift Vacancies

The biggest difference between a vacancy occurring at the beginning of the shift versus all other times is that the system has the option of using off-going personnel to fill the vacancy. When there is a vacancy midday, the off-going shift is not available and a vacancy that occurs well after shift change will require the use of off duty, overtime personnel.

One of the first things to determine when somebody is going to be vacant at shift change is the amount of time they be missing from work. For scenarios occurring at shift change in which a position on the company will be less than 15 minutes vacant, the Company Officer will typically coordinate staffing the apparatus with the off-going shift and nothing official will be put into motion in order to maintain an adequate staffing level. Vacancies lasting over 15 minutes should be documented officially into the system with some sort of official leave being taken. This holds all members accountable for their time off and it also takes a leave management load off of the Company Officer. There will be more on this later.

As we had 4-person staffing in Phoenix, if 1 position was vacant on the company, we could run with 3 people for up to 4 hours without having to pay overtime or without needing to have someone hold-over for the missing member at shift change. This is probably common for all departments with 4-person staffing levels. However, to maintain a minimum staffing level of 3 people at all times, there are several different considerations and options when filling a position that will be vacant during a shift. 3-person minimum staffing considerations and options include:

- The type of MOU or CBA that is in place on the department (if any) between labor and management
  o Most systems have agreements in place that provide if a member has to work any overtime past their normal shift (usually in15 minutes increments), they must be compensated (usually at time and a half of their regular pay).
- All positions staffed on an apparatus should be staffed based on the rank or qualifications of the missing member's position on the unit.
- In most systems, the missing position must be filled by an equally ranked or qualified member in that position.
- A higher ranked or more qualified person can fill a lower ranking position when needed. This means that if a Firefighter is missing, all other ranks of the off-going shift can cover for this missing member because it is the lowest rank on the apparatus. This method costs the most in overtime rates but is sometimes necessary to keep a unit in service.
- If the Engineer or the Company Officer is missing, an equally qualified person must fill their position. Filling these positions depends on your local system and how your members cross-train and move-up into higher ranks or classifications.
- Other combinations can be used to fill a higher-ranking vacancy. Example: the oncoming Engineer will be 2 hours late to work. The oncoming Firefighter is certified as a driver/pump operator and is qualified to move-up into the position of the missing Engineer. The off-going Firefighter is then paid overtime to fill the Firefighter's position while their counterpart is moved-up to Engineer. This method saves the department the most money in overtime costs because they are paying overtime to a lower ranked member at a lesser pay rate per hour while filling a higher-ranking vacancy.
- Filling vacancies for classifications such as PM, Hazmat Technician, ARFF members, TRT members, etc., confuses the matter even more and could cause the system (usually above your head) to move even more dominos around in order to maintain minimum staffing and service delivery levels
- Off-going personnel usually feel okay about holding over for people who will be missing for about an hour. After this amount of time, the vacancy should be filled with another off-duty member willing to be paid overtime for the remainder of the vacancy (unless the off-going shift member is willing to fill in for the entire vacancy period – some are happy to, while others are not).
- Some departments have "mandatory" overtime rules, where under certain circumstances, they can require a member to work so many mandatory overtime hours

in a year's period. Most mandatory overtime occurs in order to fill long term shift vacancies.

Background: When I had 4 years on the job, I got my first permanent firefighting spot at a southside station. At the time, I was also taking 2-3 fire science classes at our local community college every semester. The fire science subjects were all geared toward Firefighters working a shift schedule, but the non-fire science classes were on the civilian time clock. One semester, I had a 2-hour civilian class (Anatomy & Physiology) that started at 8:30 in the morning, 3 times a week. The college was over 20 minutes away from my station and there was no way to get to work on time and then to get to class on time. This caused me to be 3 hours late to work at least 1 shift per week throughout the semester.

A couple of weeks before the semester started, I sat down with my Captain and covered the 16 shifts I would be late for. For 12 of these 16 shifts, I took 3-hour blocks of official vacation time and the company would run short with 3 people. The other 4 shifts involved some sort of morning drill or exercise and the Captain wanted a 4-person company. For these 4 shifts, I had another Firefighter at the station (on a different shift) cover for me with an AWR (Away With Relief – described later in the chapter). AWRs had to be paid back, hour for hour. During that semester, the shift before I was going to be late, I would remind my captain that I would be late for the next shift and whether I was taking vacation time or using an AWR - where I would remind him of the person who would be filling in for me.

Predictable, acceptable circumstances caused me to be late over a 3-4-month period, but it was not a surprise to anybody. All parties were informed, and both the Company Officer and I had a plan to deal with it.

Electronic Staffing Systems (ESS)

An ESS is a great tool in assisting a Company Officer with managing vacancies. These systems provide the entire department access to the department wide company activity calendar along with membership vacancies, overtime personnel working, and rover assignments being posted.

I would mostly use an ESS to see who was filling in for missing personnel for not only Station 201, but for any unit L-201 had the possibility of running a call with during the shift.

Many ESS are also tied to the company accountability roll call system. It is imperative that all accountability hardware and data entry are current and up to date throughout the entire shift, especially if these systems are associated with any ESS.

Different Leave Types

Let me start this section out by saying that a Company Officer is in NO WAY in charge of granting any of the following leave types (minus an AWR) for any of their crew members. This is a GOOD thing. All leave types (minus an AWR) must go through the chain of command using any in place MOU or CBA. While not being responsible for granting leave, the Company Officer must be well aware of all leave being taken (and the reason for it).

The type of leave that is used when a member is absent from their work shift will depend on several different factors. All leave of any significant time MUST be documented by the department and by the Company Officer. Charging people for the time they take off holds them accountable for their time away from work and it also gives everyone in the organization an official record that they can fall back on if any situations concerning their absence comes up in the future (for all sorts of reasons – most of these reasons are to protect the employee and their boss).

Most leave types are planned. As stated in a previous chapter: to remind yourself and to plan around shift vacancies, all vacancies should be inserted into the company activity calendar as soon as they are known.

The following are some of the most common leave types taken, the reasons for taking the leave, and how the Company Officer fits into the process for managing the vacancy:

City/Department Business: This is leave that is taken by employees in which the department or city sponsors the time off (not taken out of the employee's leave bank). This usually concerns crew members having to be individually off for:

- Certification specific trainings (Paramedics, hazmat, TRT, etc. that do not apply to the whole company)
- Classification meetings (Firefighter, Engineer, Company Officer)
- To deliver a class or presentation inside or outside of the department
- To attend seminars, conferences, and/or workshops

A Company Officer has NO say in the city business granted to members by administration - they just have to manage around it.

Vacation: This is the most common type of leave taken. Vacation is typically an accrued leave. Scheduling or taking it is usually coordinated by a higher up leave managing authority. Taking vacation depends on several different factors, such as seniority, availability of open spots, and maintaining minimum staffing levels department wide, etc.

Again, a Company Officer has NO say in the vacation granted to members by administration, they just have to manage around it. Company Officers must be well aware of ALL the vacation time being taken by a crew member. All vacation taken should be documented into the company activity calendar and planned for before the occurrence happens.

I would like to cover one more item on the vacation leave topic before moving on: managing short term vacation time abuse. This all starts when a member of a 4-person crew needs a short period of time off (undocumented) to run a quick errand that takes less than 15 minutes. It all sounds normal and logical the first time they ask, so you grant it. Hopefully, there was a very legitimate reason for it and it only happens again on very rare occasions. But sometimes the same person will ask again a couple of weeks later for another short amount of time off, then in another couple of weeks there is some other reason for some time off, and so on. You now have a monster on your hands who thinks they can take time off at will and that their Company Officer is now their official leave manager.

To avoid creating a leave abuse monster, state to all members the FIRST TIME they ask for any time off, for any period of time: "I am not in charge of your vacation time. If you need time off, call the Chief and take the appropriate type of leave. Once approved, be safe while away from the station and please make sure you are back to work on time." Say this every time! If they really need the leave time off, they will go through the motions and proper channels to get it.

Emergency Vacation: This is usually taken for immediate family member emergencies, home or vehicle breakdowns, or weather that prevents a member from getting to work. This is another type of leave the Company Officer does not have much say in, but the Company Officer (and rest of the crew) should be quickly informed of these situations so they can provide any necessary help or support to the off-duty member and/or their family.

Sick leave: This is also an accrued leave. This is another type of leave a Company Officer has No say in, but they should be acutely aware of it. One long occurrence (usually for 3 or more shifts in a row) or a maximum number of occurrences per year (usually 5 or more) could require a doctor's note to ensure the leave is not abused. Typically, sick leave abuse is an indicator something else is going on in this person's life that is out of balance and this subject will be covered later on in the book.

Industrial (Workman's Comp) leave: This is the type of leave taken when an employee is injured in the line of duty or acquires an occupational illness that is work related. The Company Officer does not have any say with this type of leave, but as with emergency vacation, all of the Firefighter's fellow crew members will want to be informed of the circumstances and duration of the time off in order to provide whatever support they can to the missing member and/or their family.

AWR: As mentioned earlier, if a person knows they are going to need time off well in advance, they can arrange an off-shift counterpart (same rank or professional qualifications) to cover their time off. These hours must be paid back hour for hour with the person you are trading time with. Payroll usually has nothing to do with this hour for hour exchange, but most fire departments have an oversite system in which all AWRs should be documented in. Most departments have a maximum number of shifts that can be traded per year (usually about 12) and a designated time frame in which a person must pay back the hours or shifts (usually within 1 year).

In most systems, a Company Officer has a say in how an AWR is used. This is enforced by the Company Officer having to sign off on all AWR paperwork that is submitted. It did not happen very often, but here are a few reasons why I would not allow a member of my crew to use an AWR (the crew was aware of these reasons):

- It was during the same time when 1 or 2 other crew members were also going to be off.
- It was during a time period in which the unit was being critically evaluated (MCS or a major department drill).
- The crew member tried to have someone who was not qualified fill in for them

Bereavement leave: The thing that sucks most about planet Earth is that all people will die. Hopefully this happens after a long and full life, but sometimes it does not and it usually is not planned, so this type of leave can be used at any time. It usually consists of 2-3 shifts off in a row when one of a Firefighter's *immediate* family members passes away. Again, a Company Officer no say in this type of leave, but as with emergency vacation and industrial leave, all of the Firefighter's fellow crew members will want to be informed of the circumstances in order to provide whatever support they can.

Immediate family members include:

- Spouse
- Children
- Mother
- Father
- Grandparents
- Brother
- Sister
- Step - Mother, Father, Sibling, Grandparent, Children and/or Foster Children

Military leave: God bless these people. They deserve whatever time off they need to serve our great country (and also to recover from their service). These are exceptional people who are sacrificing a lot for their fellow Americans and all of our organizations should support them and their families in whatever ways we can.

Administrative leave: This type of leave can be used for many different reasons (such as family medical leave). This is another type of leave the Company Officer has no say in, but they are usually well informed on the status of one of their subordinates who is using this type of leave.

Mandatory Overtime: Mandatory overtime can be a requirement on some departments. If it is required, the rules and regulations will vary greatly from department to department.

For departments with 3-person staffing, at the morning shift change, NO position on the apparatus can be vacated until it is relieved of duty by a qualified member. If your relief is late (for a variety of reasons) you cannot vacate your position until your properly relieved. This equates to mandatory overtime (but look at the bright side, you get overtime!).

Kelley Days (Furloughs): A Kelly day is a designated day throughout a Firefighter's shift cycle that they would normally work but instead have off on a routine, rotating cycle. Typically, the days are bid on and taken on a seniority basis (the senior people get the Fridays, Saturdays, and Sundays).

Whenever possible, having the same person fill in for these predicable vacancies will go a long way in maintaining company continuity (described next).

Managing Long Term or Predictable Vacancies

Sometimes, a Company Officer can coordinate getting the same person to replace a member of the crew who will be on some type of a long-term vacancy (Kelly days, military, industrial, long term injury or illness, etc.). This helps build/keep continuity on the crew, and it is also good for the person replacing the member who will be off duty for a long period (they can leave all bedding and PPE in one place).

Cases where there is a different employee filling in every shift for a long-term missing member can be very frustrating. This is especially true when a lesser competent member is replacing a more competent member. I do not mean this in a bad way. It will be explained in much more detail in an upcoming chapter.

Whether it is a different member filling in every shift or one-member filling in the whole long-term vacancy, the Company Officer must start the first shift with the new member by communicating their expectations for the riding position they are filling in for. From there, the Company Officer will have to determine the needed level of supervision and necessary drills to get the new member up to company speed.

Background: I was always distressed when any of my full-time crew members were taking time off. We were on auto pilot. I did not have to say a word to my crew when delivering service because we had worked and drilled together for years. On top of all of this, a Ladder company has twice the tool array and MCS check offs than an Engine company. It was an absolute pain having someone fill in on the truck with a low Ladder company competence level.

Because my crew took time off, I was forced to develop a "new person on the rig" routine.

Minimum activities covered with all new personnel filling in on L-201 included:

- *Identifying riding position, PPE equipment, and storage areas*
- *Equipment the riding position is responsible for checking, operating, and maintaining*
- *Entire crew covers their role and functions to be performed on EMS and fire incidents (MCS stuff)*
- *Station areas the riding position is responsible for checking, cleaning, and maintaining*
- *Run-down on the company's activity calendar for the day*
- *Designated dorm bed and locker*
- *Chow and PT routine*
- *If one of the 2 Engineers were off, the other Engineer would always drive the truck, even if it was not their turn*

Unless I had worked with the new member before, myself or another crew member would closely supervise any new member of the crew until their competence level was evaluated and established. We could not train people with a low Ladder competence level to a high Ladder competence level in a shift or 2 (it takes literally months), but if time allowed, the first shift they worked on L-201 we would:

- *Have them set-up and operate all the power tools on the truck*
- *Have them deploy all ground ladders*
- *Have them go through the safety routine and operation of the aerial device*
- *The above activities would take about 60 to 90 minutes to complete. If the same person came back the next shift, we would to continue to expand on their role and responsibilities.*

To avoid having the continuity of the crew being broken up, whenever I knew a member of the crew was going to be off (based on the company activity calendar) I would call division the shift before and request a rover that had worked with us before, knew our routine, and was Ladder company competent.

Again, there is wide gap of staffing levels across the US due to all the different department types and configurations. This book has provided general scenarios for the major staffing routine used by most professional/paid fire departments, but a Company Officer must use and follow their AHJ's SOPs (and other agreements in place) whenever considering and managing local staffing and methods.

Chapter 9

Equipment and Facilities

The most important thing a department must maintain in order to deliver the best possible service is: **ALL** of the **PEOPLE** who work for the organization. It all starts with the people of the department and a great portion of this book will deal with this.

Service Delivery Equipment

Past the mental and physical wellness of the department's members, the most important equipment to care for are **the trucks and the service delivery equipment they contain**. Next comes the fire station and its associated parts, pieces, and infrastructures. BUT! The trucks and the equipment they are filled with come FIRST! These are the things we directly use to deliver service to our communities while keeping us safe. This equipment has to be ready to go and in proper working condition at all times.

Trucks and Allied Service Delivery Equipment

Every riding position on the company has a set of service delivery equipment assigned to it. What needs to be checked and who will check it will vary based on:

- ALS company versus a BLS company
- Engine versus a Ladder company
- 3 or 4-person company
- Any other co-staffed units to be checked-off in the station

The typical riding responsibilities include:

- Firefighters typically check all the EMS gear, hoses, nozzles, and any power tools.
- Engineers (driver/operator) typically check the engine, drivetrain, and fire pump.
- Company Officers are typically responsible for the accountability equipment, electronics, and possible EMS equipment if they are a PM.
- The Company Officer is also the person responsible for ensuring that all other members properly carry out their morning checks.

Getting into a Ready State at Shift Change

The reason why we do our morning checks is to get things in a ready state for the start of the shift. If everybody was perfect and did their job to perfection, we would not need to check anything because the last person would have done it correctly. People who actually believe this need to wake up because they are living in a dream world.

My crew quickly learned that complaining about the off-going shift was not going to get their jobs done any sooner and most of the time my response was the same: "fix it and quit worrying about A-Shift." Once the off-going shift left the station, all of the equipment/station problems belonged to B-Shift. A-Shift was far from perfect and B-Shift was not going to fix them (they all went home well before 8 AM). The only person who could fix A-Shift was the A-Shift L-201 Officer. Their boss was the A-Shift Battalion Chief at Battalion 201, not me. I quickly figured out that there was nothing I could do about A-Shift. The only things that I could manage were myself, my crew, and the 24-hours B-Shift oversaw.

I did not look upon a non-functioning piece of equipment after 8 AM very kindly or lightly. My crew knew this about me. Many times, my crew members would look at me with fear in their eyes when something was either missing, broken, or not working on a call after shift change. I did not like to look bad in front of my peers or the people who were paying our salaries (the citizens) because something did not work. Our jobs are to deliver service with a certain set of tools. Some of this service delivery takes place in a hazard zone that could kill us. We are not acting like professional Firefighters when the tools we use to do our jobs with do not work. Especially when they affect our safety!

The morning checks and getting your company in a ready state is one of the most important things that you will do the entire shift because it is so critical to your safety and performing your job at a high level. Managing this in the proper way will set you up for success for the entire shift and it will keep your crew safe. Get to work early and make sure it happens the same time and the same way every shift.

Managing Readiness Throughout the Rest of the Shift

A Ready State - *in a state of completion or preparedness, as for use or action.*

The primary goal when arriving to work needs to be getting into a "ready state." Once this has been achieved, it is the Company Officer's goal to maintain this ready state throughout the remainder of the shift.

The longer a person works throughout the shift, naturally the more tired or bored they will become. The more tired or bored a person becomes, the less their situational awareness and attention to detail is. When this happens, things get missed, overlooked, or just plain un-done. This is an example of the difference between public safety versus the rest of the working world. If waiters are too tired or they forget to refill the saltshakers at the end of their shift, no one will be injured or killed because of it. When a Firefighter runs out of air in a hazard zone because they did not change/refill their SCBA bottle since "they did not use that much on the last call" the consequences are much more serious.

Company Officer Expectation #3 - Someone who will keep their entire crew's focus on delivering excellent customer service throughout the shift. The Company Officer is the person responsible for making readiness the company's focus throughout the entire shift, not just in the mornings. Here are just a few readiness guidelines to follow and enforce throughout the shift:

- When a piece of service delivery equipment is not in a ready state, place it in a ready state as soon as possible.

- If a piece of service delivery equipment is broken or not working properly, replace it and/or repair it as soon as possible.
- If any equipment is used during the course of the shift, place that equipment back into a ready state as soon as possible after using it.
- Always keep your booster tank and SCBA bottles 100% full.
- If any EMS supplies are used during the course of the shift, clean and/or replace those supplies as soon as possible after using them (your next patient will appreciate it).
- After preparing and eating a meal (or snacks), place the kitchen and the other associated areas of the station back into a ready state as soon as possible.
- Clean up after yourself whenever using any facility in the fire station.

Facilities and Grounds

After the trucks and service delivery equipment are checked out and ready to go, the work should then shift to the maintenance of the fire station and the property it sits on. I think we are all born janitors and the last thing you need from this book is proper station cleaning techniques. We all know what needs to get done around the station.

"Days" of the Week

The official set of things a Company Officer has to manage concerning equipment and facilities is usually based around certain "days" of the week. Most departments use certain "days" of the week to identify specific activities that occur on a consistent basis that address maintaining and inventorying the different elements of our equipment or facilities.

During these "days," extra time and care is taken to clean, inventory, and sometimes inspect these specific areas/items. The "days" are always the same during a week, so they rotate equally among all 3 shifts. On the workweek "days," a Company Officer will usually provide official reports, data entry, and/or inventories to the proper divisions in charge of each specific area. Where these official reports and RMS data entries are directed to will vary from department to department.

The shift schedule made it so that the "days" are evenly distributed between all of the shifts. In my department, you worked 7 days out of 21 (1 on and 2 off). This meant that over a 3-week period, B-Shift worked each, separate 7 days of a week.

Managing the "days" is a perfect chance for a Company Officer to lead by example. I understand that there may be many administrative duties that an Officer has to do associated with each of the days but helping your crew with station and apparatus duties in some fashion shows that a Company Officer is getting their hands dirty (leading my example) and that they care about that certain "day" and their crew.

The Most Common Official "Days"

Station Day – This is the day the grass gets mowed, the fridges and cabinets are cleaned out, the bathrooms are scrubbed with stronger cleaning agents, the corners are all vacuumed, and everything gets dusted. Some systems have the Battalion Chief come to the station to "inspect" its condition and cleanliness. Documenting the condition of the station and putting in maintenance request orders are some of the administrative duties that are associated with station day.

Apparatus and Allied Equipment Day – This is the day that all compartments are emptied, all the equipment is cleaned with a fine-tooth comb, and everything is inventoried. The trucks themselves are also cleaned from top to bottom, along with performing all scheduled maintenance. Apparatus Day comes with a lot of paperwork. Apparatus day could also include a monthly inspection from a higher up response or Logistic Chief.

Supply Day – This is they day when everything (minus the trucks and their allied equipment) associated with the stations and grounds gets inventoried. This stuff mostly supports living in and maintaining a fire station. Every department is different, but Station 201 would get a supply delivery every 3 weeks (delivered on Supply Day) when both the order requested and the order sent would be compared and validated. Lots of paperwork comes with this day.

Conclusion

I know the "days" are always a pain, but they need to be taken seriously because they are the processes a department uses to ensure that all of our equipment and their associated facilities are maintained and are functioning at their peak proficiency - just what the taxpayers are paying for.

Chapter 10

Physical Fitness

"Firefighters are basically professional athletes that don't get any warmup." – Alan Brunacini

Because a Firefighter's level of fitness will impact their ability to do the job, I really do not want to candy coat this section. Firefighters who are out in the field delivering service must be in good physical condition. To me, there are no excuses not to be in good physical condition if you are a Professional Firefighter – it is your JOB! If a Firefighter has a medical issue/reason that prevents them from being in the physical condition required to perform the different activities of their job, they should not be delivering service in the field until that medical condition is resolved and they are back to the physical condition required to deliver emergency service.

The activities involved in firefighting are very physically demanding and also create a huge amount of stress on the human body. The only way to perform these activities while combating the stresses inflicted on the body is by being in good physical condition by typically undergoing regular periods of exercise. Therefore, it is the Company Officer's responsibility to create a fitness culture in the fire station. To intentionally sound like a broken record, let's start this section out with the book's cliché phase: "Lead by Example."

It is hard to create a fitness culture if you are clinically obese. It is also hard to tell everybody else to work out unless you are working out, as well. It becomes very difficult to manage everybody getting their annual physical when you refuse to get one yourself. I would like to end my very legitimate judgements on out of shape Professional Firefighters with one other judgement - the most important one: the "public we serve" judgement. They do not have much confidence when the 911 help that shows up is visibly out of shape.

Job Performance Requirements (JPRs)

A JPR is the combination of an expected activity, the description of the tools, equipment and materials required to perform and complete the activity, and the details of the performance measures required for the activity (checkoffs) with the successful completion of an identified outcome.

As agreed upon by the NFPA (NFPA 1582 & 1583 – thanks Dad!) and the IAFF (Wellness and Fitness Initiative), a JPR that all Firefighters need to meet is to possess and retain the following fitness level:

- Body Composition (body fat%) - men: less than 20% and women: less than 30%
- Aerobic Capacity – minimum of 42 mL
- Muscular strength and endurance to perform a set number of firefighting tasks under a certain time frame - CPAT
- Flexibility – measured in many ways

The best way for a Company Officer to evaluate this level of fitness is through the performance of the actual, physical, job-related activities that can occur at the typical fire scene, such as stretching hose, raising ladders, pulling ceiling, etc.

Most Company Officers are not doctors, kinesiologists, physical trainers, personal trainers, dietitians, etc., but they must sort through a number of these issues to maintain a minimum fitness level on their crew. Again, this all starts out with the Officer being in good physical condition and setting the example of working out. It all starts with YOU!

Managing Crew Members' Fitness

To manage members' fitness, a Company Officer will have to consider the following:

1. Department support and resources available
2. Different levels of fitness
3. Different age groups
4. Different workout program preferences
5. Different workout time preferences
6. Members who work out on their days off and do not want/need to work out at work
7. Preventing over exercising
8. Fitness activities in house versus out of house
9. The competitive nature of Firefighters playing a team sport (the higher the competition level, the higher the chance of sustaining an injury)

1. Department Support and Resources Available

The amount of complications that a Company Officer will have to manage with physical fitness will be based on the overall commitment to physical fitness of the fire department they work for. A Company Officer will have to manage PT around the resources available to them inside their own department. This could include:

- Doctors available
- Annual physicals
- Rehab staff and facilities
- Physical fitness equipment available in the station
- Peer fitness program
- Whether PT time is mandated during the shift by the department
- Local facilities available (first due area) (e.g., gyms, parks, courts)
- Whether there are annual minimum fitness standards and evaluations required

CPAT does not allow its use for annual requirements of incumbent personnel. Some departments have developed a similar type of annual job-based requirement and numerous fire departments are moving to FMS to determine fitness level and the employee's propensity to injuries.

All of these resources will greatly assist a Company Officer in helping to maintain their crew's fitness level, while not having to "go at it alone."

One of the best items on the resource list that will help a Company Officer in managing their members' fitness is having Physical Fitness equipment available at the fire station. This does several things for the Company Officer:

- It sends a message from the top of the department down that they care about their members' fitness.
- It gives members who are out of shape NO EXCUSE NOT TO WORKOUT!
- It provides an onsite gym that is located right next to the 911 response vehicles. This facilitates the most rapid response times while performing PT.
- Most fire station gyms provide enough equipment to accommodate several different workout routines.

Peer fitness trainers are also a tremendous resource for a fire company. These people are actual Firefighters who have been trained and certified as personal trainers with the single focus of the physical requirements and ergonomics of performing the routine tasks of firefighting. They do a great job of customizing individual and company workouts that specifically help members perform their jobs better and safer based on their fitness level, body type, and scar tissue limitations.

Hopefully, all of your crew members are in good shape and because of your example, they do not require much motivation to perform PT on a regular basis. If this is your situation, you probably will not have to dig too deeply into the department resource bag to help manage physical fitness. In this case, probably the biggest things to facilitate are ensuring that everyone is getting their annual physicals and limiting PT activities that overexert or have a high possibility of causing injuries. Past this, it is a piece of cake (no pun intended).

If you have a member of your company who is headed in the wrong direction of not being able to perform their job physically (bottom tier fitness level – covered next) you are probably going to need to access most of the health and fitness resources available on your department. I really hope that every professional fire department has a standard set of resources that are available so that Company Officers do not have to "go at it alone" when dealing with an unmotivated, out of shape member. There will be much more on managing "Fit for Duty" later on in this book.

2. Different Levels of Fitness

Every member of the crew will have a different fitness level. The key element to manage here is ensuring that everyone on the crew has the minimum level of fitness required to perform their jobs safely. The Phoenix Fire Department used a tiered system to classify a Firefighter's overall physical fitness level. Here is a very basic rundown of the classification system:

- Tier 1 – Low body fat (below 10%) – higher than normal aerobic capacity – superhuman. People in this category were mostly younger than 30 years old and you could see their abs.
- Tier 2 - Medium body fat (around 15%) – high to average aerobic capacity – a normal human in good shape – This was mostly everyone over 30 years old on the job.

- Tier 3 - High body fat (20%+) – low aerobic capacity – the absolute minimum physical condition that a member can be in and still operate in the field. Members in this category must be making progress to get back to being in at least the Tier 2 category.
- Tier 4 – A member's physical condition does not allow them to be a Firefighter in the field. This can be due to a medical issue/condition or from being grossly out of shape.

There was much more that went into the tier system. It was all managed by doctors. It included blood tests, strength tests, endurance tests, EKGs, full medical exams, past exposures, etc. The big things to take away here are:

- If everybody is in the same, similar condition, the entire group can participate in the same activities.
- If there is a mix of Tier 1s and 2s, each group might want to do their own thing.
- If there is a Tier 3 member on the company, the Officer will probably have to modify the PT routine in order to help the member get back to a Tier 2 status, while causing the least amount of stress and embarrassment as possible.

3. Different age groups

"Firefighting is a young person's job." – 30-year veteran Firefighter

Generally, younger people are naturally in better shape than older people. Younger people should also have much less scar tissue inside their bodies and have most of their body parts working near 100% capacity. Older, middle aged Firefighters who have had active firefighting careers will naturally have some nicks, deep scratches, big bruises, strains, sprains, and tears, along with the possibility of having one or more of their body parts being surgically repaired that resulted from an on-the-job injury. From my own experiences, once something has been surgically repaired, it is never 100% again.

Having said this, it is easier to manage fitness activities when everybody is in the same age and condition range. During my career, it seemed like station and crew age levels were divided up into quarters:

25% – Young Firefighters in their early 30's or younger (E-201 & A-201 crews)
25% – Middle age Firefighters from mid-30's to mid-40's (L-201 crew)
25% – Firefighters are all over their mid-40's (you know the stations I am talking about)
25% - Mix of all age ranges

If everybody is in the same age range on the company, having everyone agree to participate in group physical activities will be much easier to manage (a bunch of 20-year-olds would love to go out and play with free weights, while a bunch of 40-year-olds would prefer to walk on the treadmill).

Some basic observations on the different age group PT routines:

- Younger Firefighters will experiment with more PT activities trying to figure out what workout type and routine is the best for them.

- Younger Firefighters tend to use more weight resistance and higher impact PT routines.
- Younger Firefighters will be more physically active in competitive PT activities (they also have a higher injury rate performing competitive PT activities).
- Middle aged Firefighters will choose between one of the groups – they will either try to keep up with the younger Firefighters or they will side with the older Firefighters.
- Older Firefighters tend to gravitate to lower-impact PT activities, while avoiding high impact and high aerobic PT activities.

4. Different Workout Program Preferences

There are literally thousands of different workout and fitness programs that a person can perform. Some people even change the program they do every day to always be "shocking" their bodies with something new and different (insane!).

Again, most Company Officers are not personal trainers and most people will choose their own workout routine. The important thing is that everybody works out and does something. It is always great when everyone on the company works out in some form or another during the shift without much needed motivation. It is even better when the whole company can perform a PT routine together as a crew. This helps build comradery and crew unity.

Background: Early in my career (1980's,) there was not much science involved in working out. Much of the stuff out there was from the individual workouts of bodybuilders (Arnold!), so it involved a lot of free weightlifting with not much stretching or cardio. This individual centered workout craze took me into my mid 30's. This workout routine is also one of the reasons there is scar tissue in my body.

In the mid 90's, when the scar tissue was starting build up and I was also having some on the job skeletal injuries (knees, neck, shoulder, upper back, etc.), I was introduced to the modernized physical fitness world. In this world, the people who were fixing and rehabbing my injuries had actual college degrees and certifications in their profession and they radically changed the way I worked out. I went from high impact and free weights to a low impact and core-based fitness routine. Core, core, core!

In the middle of all of this, I was the Company Officer on L-201 and everyone on my company was older than I was. The range was 5 to 15 years older. Everyone had about the same amount of scare tissue in their bodies as I had (if not more). Despite this, we were all active and in good physical condition.

The first 3 or 4 years of being the Company Officer of L-201, everybody pretty much did their own workout routine at the station or while off duty. After a few of my own injuries and the rehab that was facilitated by highly qualified people, I consulted with one of the Peer Fitness Trainers on the department. He came out to the station and designed a core fitness workout routine for the entire L-201 crew that involved:

- *We would perform the routine after morning checkoffs, fellowship, and getting the station cleaned up (around 9 AM).*
- *We had 5 people on L-201, so there were 4 core exercise stations with a 5th station as a rest area.*
- *A 5-station example: 1) push-ups 2) side bends 3) planks 4) jumping rope, and the 5th station was for a rest period while the other 4 members completed their station.*
- *Each station would last 45 seconds with 15 seconds to switch stations and start the next activity.*
- *We would rotate 3 times through all 5 stations.*

- *When we first started, it would take 15 minutes to get through the whole routine.*
- *After finishing, we would go out drilling or shopping for chow.*
- *Each month the Peer Fitness Trainer would come to the station, change the core activities on all of the workout stations, and then work with all of us going through the new routine for the first time on the proper form to use for all of the stations.*
- *We would feed him breakfast burritos and he would come out again every month to change up the routine for the next 4 to 5 years that I was on L-201.*

Station 201 had an Engine, Ladder, and Ambulance company with a total of 11 people working at the station. As referred to previously, by setting the example of having a professional resource of the department come out to the station to set up an "old" person core training routine, all 11 members at Station 201 started participating in the routine within the first month of it starting.

With the whole station now doing it, we would switch off month to month between having 2 sets of identical stations, to 1 long set of 10 stations with 1 rest period station. Because we were all getting, or already into, the middle fitness bracket at the station (Tier 2,) the new workout routine motivated everybody to eat heathier and make healthier choices on our days off. Over the course of the next 4 to 5 years, we all lost weight and got into and maintained a better physical condition the rest of the time I was at Station 201.

Let me end this background by saying that if there was a morning 911 response or something scheduled in the morning that interrupted or cancelled the morning core fitness routine, the entire station would complain about missing it. It became so popular that even if a morning activity made us miss the routine, we would often do it later in the shift. The station was so committed to it that sometimes we would even do it after dinner (all 11 of us).

5. Different Workout Time Preferences

Again, the important thing here is that most of us do some type of a PT routine during the shift. The time it takes place really does not matter (mostly) as long as the person is actually working out. The biggest thing to manage here is preventing somebody from performing a PT activity that will disturb somebody else who is sleeping. It is fine if a member prefers to run on the treadmill at a high-speed during afternoon nap time, but do not let them do this if it is going to shake the dormitory (or the Company Officer's office).

Some fire departments actually designate a set time period during the day for a company to perform PT (usually in the morning). This is a very good thing and it demonstrates a department's commitment to their members' health and fitness. While managing this, you might have a person on your crew who fits into the next bullet point. If this is case, I would not worry too much about that person, especially if they are keeping busy and being productive while everybody else is working out.

6. Members Who Work Out on Their Days Off and Do Not Want/Need to Work Out at Work

At almost every fire station I worked at, there was someone who would do all of their PT on their days off and they had no set routine to perform while at work (they were usually in great condition).

Keys to managing this situation are:

- If the person is in good shape, my hat is off to them and leave them alone.
- If the person is in good shape, it would be nice if they would still participate in group PT activities (most of the time they have no problem doing this and they even look forward to it).
- If the person is in bad shape, call them out and tell them to get moving.

If the Company Officer is this person, you still must work out and/or facilitate company group PT activities. You do not get the luxury of taking the shift off. Sometimes, it is a pain being in charge and setting positive examples.

7. Preventing Over Exercising

Company Officers must not allow themselves or their crew members to overexert themselves during PT activities either before the start of a shift, as well as throughout the shift. All members of the company must have enough "gas in the tank" to make it through at least two work cycles (2 SCBA cylinders) during the course of a shift. This equates to performing PT while on duty in the following manner:

- Keeping your heart rate below 75% of its maximum as much as possible throughout the activity
- Limiting the time of the activity to 30 to 45 minutes
- Performing regular periods of rest and re-hydration while performing the activity

8. Local Facilities Available (First Due Area) (e.g., Gyms, Parks, Courts)

Let me start out #8 by stating that anytime PT can be facilitated at the station, IT SHOULD BE. Doing PT on the station grounds puts the company in the best position to respond to 911 calls for service.

Having said this, I agree with performing team building, low risk PT activities that involve the entire crew and that these activities may occur at a location outside of the fire station. While I highly encourage these team building activities, the following guidelines should be followed when performing PT outside of the fire station:

- Never go outside (or far from the center of) your first due area to perform PT or any other in-service activity whenever possible.
- Never place any member of the crew where they are over 60 to 80 seconds from getting into the proper response gear, onto the truck, and into a belted position for a 911 response. If everyone is awake in a fire station (and close to the trucks), this set of actions should take about 30 seconds. This gives you an extra 30 seconds when performing a PT activity away from the station and crew members are much further away from the apparatus.
- A person can quickly walk about 100 yards in about 30 seconds.

- This should equate to a rule of thumb of always trying to perform any in-service activity where your response vehicle is no more than 100 yards away from the furthest member of the company.
- When the truck is parked and before performing any activity away from the truck, set up both EMS and fire PPE outside your riding position (just like back at the fire station) to facilitate a quick 911 response (being in the proper PPE and belted in before the response).

9. The Competitive Nature of Firefighters Playing a Team Sport (the Higher the Competition Level, the Higher the Chance of Sustaining an Injury)

One quote on this subject will provide a lot of insight. It was from a person who managed over 2,000 type-A, competitive, Professional Firefighters for over 40 years.

"If you want to produce a Firefighter injury, give a group of Firefighters a ball of any type and they'll figure out a way of hurting themselves playing with it." - Alan Brunacini

Company Officer Expectation #5 provides that a Company Officer is "someone who acts as the overall safety manager of their crew that will not hesitate to stop unsafe or dumb acts." One of the best ways to manage this expectation is to not create the very conditions where it could possibly happen. Having said this, ALL sports with high potential for injury while on duty should be AVOIDED. This includes:

- Any competitive sport where Firefighters have to aggressively compete against each other
- Any high impact sport or activity (cross-fit training using non-job related very heavy objects like a large tractor tire)
- Any sport or activity that involves using a stick/bat
- Any sport or activity that involves a device using wheels or is motorized
- Any sport or activity performed within 100 feet of something fragile (if it can be broken, it will be broken)
- Any sport or activity that will embarrass a crew member who cannot play it (for a lot of different reasons)
- Any other sport or activity a Company Officer deems to be unsafe for the crew

Closing

To end, I want to note that I did not like forcing a subordinate that was not in good shape to workout. However, I knew that one of the greatest pieces of workout equipment was a fire truck, so instead of forcing a person to work out, I would force my entire crew to go drill (described in the next chapter), which is the best form of exercise there is! Use it to your best advantage.

Chapter 11

Company Drilling

Managing readiness establishes the Company Officer as the person who is "In-Charge" of the company. It is a coach's job to get the team ready to play the next game. Coaching the team establishes the coach as the person who is in charge of the team. If the star linebacker or point guard is the person who drives the practices (the team's readiness), then they are the ones who are basically in charge of the team (the informal leaders) - not the coach. Getting the team ready and calling the next play at the game puts the coach in charge of the team - not the players.

Most Firefighters (the "players") want to perform at a high level and make their bosses happy. Managing readiness goes a long way in providing your crew members with the opportunities to do just that. There is no magic fairy dust that is sprinkled on us to make us ready at all times to perform at 100% competency. It ALL starts with the hard work that must be put in **PRIOR** to the call.

There is NO activity that does more for making the Company Officer "In-Charge" of the company than company drilling. It is THE most important activity that needs to take place on the company level. This not only puts the Company Officer in charge of the company, but it is also the most effective way for a Company Officer to ensure the overall safety, wellness, and performance of their crew.

Background: At Station 201, we were constantly drilling to meet our department's MCS. We would perform the standard evolutions we delivered in the field five times more often in the drill setting than we would perform them in real life. This provided Station 201 personnel with unlimited opportunities to impress their bosses and co-workers with their skill sets and abilities. As the Company Officer, sometimes my crew would be resistant to get out and train when it was announced first thing in the morning. However, as we got started, they would always fall into the groove and start to enjoy it (proven by all the high 5's given), while also letting the endorphins flow. I would call it training therapy. Never let the crews initial attitude deter the Company Officer from getting out there to train. There is no fairy dust! Just plain old hard work - all directed by the Company Officer.

Company drilling addresses the Company Officer's job description for 3 out of the 8 expectations. This includes:

#5. Someone who acts as the overall safety manager of their crew that will not hesitate to stop unsafe or dumb acts
#6. The overall training officer of their crew
#7. Someone who keeps their entire crew's focus on delivering excellent customer service throughout the shift

When it comes to performing any high risk activities that could cause serious injury and/or death, drilling and Firefighter safety are synonymous. You cannot have one without the other. The best way for a Company Officer to protect their crew working in a high risk environment is by focusing company drills on the high risk, low frequency tasks that we perform. This set of tasks must be drilled on to the point where they can be performed by your crew on the "auto-pilot" mode.

Managing Company Drilling

A Company Officer will have to consider the following when managing company drilling:

1. Minimum Company Starts (MCS)
2. Crew competence level
3. Prioritizing your drilling
4. Training in context
5. Scheduling drills
6. In service versus out of service drills
7. In station versus out of station drills
8. Battalion/department wide training
9. Certification maintenance
10. Documentation of training

1. Minimum Company Standards (MCS)

MCS represent a standard set of tasks and evolutions that a fire department uses on a routine basis to control working fires. All these tasks come with a complete set of JPRs and they are usually institutionalized at the state level because they are tied to a Firefighter 1 & 2 certification.

These tasks are originally taught in the recruit academy and all recruits must pass them in order to graduate. Companies are evaluated in performing these same tasks on a quarterly and annual basis out in the field. There are usually about 15 individual tasks or evolutions that are evaluated in the following areas:

- OSHA confined space (SCBA skill sets – search and rescue)
- Offensive hose stretches
- Defensive hose stretches
- Master stream set-up
- Ground ladders
- Power and hydraulic tool set-up and operation
- Overhaul and salvage

Most drilling done in the field should be structured and performed around successfully completing all MCS evaluations, especially the high-risk activities that involve offensive water application and the use of an SCBA.

2. Crew Competence Level

Unlike most other professions, Firefighters routinely engage in service delivery activities in which they must make critical decisions under extremely hazardous and dynamic conditions that are fast paced and rapidly evolving. These conditions cause a high amount of stress for the decision makers. When people are under a high amount of stress while making decisions, the human brain will go into a survival decision making and action mode. There is a lot of science and studies that have been performed over the past 50 years that document all the chemicals, hormones, and the brain activity of people who are making decisions under a high amount of stress. All of it really boils down to this: under extreme stress, people will make decisions and base their actions on their lowest level of competent training and/or based on similar experiences.

There is a famous saying that sums all of this up: **"Under stress, you will not rise up to your highest expectations, you will fall down to the lowest, best level of your training."** As a Company Officer, you want the lowest, best level of training for your crew to be pretty damn high.

Because a person's level of competence is directly connected to their level of **SAFETY**, a Company Officer must evaluate the competence level of all of their crew members performing MCS (high risk, high stress tasks) and then take the necessary steps to either maintain or increase their crew members' competency in these areas to the highest level possible.

The Four Levels of Competence (0-1-2-3)

Mastery of a skill or a subject can be measured within 4 different levels of competency. **The 4 levels of competency also correlate to the level of risk and responsibility a person should be exposed to and be able to manage in an organization.**

Level 0 - This is the lowest level of competence. At this level, people are entering into a class, subject, or a profession they know little about and this is where they start to study the new information about the subject and everything that goes with it. These people are best described as ignorant (but not oblivious), as they have very little cognitive or practical knowledge about the subject. This level of competence describes people who are in a training academy trying to become Firefighter 1 & 2's.

The people at this competence level should be exposed to minimal hazards while being highly supervised by competent instructors. This group should be given **NO** responsibility or exposure to "real life" hazards outside of a highly controlled and supervised academy-like setting.

Level 1 - Study and frequent hands on application in a drill/testing setting brings a person to the next level of competency - the level of theoretical knowledge. This group understand the concepts, but to apply them, they must continue to think critically about them while they are performing the related tasks. These people have had very few repetitions in the real life setting on the subject's skill sets. These people are best described as "Green."

People in this competence category represent a group of recruits who are just finishing their entry level firefighting training (the academy) and are entering the field. This group should be given **VERY LITTLE** responsibility dealing with "real life" hazards, while being closely supervised during real-life high risk activities until their competence increases to the next level.

Level 2 - When people can do a critical activity/task without thinking about it, they have made it to Level 2. At this level, theoretical knowledge is transformed into practical, applied knowledge. Study, demonstrations, and walk throughs might get you to Level 1, but only a lot of practice (drilling), real-life experience, and application will get you to Level 2. This level cannot be achieved in a training academy setting alone - you need real life experiences.

I would call people in this competence category Senior Firefighters on "auto-pilot" mode. This group of people can be given **A LOT** of responsibility when dealing with real life hazards. This group of people can also be given supervisor responsibilities of directly overseeing Level 0 and Level 1 people while performing tasks in a hazard zone.

Level 3 - The highest level of competence is the ability to do something without thinking about it while retaining a high level of awareness of how the activity is performed and how it fits into solving the overall problem. This level of competence describes a person who knows the "How's" and the "Why's" of the activity. This level of understanding also enables a person to teach the skill to someone else.

The group of people who are at this level of competency have **ALL** the responsibility for conducting safe operations in hazardous situations. This group is who I would call the supervisors, managers, and leaders of the organization.

A Company Officer must be at Competency Level 3 for most of the activities and/or skill sets that will be performed in the field on the company level. When a Company Officer is at a Level 3 for most activities, it puts them in the best position to have the most personal authority within the crew and it also goes a long way in making them the "coach" of the team.

Coupled with this, a Company Officer's major goal needs to be getting any permanently assigned member of their crew trained to no less than a Level 2 on the competency scale. As discovered and researched by highly intelligent people, the only way to do this is with constant repetition of the critical tasks required to keep us safe and effective. In the fire service, we call this drilling.

Managing Qualifications and Competencies beyond MCS

Company Officers must also assess what other applicable skill sets each member of the crew possesses outside the MCS competencies for their current riding position. This includes knowledge, expertise, and/or experience in the following fields/trades:

- Any fire department certification beyond a crew member's current riding position including Hazmat Technician, TRT member, USAR member, Arson/Fire Investigator, being certified in the riding positions above their current rank (Engineer and/or Company Officer), etc.
- Construction fields including framers, masons, electricians, plumbers, dry-wallers, roofers, etc.
- Mechanical fields including small motors, large motors, diesel motors, drive trains, pumping equipment, hydraulic equipment, operation of heavy machinery, etc.

- Medical fields involving medical certification above their current riding position, including being a PM, Registered Nurse, Nurse Practitioner, Physician's Assistant, Respiratory Therapist, Physical Trainer, etc.

Company Officers must have the self-confidence and emotional intelligence to know that they do not know everything, along with the need of using and deferring to the different talents and capability levels of their crew members whenever the situation requires them to do so. When managing in this fashion, a Company Officer is NOT giving away any of their authority or responsibility for the incident, but rather they are enhancing their overall authority and position on the company by having the right person for the situation be front and center for directing the completion of the activity. Always use your crew's talents to the company's best advantage!

3. Prioritizing Your Training

Naturally, the majority of company drilling time should be focused on the high risk activities we respond to on a shift-to-shift basis. However, there is only so much training time available during a 24-hour shift. Some shifts will offer very little, if any, training opportunities due to the unscheduled service delivery events that occur throughout a shift (911 service calls). However, every day should be taken advantage of as a training day whenever there is time available to master the proficiencies of our high risk jobs.

ISO requires all professional/paid fire department members to perform 2 hours of training per shift. While this may seem excessive, it can be performed in many different ways. This includes:

- Any formal training scheduled by your department
- Any classroom training
- Hands on drilling
- Tabletop exercises
- Simulation based training
- Any riding position specific training
- All activities performed in a clinical setting
- Etc.

Short training sessions that last only 15-20 minutes (throwing ladders, stretching just 1 handline, setting up set of extrication tools, breaking down power tools, donning PPE, etc.) add value to every shift and over time they add up to a lot of hands on training experience.

Background: Right after completing the Company Officer promotional testing process, but before getting promoted, my father introduced me to one of the best Risk Managers in public safety: Gordon Graham. Other than my Dad, Gordon Graham has had the greatest impact on my professional career. He, like my father, is an incredibly smart person with immense street credit.

During our first meeting, Gordon explained to me that the best way to protect my crew was by performing all training in context, associated with the least frequent, highest risk tasks or activities that we perform. In other words, focus training on high risk, low frequency events while keeping the training as "real" as possible.

What will follow is a graphic that Gordon Graham uses to illustrate where high risk occupational training needs to be focused (I will not be doing Gordon Graham's in person, Elmo graphics justice). Before looking at his toned-downed artwork, here is a description of the different terms he uses in the upcoming graphic:

The Level of Risk Associated with an Event, Activity, or Task

The graphic starts by dividing the activities that a fire company could possibly perform during the course of a shift into two basic categories:

- Low Risk Events, Activities or Tasks
- High Risk Events, Activities or Tasks

I would consider low risk activities as being able to hurt someone a little, but everyone involved will eventually recover. I would consider high risk activities as being able to severely injure or kill someone involved in the activity to the point where someone might not recover from the event. This could be either physically, emotionally, or professionally (job status).

The Frequency of an Event, Activity, or Task

The next set of definitions for the graphic examines how frequently these activities are performed. They also create two basic categories:

- Low Frequency Events = LF
- High Frequency Events = HF

When performing anything very few times (low frequency) humans naturally will not be as good at the activity as when compared to performing activities that occur with a higher frequency. Even if the higher frequency activities/tasks/events are more difficult and/or complex to perform than the ones that are done less frequently.

The Decision-Making Time Associated with an Event, Activity, or Task

The last set of definitions in the graphic look at the amount of decision-making time the people performing these activities usually have. This amount of time is defined as:

- Discretionary Decision-Making Time = DDMT
- Non-Discretionary Decision-Making Time = NDMT

Discretionary Decision-Making Time (DDMT) equates to having an extended amount of time to decide on what to do for a particular situation, before actually having to do it or act.

Non-Discretionary Decision-Making Time (NDMT) equates to the person having very little time to make a decision when presented with a particular situation.

Gordon Graham's Training Focus Graphic

Now that you have the vocabulary for Gordon's graphic, let's look at each category highlighted inside the graphic and how it correlates to the training time and focus a Company Officer should devote to each particular category. It rates each of the categories on a color-coded scale of how a Company Officer's training time should be devoted to it:

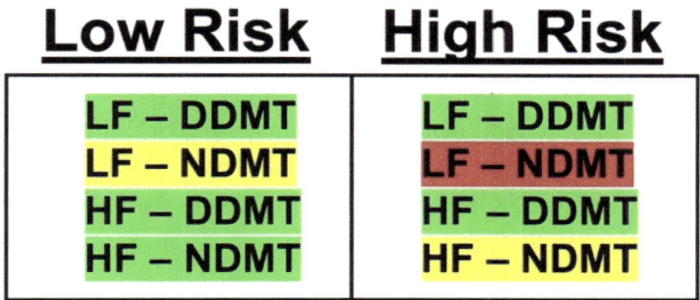

Each color represents the amount of training time that should be devoted to the activity:

- **Over 50% of your training time should be devoted to these activities**
- **About 25% of your training time should be devoted to these activities**
- **The rest of your training time should be devoted to these activities**

Training Time Devoted to Low Risk Events, Activities, or Tasks

LF – DDMT – Low Risk - Low Frequency Events with Discretionary Decision-Making Time. Because you have a lot of time to think about something that does not present much risk, do not waste much company training time on these activities. These situations include:

- Employee gradings
- Public events (station tours, ride alongs, appearances)
- Performing quarterly/annual inspections (hydrant, hose, PPE, etc.)

LF – NDMT – Low Risk - Low Frequency Events with Non-Discretionary Decision-Making Time. Even though this is a low risk event category, it gets a yellow highlight because these tasks or activities are not done very often, coupled with little or no discretionary decision-making time. All yellow highlighted categories should get about 25% of your training time devoted to them. These situations include:

- Dealing with upset customers outside of an emergency setting
- Minor issues with crew members that must be addressed immediately

HF – DDMT – Low Risk - High Frequency Events with Discretionary Decision-Making Time. Because you have both a lot of time to think about something that does not present much risk and you perform these activities on a high frequency, it puts this in the green category for a company's training time. Again, do not waste much training time on these activities. This category is the very lowest ranking on the training time scale. These situations include:

- Checking your equipment
- Attending classroom training
- Structuring your company's daily activities
- Responding to most administrative duties

HF – NDMT – Low Risk - High Frequency Events with Non-Discretionary Decision-Making Time. These tasks/events represent what we should really excel at as an organization. All low risk events that happen frequently with not much decision-making time should have a formal safety response (SOPs) developed for the situations we routinely deal with. Because we respond to these types of events so often, very little company training time should be devoted to these activities. These situations include:

- EMS service delivery on non-critical patients (75% of the EMS calls)
- Driving with no lights or sirens

Training Time Devoted to High Risk Events, Activities, or Tasks

LF – DDMT – High Risk - Low Frequency Events with Discretionary Decision-Making Time. Because you have a lot of time to think about something before making a decision, it puts this category very low on the training time scale. Again, do not use up much training time on activities that give you plenty of discretionary decision-making time. These situations include:

- Most personnel problems (once they are stabilized)
- Most hazmat incidents

Most of the risk in this category does not involve managing service delivery or readiness. Instead, the risk is related to dealing with and managing personnel problems or people issues, in which the Officer has plenty of time to consider their options prior to directly addressing the problem or issue. Company Officers should be trained in HRM in order to equip themselves with the tools, procedures, and confidence to properly address these types of issues. This type of training should take place outside of the company training setting and should occur prior to putting Officers into these positions. There will be much more on this in a later section of this book.

Another event that occurs often in this category are most Hazmat incidents, in which we initially take a defensive posture. This allows responders the discretionary decision-making time needed to reference the "manuals" that refer to the thousands of chemicals that we could possibly deal with prior to taking any action to mitigate. Hazmat calls are usually long and boring for a good reason: responder safety.

LF – NDMT – High Risk - Low Frequency Events with Non-Discretionary Decision-Making Time. These types of events require the Company Officer (and the rest of the crew) to make split second decisions for a set of activities that do not occur frequently and they could possibly injure or kill a civilian, a Firefighter, or a fire department organization. Because this category is a public safety killer, it should be where a Company Officer and the rest of the department spends the majority of their training time. These situations include:

- Issues involving immediate safety concerns
- Serious personnel issues that must be addressed immediately
- Any work performed in an IDLH atmosphere requiring the use of an SCBA - MCS
- Operating any piece of equipment used on an infrequent basis that can harm or kill the user or another person in their general vicinity
- EMS incidents that involve trapped patients that require extrication equipment
- Any incident involving violence

Another major benefit of devoting the majority of your company training time to this risk category is that it will produce excellence at all other levels of service delivery. Most people who are good at performing the difficult, quick thinking stuff are just as good at performing the easy stuff. As this type of training touches everything else we do in terms of making us competent, these activities should utilize the most training time.

These events/activities require the Officer to be trained to Level 3 on the competency scale. This not only allows for the Officer to deal with these situations as they occur in real life while keeping their crew safe, but also to use their competence to help train the rest of their crew to no less than Level 2 on the competency scale for these high risk activities.

A Company Officer must be prepared at all times to stop unsafe and dumb acts. High risk, low frequency events with little to no decision-making time also require a well-trained, well informed officer who will **ACT DECISEVELY** (and correctly) when presented with these types of situations. There will be more on acting decisively later on in this book.

Background: Being involved at our training academy for several years, along with following Gordon Graham's training advice, I personally felt that Firefighters (at all ranks) needed to perform the following training to maintain at least a Level 2 competence:

- *Perform all high risk, low frequency tasks 100 times in the training academy setting before working out in the field*
- *Probationary Firefighters in the field should perform all high risk, low frequency tasks at least 100 more times in their first year*
- *All high risk, low frequency tasks should be performed at least at a 2 to 1 ratio of drilling - twice for every 1 time the task is performed in the field*
- *If the frequency of the task is so low that it is performed less than 2 or 3 times a year, it should be trained on at least once a quarter*

HF – DDMT – High Risk - High Frequency Events with Discretionary Decision-Making Time. Because you have a lot of time to think about something before reacting and you perform these activities at a high frequency, not much training time should be devoted to these activities even though high risk is involved.

Again, these tasks/events represent what we should really excel at as an organization. All high risk events that happen frequently with decision-making time should have formal SOPs, policies, and checkoff systems developed for the situations we routinely deal with. These situations include:

- Preparing and filing incident reports
- Company drilling on critical hazard zone tasks - MCS (hopefully this happens on a high frequency)

HF – NDMT – High Risk - High Frequency Events with Non-Discretionary Decision-Making Time. These tasks/events also represent what we should really be good at as an organization. Because these events happen so often, there should be automatic safety responses developed (SOPs) and drilling systems in place for the high risk situations we frequently deal with. Coupled with high frequency, but with no discretionary decision-making time, about 25% of a crew's training time should be devoted to these activities. Some of these event types include:

- Driving with lights and sirens
- EMS calls with critically injured/ill persons
- Working on a freeway/busy roadway

4. Training in Context

Whenever possible, all training should be performed in the context for the activity/tasks that are being drilled on. Training in context has been proven to be the best transference learning method (where participation leads to understanding, which leads to higher performances in a live setting) that high risk occupations can perform. The more real the training setting, the more that will be absorbed and learned by all the participants.

Training in context includes:

- Creating a similar setting where the activity/task will take place in real life. This can include several different settings that can range from indoor, outdoor, in the light, in the dark, confined settings, wide open settings, structures and/or props being used, etc.
- Using the same equipment designed for the full completion of the activity that would be used in real life. This includes EVERYTHING that will be used to perform the activity in real life. Example: if you are pulling hose, fill the hose with water after it is stretched and have the Firefighter flow water for 60 seconds while they move around to different target areas (just like they would do in real life).
- Use the same uniform/PPE that will be used to complete the activity/task that would be used in real life. This includes EVERYTHING that will be worn to perform the activity in real life. If performing any IDLH training activity, all PPE for the activity should be worn. This includes wearing an SCBA.
- Avoiding performing a "talk through" where everyone stands around and talks their way through the activity/task without actually performing them in context after doing the "talk through."

5. Scheduling Training

Now that a Company Officer has a good idea of how to prioritize their company's drilling time, the next biggest challenge is scheduling it. Drilling time always must be balanced with service delivery. As covered in a previous chapter, all known scheduled events should be inserted into the company activity calendar. This includes all drilling activities.

Background: To recap, Station 201 housed E-201 (a 4-person ALS company with 2 Paramedics), L-201 (a 5-person BLS company), and A-201 (a 2 person BLS ambulance).

L-201 had a new Probationary Firefighter rotate onto the truck every 3 months. The Probationary Firefighter is what drove our drilling schedule. I will list my priorities in the order of the things I had to consider when scheduling any drilling for the company:

- *Training in service versus out of service - having 2 response units at Station 201 made it much easier for L-201 to be out of service rather than E-201, because they provide ALS coverage for our first due area.*
    - *This becomes a huge consideration for a 1-unit fire station that still must provide service delivery to their first due area (more on this later in the chapter).*
- *If the drill required a unit to be out of service, it had to be highly coordinated with the Brass (more on this later in the chapter).*
- *Did the drill involve any water? If this was the case, we would need an Engine company to participate in the drill (L-201 was not equipped with a pump). 50% of the time it was E-201, the other 50% of the time it was another Engine company we often ran with in our battalion and their unit also had a probationary Firefighter.*
- *If we needed water, those drills were usually scheduled for weekend mornings when 911 service delivery is typically at its lowest. This was because the Engine company needed to be placed out of service during the drill because they had hose off the truck and were flowing water. Water drills lasted less than an hour in order to get back into service in a reasonable time frame (usually we would get 5 or 6 water application drills performed in an hour).*
- *Where was the drill located? Well over 50% of L-201's drills occurred at the fire station. Water drills had to occur off-site (most fire station properties are not big enough to accommodate laying supply hose and stretching handlines).*
- *A-201 (the Ambulance personnel) would attend and participate in all drills possible while they remained in service. This was because we did not need their response vehicle involved in the drill and they could quickly disengage from the activity and respond. Because of this, A-201 were some of the best trained Firefighters on the department.*

Knowing and considering all of this, I would:

- *Produce L-201's training schedule for the quarter based around our current Probationary Firefighter (after the first year or 2 at L-201, it was a copy and paste).*
- *This included:*
    - *Type of drill*
    - *Where it was located*
    - *Was there any other unit involved?*
    - *If I had to coordinate (well in advance) any out of service time for any unit*

- o *Who is the lead trainer for the drill?*
  - *Company Officer*
  - *One of the Engineers*
  - *Another Company Officer at the drill*
  - *Subject matter expert*
- *From here, I would put all this information into L-201's company activity calendar (where everyone could see it and plan on it).*
- *I would then sit down with our new Probationary Firefighter and go over in detail what L-201 was going to train on over the next 90 days (30 shifts).*

There was never a training quarter where L-201 accomplished everything on our training schedule (but we always did most of it). This was predominantly due to 911 activity and other events that seemed to come up.

6. In Service versus Out of Service Drilling

Whenever possible, most single company drilling should be performed while remaining in service and available for 911 responses.

Engine companies:

- About half of MCS drilling can be performed while in service.
- The other half of MCS drilling requires engaging the Engine's pump and flowing water.
- When flowing water, the Engine should usually be taken out of service due to the delay of disengaging the pump, hoses, and any appliances attached.
- An Engine company can still stretch hose and remain in service by not pumping any water. Pull dry hose, load dry hose. If a 911 response comes in, disconnect the hose, make the response, and then come back and re-load your hose and keep on drilling.

Ladder companies:

- Most of a Ladder company's equipment can be used to drill with while remaining available for 911 responses.
- All of the set-up and operation of the power tools can be drilled with while in service, but using them in the actual application of performing forcible entry and vehicle extrication drills will usually require the company to be taken out of service.
- Flowing water through any appliance on a Ladder company will usually require that the unit be taken out of service.

If a company is going to perform an in-service drill, there is really no need to officially notify the Brass unless the training is going to place the company significantly away from their fire station, affecting 911 response times. In these instances, the system needs to be informed of, and also approve of, your response status.

Scheduling Out of Service Drill Time

As stated earlier, all training was planned out well in advance at Station 201, so any out of service time was coordinated well before it happened. Coordinating out of service drilling considerations include:

- Usually, there will be a maximum number of units that can be out of service for any reason at one time on a department (minus service delivery – 911 activity).
- Keep in mind while being out of service for drilling that other fire stations do not like making routine 911 responses into another fire station's first due response areas when that unit is unavailable or out of position in their own first due area for "non-911 activity."
- Any out of service time request needs to go to the supervisors above you. This can include several different people.
- In smaller departments (5 stations or less), the person you make the request to is usually your Battalion Chief that will personally handle all the movements.
- In larger departments, the request may need to be managed by your boss, Shift Commander, Alarm Room/Dispatch Coordinator, Training Chief, Operations Chief, and/or a time management/event coordinator.
- Use the chain of command to request the out of service time in the appropriate time frame needed to have the activity granted.
- Try to keep all MCS out of service training drills to 60 minutes or less.
- Most out of service training will be scheduled for the weekend mornings due to low 911 activity and all the 40-hour administrators are all off, not demanding any of your time.

6 out of the 60 fire stations of my former fire department had 2 Engine companies housed at their station. The 2nd Engines at these fire stations were called "Adaptive Response Units." These companies would fill in for other companies throughout the city that were out of service for:

- Extended 911 responses (usually big fires)
- Extended out of service times caused by mechanical issues
- Other units out of service while performing training (scheduled well in advance)

7. In Station versus Out of Station Drilling

Over 50% of a company's drilling can be performed while in service at the fire station. If you work at a station on a large piece of property with a fire hydrant on it or if your fire station is next to the academy, you can probably perform 100% of your drilling while at or very close to the fire station (this is the very best scenario).

Selecting an off-site drill location has several considerations that include:

- All in service drilling performed outside of the fire station should be performed as close to the fire station as possible.
- City/District property is always the first and best choice. This includes non-major roads, parking lots, training facilities, etc.

- Non-city owned parking lots with hydrants that are close to them offer the 2nd best location choice. If these are going to be used, the company MUST get formal permission from the RP who owns/manages the property before using any privately-owned property.
- When flowing water, always flow it in a manner that does not upset the public. This includes NOT:
  - Having a roadway blocked with supply hose (whenever possible)
  - Getting a building wet (including the roof)
  - Getting parked cars wet
  - Disturbing landscaping with fire streams
  - Getting a busy roadway soaked with water where freshly washed cars get unwashed driving through it
  - Creating areas of mud that cars or people on foot must travel through
  - Avoid drilling with any type of foam system in public settings
- One of the main reasons to go out of service to do company level drilling is to flow water. It is very hard to disengage and make a timely 911 response with an Engine company that has a supply line hooked into it while flowing water through various hose and appliances.

8. Battalion/Training Academy/Department Wide Drills

In many fire departments, MCS drilling is pre-scheduled on a routine, consistent basis and the Company Officer does not have to take any action facilitating the drill other than showing up. This makes it very convenient for the Company Officer, as they do not have to personally schedule all of their water flowing drills. These drills can be structured in the following ways:

- Around a pre-determined area of MCS skill sets
- To have 2 or more companies participating
- Centered around a specific tactical situation (brush fires, high-rise, special ops, etc.)
- Using an SME, Training Chief, or a Battalion Chief as the drill's proctor
- To be mandatory with MCS checkoffs being performed

Again, these are great drills that take some of the coordination management load off of Company Officers, but generally, formal department drills are not enough to maintain (or increase) the competency level of Firefighters in the field.

- Low frequency – high risk drills performed once every 3 weeks is the bare minimum drilling required to maintain any competence level.
- Low frequency – high risk drills performed once every 2-3 shifts is the bare minimum drilling required to increase competence levels.
- Trying to facilitate some sort of drill every shift (there are lots of them) will facilitate the highest company competence level possible.

Most of the drilling required to reach a high level of competence will have to occur on the company level and most of it will be scheduled and facilitated by the Company Officer. Company Officers who feel that their departments formally scheduled and facilitated training sessions are all that are required to maintain or increase a company's competency level better get ready for some long, painful shifts.

9. Certification Maintenance

While it is the primary responsibility of the Company Officer to facilitate the maintenance of their company members' Firefighter 1 & 2 certifications (MCS), there are several other certifications their members may possess that the Company Officer will not be the primary trainer or facilitator for. These other certifications include:

- EMT
- PM
- Driver – Apparatus Operator
- Hazmat
- Technical Rescue
- Blue Card Hazard Zone Incident Command

Some of the drilling or CE for these certifications will have to be attended by the entire crew, while others may only require 1 crew member to attend. If this is this case, most of these drill and classroom sessions are scheduled far in advanced and both the event type and how the vacancy will be filled/managed should be inserted into the company activity calendar.

10. Documentation of Drilling

All training should be documented. This comes in a variety of different formats and documentation systems (most do not hook up to each other). All Company Officers will need effectively input and document whatever information that is required into whatever system that is currently being utilized by their agency.

Closing

"Through training and discipline, we become the masters of our own fates." – Marine Drill Sergeant motto

As stated previously, Firefighters have very physically stressful jobs, in which they perform a set of physically demanding activities that if not correctly performed, could injure or kill a Firefighter. Civilian lives (and their overall wellness) also depend heavily on the fitness and competence levels of the Firefighters trying to intervene on their behalf. This makes it critically important for Company Officers to continually manage the drilling required that facilitates their crew members having the highest level of competence and performance possible. The fate of your crew members rests in your hands. Drill, drill, drill.

Chapter 12

Chow

"An army marches on its stomach." - Napoleon

This is a great quote to start this chapter. I am sure that knowing how much battlefield success depended on how well fed his army was, Napoleon took great care and put much attention into the management of this phase of his troop's readiness - and so must a Company Officer. Chow becomes a critical component of performance when working 24 hours, during which all crew members need to be on their A-game during the entire shift.

The 3 biggest considerations in managing chow include:

1. Hydration
2. Nutrition
3. Eating together

1. Hydration

We start with hydration because between hydrating during a shift and eating anything during the shift, hydration wins hands down every time (you still need to eat though). All nutritional health starts with proper hydration. Ask any professional athlete - their performance depends on how well they hydrate. A Firefighter's body is subjected to much more physical stress when performing tasks inside a burning building than it would be in a professional athlete's environment (heat, toxins, air limitations, etc.), so being properly hydrated becomes even more important.

When the body is dehydrated, so is the brain. Hydration, physical performance, and cognitive thinking are all linked together. Dehydrated adults show signs of increased brain activity when performing cognitively engaging tasks, indicating that their brains are working harder than normal to complete a task. This additional effort typically manifests as fatigue and changes in mood (irritability). Dehydration causing more than a 2% reduction in body mass (200 lb. person loses over 4 lbs. of water – ½ gallon) is associated with moderate to significant impairments on attention, executive function, and motor coordination. [1]

Properly hydrating Firefighters is important no matter what part of the country you work in. Firefighters working in climates that promote dehydration (hot, humid, dry, windy, etc.) must put a heavy emphasis on keeping hydrated during the shift. No matter what climate you are working in, Firefighters under the physical stress of working in full turnouts have a much higher chance of experiencing rhabdomyolysis ("rabdo") if they are not properly hydrated.

Rhabdomyolysis is a serious medical condition that occurs due to a direct or indirect muscle injury. It results from the death of muscle fibers and the release of their contents into the bloodstream. This can lead to serious complications such as renal (kidney) failure and in some cases, it has even caused death. This injury causes the kidneys to go into a state of failure (because they are backed up with muscle tissue) to the point that they cannot remove waste and concentrated urine from the bloodstream. The most common causes of rhabdomyolysis are overexertion, **dehydration,** crushing injuries, and alcohol abuse. Certain medicines and toxic substances will also cause this muscle breakdown.

The best thing a Firefighter can do to prevent rhabdomyolysis is to **be properly hydrated and well-conditioned** while performing any activity in which the Firefighter will be under extreme physical stress.

Background: Hydration was a very big deal on the Phoenix Fire Department. This all started in the academy with the recruits, in which the department started its hydration culture with its new members. Every recruit weighed in every morning and throughout the rest of the day. All recruits were taught to stay within 1 pound of their "hydrated weight" (going over it a couple of pounds was also a very good thing while being on duty). All water weight loss needed to be replaced pound for pound. A gallon of water weighs just over 8 pounds. Therefore, if a person loses 4 pounds of weight during a 1-hour drill, that person would need to drink at least a half a gallon of water to get back to their normal hydrated state. Any weight loss of over 5 pounds would put that recruit in time out until they were within 1 pound of their normal weight again. This was usually cured within 15 minutes by the recruit drinking 2 quarts of water or a department approved sports drink (while being out of full PPE and "cooling down").

The hydration culture would continue to be facilitated in the field by all the fire station bathrooms having a doctor's scale for all members to weigh themselves throughout the shift, along with having urine color charts that also help gauge how well you are hydrated. The department provided all the ice, bottled water, and sport drinks a fire station could consume. In addition, the department also provided staffed rehab units filled with hydration supplies that were dispatched to all working incidents and every fire truck carried at least 5 gallons of iced down water.

During my 26-year career, despite all of the precautions taken to prevent it, I witnessed rhabdomyolysis still send several Firefighters to the ER. Proper hydration is a big deal for a Company Officer to manage. There is already a long list of bad things that can happen to us – do not let rhabdomyolysis due to somebody on your crew not being properly hydrated be added on to the list!

The only proven hydration substance with no side effects is:

- # WATER

The only proven hydration substitute other than water with no side effects when used under extreme physical stress are **sports drinks** that contain only water, electrolytes, and glucose (sugar) with no other artificial sweeteners, caffeine, or any other additives.

Energy drinks (not sport drinks) have become quite popular with the youth of the fire service. Firefighters that routinely consume energy drinks need to be informed that energy drinks are not designed for fluid replacement (hydration) and they can be potentially harmful for a person who is under the extreme physical stresses that a Firefighter has the potential to be under. I would define a Firefighter of having the potential to be under extreme physical stresses while being in a training academy setting or while being on active duty during a shift. Consuming energy drinks prior to, and while being on duty, should be avoided at all costs (in fact, some fire departments and divisions of the US Military have banned the use of them).

Firefighter hydration guidelines:

- Use only water or an approved sports drink with no caffeine or other non-hydrating additives.
- Generally, a Firefighter should drink at least 1 gallon of water a day while on duty (more with vigorous activity throughout the shift).
- A properly hydrated Firefighter should need to urinate about once an hour.
- Ingesting cold water will also assist in lowering a person's core body temperature.

Great ways to help facilitate hydration throughout the shift:

- Keep the station fridge full of bottled water and sports drinks.
- Keep a 2-3-gallon pot full of ice water with a ladle in it on the kitchen countertop and stack a bunch of cups next to it. Keep it full during the shift.
- Keep a 2-3-gallon pot full of an approved sports drink with a ladle in it next to the ice water pot and stack a bunch of cups next to it. Keep it full during the shift.
- Ensure plenty of cold water and drinking cups are stored on the apparatus (at least 5 gallons and 100 6-ounce paper cups).
- As the supervisor, ensure that when performing physical activity, you and the crew are taking 5-minute hydration breaks about every 10-15 minutes while drinking at least 8-16 ounces of water during each break.
- Lead by example. Let your crew members see you hydrating often throughout the shift.

Background: My favorite beverage vendor at the Arizona Diamondback baseball games uses the following sales pitch to sell his beer and water (he shouts it out very loudly):

"Ice cold beer and water for sale! Hydrate or die!"

He's right...

2. Nutrition

Let me start this bullet point with the timeless phrase: "You are what you eat."

- Firefighter W works out at least 6 times a week, they have excellent overall body strength, endurance, and can perform all aspects of the job, but they have a body fat percentage between 15 to 20%. They have a diet consisting of mostly good foods, but they also eat a lot of bad foods a person should not eat (clinically proven). They are 100% physically competent and look okay physically.
- Firefighter X works out about twice a week and it always involves a sport (no gyms), they have good overall body strength, endurance, and can perform all aspects of the job and they have a body fat percentage that is below 10%. They have a diet consisting primarily of all the good, healthy foods that a person should eat (clinically proven).

All firefighter W needs to do is change their diet. In less than 4 months, they will see a significant reduction in their body fat.

Background: My father was so committed to fitness that he built a full-sized gym in his own backyard (Bruno's Gym). It contained both free weights and several cardio machines. For a number of years, I lived across the street from my parents, so I would work out in my dad's gym just about every day I was off duty from work. My favorite piece of cardio equipment was the stair climbing machine, with which I would climb floor after floor of steps to achieve the most calories burned as possible.

I was always in good shape out in the field, but I was firefighter W. I had about 16% body fat with a nice little roll around the waste. The reason for this was because I was addicted to salty snacks - potato chips being my favorite. My reward for walking on the stairs for 60 minutes was a nice fresh bag of sour cream and onion potato chips because I had just "earned" the right to eat that entire bag of chips.

My father decorated his gym with all sorts of motivating phrases. A smaller poster on the wall, almost directly in front of the stair machine, had the following saying by Albert Einstein: "The definition of insanity is trying the same thing over and over again and expecting different results." It only took me about 10 years of looking at that poster before it finally sunk in. My goal was to get rid of my belly fat roll and look like a proper A-Shifter. I climbed enough steps to reach the moon, but my fat roll was still there. Einstein's quote finally sank in and for the first time in my life. I went on a diet.

The word diet is probably not the best word to use, as I did a lifelong dietary change - it was not a fad. I cut out all sugar from my diet that was possible without having to eat like a bird. It was kind of easy – just no more salty snacks, white flour, sugar, processed and fast foods (well, maybe sometimes). Within 4 months of making this lifestyle change, I went from 16% to 10% body fat, I lost most of my fat roll, all of my bloodwork improved, and I have pretty much maintained the best "rest of my life weight" since. During this time, I also decreased my cardio workout times, I did more core training, and most of my exercise was performed outdoors, away from the gym.

I had no genetic predisposition to having a fat roll around my belt line. A third of my diet consisted of foods that were not good for me. Once I cut them out, the roll went away. I am what I eat. Other than hydrating, eating right is the most important thing a person can do for their overall health and the way they look (much more so than just working out). Go ahead, climb stairs all day long trying to lose the weight - or lose it in combination with changing your diet and doing different forms of exercise that are a lot more fun.

The best official Firefighter calorie guide comes from the US Forest Service. They recommend that a Forest Firefighter working on the line consumes:

- Between 4,500 to 6,000 calories a day
- Moderate work requires between 350 to 490 grams of carbohydrates a day
- Hard work requires between 490 to 700 grams of carbohydrates a day
- Food should be eaten throughout the day in regular intervals with less than 2 hours between meals and hearty snacking. This is to maintain proper glucose and energy levels.

Because a red carded Firefighter working on the line of a forest fire has a similar work schedule as a soldier on the march, I am sure that this is the same basic calorie formula that Napoleon used for his troops. However, troops marching and/or working a fire line all day is much different than working out of a fire station on a fire company (however, there will be shifts when a company will be out working in the field for extended periods of time).

Here are some typical peak working times for a Firefighter when they will need the proper number of calories to maintain their energy levels:

- From morning shift change to about lunch time - this was the most consistently active period at Station 201, in which we would: relieve our counter parts, maintain response equipment and the station, do some sort of PT, go drilling, go shopping, along with responding to any 911 responses. Firefighters should show up to the station well fed and do some heavy snacking during fellowship and throughout the morning routine.
- After lunch, nutritional energy needs would vary based on the amount of activity that is performed the rest of the shift.
  - Light activity during the rest of the shift (EMS runs, low calorie service calls): eat and snack normally throughout the rest of the shift, choosing healthy foods
  - Heavy activity during the rest of the shift (working fires, etc.): eat and snack heavily throughout the rest of the shift in order to consume enough calories needed to maintain peak energy levels, choosing healthy foods whenever possible

Company Officers need to worry more about their crew eating enough calories throughout the shift than managing what they are actually eating. Most Company Officers are not nutritionists or dietitians, but they should know the difference between foods that are good for a Firefighter trying to maintain peak energy levels (complex carbs, protein, and good fats) versus the foods that are bad for maintaining long term energy levels (simple sugars and bad fats equal crash and burn energy levels). This should help guide your own nutritional choices and sources, as well as your crew members'.

There is also the problem of trying to dictate what other people should eat when the only food you can really control is the food that you eat. It is very unrealistic to tell somebody else what they should and should not eat. This is becoming even more problematic as humans learn more and more about the science of what they are eating. I would say a 100 years ago, there were 3 basic diets: eating less, eating the same amount, or eating too much. Today there are hundreds of different diets and eating lifestyles.

Because of people's eating independence, coordinating everyone at the station to sit down together to eat a meal is getting tougher to do.

3. Eating together

"Food brings people together in a way like nothing else can." - Yotam Ottolenghi

I am going to start this section with a previous saying used in the book: "If you follow a bad fire company home, you will most likely find a bad Company Officer." Let me add to this with: "and the crew probably does not eat together either."

Background: I have been in the fire service for over 40 years. Over this time period, fire station design and layouts have changed significantly (along with a lot of other stuff, such as computers, cable TV, internet, cell phones, social media platforms, etc.). One of the biggest changes that has happened to fire station layouts is in the dormitories, as the once common and open dorm room has been replaced with a set of individual bunk rooms. I personally feel that most of these changes have been for the better, while many others feel these changes have created an atmosphere that leads to less crew interaction, unity, and comradery because crew members can now retreat to their dorm rooms and not "engage" in team activities.

I want to get this out of the way: I think it is totally ludicrous that people think that the new dorms have "separated" a fire crew when the real issue is usually that the Company Officer is not facilitating the activities required to promote crew unity (many times they are the ones hiding out in their office). One of these activities is eating together. I hear Company Officers complaining about and blaming the new environment when not facilitating eating together because "it's too hard," or "the department is pulling the rug out from under me," or "what can I do about it?" What a joke - all of these changes are for the better!

Instead of up to 8 people now in 1 dormitory, there are 8 separate bunk rooms. This promotes the following:

- *You are not kept up or are awoken by somebody coming in and out of the dorm to go to the bathroom, snoring, passing rancid gas, turning on the lights, rummaging through their locker, phone or tablet noises, another unit's 911 call, and/or another unit coming back from a call and getting back into bed.*
- *You can now adjust the temperature in your sleeping area that promotes your best sleep (no more thermostat wars).*
- *You now have the privacy to talk to your family members and friends on your cell phone, read a book, work on homework, study for a promotional exam, etc.*

There will be times when the entire crew (including the Company Officer) is in their dorm room getting some quiet time away from everybody else. This is a completely natural thing that happens when you work a 24-hour shift. There are still plenty of hours and activities during the course of a shift that the crew will be working and interacting together that does not involve 911 activity.

I agree with Yotam Ottolenghi: one of the best ways to bring people together and build an effective team is for everyone to eat together. Instead of a Company Officer complaining about new fire station layouts, get proactive and facilitate crew activities that promote teamwork and unity. One of the biggest is everyone at the station preparing and eating meals together.

Preparing and eating meals together at the fire station does 3 major things:

1. It greatly facilitates team building and unity.
2. It promotes mental health.
3. It facilitates eating the proper nutrition necessary to maintain peak energy levels.

1. Station Meals and Team Building

Fire station meals are viewed by some people as a burdensome chore, but the effort in preparing and sitting down together to eat a meal with the entire group is well worth it for the numerous benefits that come from facilitating this activity. Eating together:

- Creates an atmosphere that promotes communication
- Gives the entire crew the opportunity to voice their informal expectations and opinions
- Provides an important context to build the collaborative trust necessary for station and unit cohesion
- Is an important means of making and reinforcing friendships
- Breaks down barriers and lowers people's prejudices or preconceived notions

The quietest time in a fire station is the first 5 minutes the station sits down to eat a meal together because everyone's mouths are full. The next 15 minutes is the loudest time in a fire station because of all the social interaction going on around the table.

Lunches are generally shorter meals and the conversations center around performance and job activities. Dinners are generally longer meals and the conversations center more around social and personal discussions. Because the dinner meal is more of a social event, it will greatly assist a Company Officer in managing their members mental health.

2. Station Meals and Mental Health

Fire station meals are not only imperative for crew bonding and unity, but for mental health, as well. The University of Oxford has researched that the more often people eat with others, the more likely they are to feel happy, feel more included in the group, and satisfied with their lives. 2 Social interaction is also important to the health of your crew because it creates a strong network of support.

Crew meals provide the vehicle for conversation and understanding of each member's:

- Personal, or away from work, life details that include:
  - o Social structure: family members, significant others, children, friends, etc.
  - o Significant personal and family events, triumphs, and setbacks
  - o Off duty interests, hobbies, vacations, etc.
  - o Any home or family stressors (divorce, illnesses, newborns, financial issues, etc.)
- Work life details that include:
  - o Goals
  - o Ideas
  - o Frustrations – therapeutic, not chronic concerns
  - o Highs and lows of the day/week
  - o Resources for those struggling

In the next section of the book, in the chapter entitled "Mental Wellness - Enhancing Crew Resilience," Tim Dietz will present the role and responsibilities that a Company Officer has in managing the resilience of their crew members (mental health). This will include:

- Creating the culture
- Knowing your crew
- Eating right
- Talking
- Life away from the fire station

All of these responsibilities can be handled around the dinner table. Meals, particularly dinner, provides the social interaction necessary to maintain the psychological health of the crew. To help make this happen, everyone around the dinner table should not be in a hurry to clean-up. Crews should spend at least 15-20 minutes after eating just sitting around the table to enjoy each other's company.

3. Station Meals Facilitate Healthy Eating and Sustained Energy Levels

In all of the studies done on the benefits of people eating together, one of the biggest benefits is that it leads to a much heathier diet. People that eat together:

- Eat heathier foods that include more fruits and vegetables
- Eat slower and ingest less
- Have fewer health problems
- Have much lower obesity rates

Having said this, a great challenge in getting everyone to eat together is having them all agree on what to actually eat. As stated previously, this is getting harder and harder to do in today's modern times with all of the different diets available. Here are just a few examples of the diets you could have to manage around:

- Food allergies
- Vegetarian diet
- Vegan diet
- Paleo diet
- Low-Carb diet
- Raw food diet
- Keto diet
- Bodybuilder diet (high protein in mass quantities)
- Intermittent fasting
- Hundreds more (there is a new one out every week now)

Company Officers may also have people on their company that are so serious about their diet that they bring their own food to work to eat throughout the shift.

I do not care!!! Sit down in the morning and figure out what you are all going to eat together!

Background: I have no idea what kind of diet my oldest daughter is on. I think it is a mix of all of them based on her own scientifically documented food allergy profile. Since this profile was developed, she examines every single molecule she ingests into her body on how compatible it is to her overall health. The list of foods she cannot eat is impressive. Most of her forbidden foods are the ones that I love the most - like butter. But whenever we get together, we manage to figure out what we can all eat together that makes everyone feel both happy and satisfied. It is painful sometimes. Sometimes the discussions on what we are going to make or where we are going to go out for dinner takes longer than making or eating the actual meal, but we make it happen and we all eat together when she is in town. It would absolutely NOT BE RIGHT for my daughter to come in from out of town and have all us eat meals separately! NO WAY!

Here are some general tips and guidelines for making and eating fire station meals that will help facilitate everyone eating and socializing together:

- We will start with Company Officer Expectation #1: Someone who respects and values their co-workers and the public they serve. Always respect other people's tastes, diet, and what they eat (and do not or cannot eat).
- It is very hard to cook 2 separate meals at once in a fire station.
- Often times, it is just 1 ingredient in a dish that a person cannot eat. If possible, cook that ingredient separately where it can be added to a person's plate on an individual basis.
- Dishing out meals buffet style helps facilitate this process the best.
- Let people dress their own salads (no communal bowls with already dressed salad).
- The more a person is involved in making a meal, the more they will like eating it.
- Do not make people cook a meal when they cannot cook. This will lead to everybody being unhappy with the meal, especially the cook.
- People who are not great chefs are usually great at chopping foods and doing dishes.
- Remember that you are in a fire station where a 911 call can come in at any time. Avoid making complicated dishes that have to come together in a small window of time or that do not taste very good cold, re-heated, or cannot be eaten the next shift.
- People who have such a specialized diet that they absolutely cannot eat a station meal still need to sit down and eat their own meal during mealtime with everyone else.
- If you are fasting (or have already eaten), still sit down with everybody else and join in on the mealtime discussion (and clean-up).
- During the meal, put all the cell phones away and talk to each other. A Company Officer can help facilitate this by asking his crew members socially based questions like "what did you do on your days off?" or "how did the football game you were taking the kids to this weekend go?" or "I saw this on TV the other day. Anyone else see it? What did you think?" There are thousands of engaging questions you can ask that force your crew to put their phones away and talk.
- No one should be in hurry to get up and start cleaning up the kitchen when everyone is done eating (this includes all junior members, as well). There should be at least 15-20 minutes of fellowship at the table before declaring the meal is officially over and allowing clean-up to being.

Paying for chow

Most of time, eating together requires shopping for chow. Before getting into the shopping guidelines, let's look at some of the possible "collection" processes that will pay for the meals prepared during the shift:

- Today, there are several different apps that allow people to electronically pay into chow and kitty accounts (I'm sure cash still works, as well).
- Kitty – This is a community collection pot that is collected between all shifts on a shift-to-shift basis. Every 2 weeks (pay days) the "Kitty Manager" of the station (A.K.A. the King) would collect kitty from all the shifts and they were the person responsible for stocking the station with condiments. This included all the major condiments that are used to cook most meals - like salt, pepper, sugar, coffee, tea, spices, flour, crackers, mustard, ketchup, etc. The list goes on and on. Here is some lifelong career advice: always pay your kitty and never complain about the amount (even if you do not use a thing from it).
- Some stations collect chow money after the food has all been purchased and the total is divided up equally amongst the crew members.
- Some stations keep a "pot" where they charge a flat fee for chow and kitty every shift based on an average price. Some shifts they go over, some shifts they go under. It all balances out in the end. Here is some more lifelong career advice: always pay whatever chow costs and never complain about the amount.
- Get ready for some possible friction when telling a station that you are out on chow. I get it, but others might not. If this is the case, pay your kitty fees anyway. When asking what the kitty fees are, you may hear something like this:
  - "I'm not in on chow today, but what do I owe for kitty?"
    - "Chow and kitty are 25 bucks."
  - "No, I just want to pay my kitty fee. I brought my own food in."
    - "Oh! No worries. Kitty is 25 bucks."

Shopping for Chow

Shopping for chow has many of the same guidelines as drilling outside of the fire station. Here are some of the things a Company Officer will need to consider when shopping for chow:

- Shopping for chow is an in-service activity.
- Most fire stations have a grocery store located in their first due area. Always try to shop at a store as close as possible to the fire station.
- Do not leave your first due area to shop for chow (sometimes you can skirt the edge of your area, but never go out of it).
- NEVER park your apparatus when at the store or when dinning out so that it blocks any civilian access or makes a taxpaying citizen think you are inconsiderate. ONLY PARK IN A FIRE LANE WHEN SOMETHING IS ON FIRE!
- Always wear the proper uniform while in public.
- Shopping as a crew can greatly speed up the process. With all crew members equipped with a portable radio, it allows the crew to split up to collect all the ingredients needed in order to reduce the time spent in the store.
- Always be on your best behavior while shopping for chow. A large percentage of the citizen complaints my dad processed while on the Phoenix Fire Department were related to how we parked and/or our behavior while shopping.
- The public often times does not understand why we are in the grocery store, even when we are on our best behavior. Try to use it as an opportunity to connect with the public in

a positive way. Many departments have stickers or other treats to hand out to the kids while always smiling and waving to the adults.

Chow and 3rd Parties

Most fire stations have a collective cooking staff that puts out great chow on a routine basis. Great fire station chefs have been featured on popular cooking networks, some even have their own TV cooking shows, and some have written their own cookbooks. The fire service is well known for our great cooking. While eating a fire station meal may be a routine activity for all Firefighters working on duty, it is not routine for any other 3rd Party that we routinely interact with who works outside of the fire station setting. At charitable silent auction events, I have personally seen the bidding for a fire station meal for 4 people go as high as $2,000 (going to the charity involved – not to the fire station). For most people who are not Firefighters, eating a meal at a fire station is BIG DEAL, a great honor, and a privilege.

A fire station meal invitation is also a great opportunity to create harmony and goodwill with the other people who we respond with, interact with, and depend on at work, along with all the other people who support all the individual Firefighters on their days off (family). These lunch and dinner invitations should be given out on a routine basis (at least a few times a month) and they should primarily go out to:

- Your Battalion Chief if they are not assigned to your station (make it an open invitation)
- Support personnel inside of your own department. These people include admin personnel, dispatchers, secretaries, mechanics, techs, etc.
- Other Firefighters who have worked at your station in the past that have moved onto other 40 hours roles on the department (staff jobs – possibly now higher ranking) who need a good meal and some fire station comradery every once in while
- Law Enforcement officers that you routinely respond with
- 3rd Party EMS personnel that you routinely respond with (ambulance staff, hospital staff, flight crews, etc.)
- If allowed, Firefighter family members
- If allowed, an occasional "auctioning off" of a fire station meal to the public

Having 3rd parties to the fire station for a station meal facilitates a bonding and co-understanding opportunity that can lead to building solid relationships with the other agencies and people that are connected to fire station personnel that we absolutely depend on – on a shift-to-shift, day-to-day basis. This replicates the same exact process that happens when Firefighters eat a meal together (breaking bread together).

References:

1. Gopinathan, PM, Pichan, G & Sharma, V (1988) Role of dehydration in heat stress-induced variations in mental performance. Arch Environ Heal 43, 15–17

2. Dunbar, R.I.M. Breaking Bread: The Functions of Social Eating. Adaptive Human Behavior and Physiology 3, 198–211 (2017). https://doi.org/10.1007/s40750-017-0061-4

Chapter 13

Sleep Deprivation

Let me begin by stating that this chapter is in no way trying to drive the AHJs, SOPs, MOUs, CBAs, and/or any shift schedules. The focus of this chapter will be making Company Officers aware of the effects that sleep deprivation has on our physical abilities, cognitive awareness, and its long-term health effects. The more a Company Officer is aware of the effects of sleep loss and sleep deprivation, the higher their capability will be in managing the negative effects of it.

Normal Sleep

The CDC recommends that in a 24-hour period, all adult humans need 7 or more hours of sleep per night for the best overall health and wellbeing. **A short sleep duration is defined as less than 7 hours of sleep in a 24-hour period.** [1]

Sleep Architecture

Sleep architecture refers to the basic structural organization of normal sleep. There are two types of sleep:

1. Non-rapid eye movement (NREM)
2. Rapid eye movement (REM)

Each type of sleep has an effect on brain waves, outside awareness, muscle tone, and eye movement. Over the course of a sleep period, NREM and REM sleep will alternate in cycles. Each period of sleep typically contains 4 to 8 NREM and REM sleep cycles.

1. Non-Rapid Eye Movement (NREM) Sleep

NREM sleep consists of the following 4 stages with each phase having its own distinct activity and physiology:

- **NREM Stage 1** – This stage lasts 1 to 7 minutes (2 to 5% of sleep) and is easily interrupted by a disruptive noise. Brain waves and muscle tone in this stage are similar to wakefulness and the typical heart rate and respirations are slow.
- **NREM Stage 2** – This stage lasts 10 to 25 minutes in the initial sleep cycle and increases in each successive cycle (45 to 55% of sleep) and requires a more intense stimulus to waken. Brain activity in this stage displays sleep spindles (low voltage waves) that are important for memory consolidation. Individuals who learn a new task have a significantly higher density of sleep spindles than those in a control group.
- **NREM Stage 3** – This is referred to as slow wave sleep. This stage lasts only a few minutes (3 to 8% of sleep) and requires more intense stimulus to waken. Brain activity in this stage displays a higher voltage of slow wave brain activity.

- **NREM Stage 4** – This stage is also referred to as slow wave sleep. Most of this stage occurs the first third of the night, lasting 20 to 40 minutes (10 to 15% of sleep) and the arousal threshold at stage 4 is the highest for all NREM sleep stages. Brain activity in this stage displays a further higher voltage increase of slow wave brain activity. [2]

Overall, NREM sleep consists of approximately 60 to 80% of the sleep period.

2. Rapid eye movement (REM) Sleep

- REM sleep is defined by the presence of low voltage - mixed frequency brain wave activity with bursts of rapid eye movements.
- During the initial sleep cycle, it may last only 1 to 5 minutes, but it becomes progressively prolonged as sleep cycles progress.
- REM is when dreaming occurs.
- Muscle tone is absent while in REM sleep.
- The increase in brain activity here is higher than in NREM sleep.
- Brain blood flow here is higher than in NREM sleep.
- Respirations and blood pressure here are higher than in NREM sleep. [3]

Overall, REM sleep consists of approximately 20 to 40% of the sleep period.

Sleep-Wake Regulation

It is believed that the sleep-wake system is regulated by the interplay of two separate processes in the brain - one that promotes sleep (S process) and one that maintains wakefulness (W process). [4] The best way to look at this is:

- When you first wake, the S process is still slightly dominating the W process.
- As you continue through the early day, the W process gradually dominates the S process (30 minutes to 1.5 hours).
- The W process is typically at its peak in the afternoon. This is when the S process is at its lowest point.
- As nightfall comes, the S process starts to compete with the W process.
- The S process begins to peak around a normal bedtime. This is when the W process is at its lowest point.
- The S process diminishes throughout the sleep period, while the W process increases through the night's sleep until wakening.
- The cycle begins again.

Circadian Rhythm

Circadian rhythms collectively refer to the daily rhythms in physiology and behavior. Animal and plants possess endogenous clocks to organize daily behavior and physiological rhythms in accord with the day-night cycle. [5] The circadian rhythm regulates:

- Sleep-wake cycle

- Physical activity
- Food consumption
- Body temperature
- Heart rate
- Muscle tone
- Hormone secretion [6]

Sleep Deprivation

Negative Health Effects of Sleep Deprivation

Over the past 25 years, extensive research has overturned the dogma that sleep loss has no negative health effects, apart from daytime sleepiness. Dozens of studies have determined that **less than 7 hours of sleep per night** can have wide-ranging effects on the cardiovascular, endocrine, immune, and nervous systems, including the following:

- Obesity
- Diabetes and impaired glucose tolerance
- Cardiovascular disease
- Hypertension
- Anxiety
- Depressed mood
- Alcohol use [7]

All studies in the past 25 years indicate that the greater degree of sleep loss, the greater the apparent adverse effects of it will be. Sleeping 5 hours or less a night on a chronic basis increases mortality risk, for all causes, by roughly 15%. [8]

Sleep Deprivation and Physical Performance

There have been more than 750 scientific studies that have investigated the relationship between sleep and physical performance. Obtaining less than 8 hours, and especially less than 6 hours of sleep, will cause some of the following to occur:

- Time to physical exhaustion drops 10 to 30%
- Aerobic output is significantly reduced
- Limb extension force and vertical jump height is significantly reduced
- Decrease in peak and sustained muscle strength
- Impairment to cardiovascular, metabolic, and respiratory capabilities
- Faster rates of lactic acid build up
- Reduction in blood oxygen saturation
- Impairment of the body's cooling system
- Chances of sustaining an injury increases

These studies also observed that recovery time from injury or illness was also significantly reduced when the subjects had at least 8 hours of sleep a night. [9]

Sleep Deprivation and Cognitive Performance

Research has revealed that sleep loss creates many negative neurobehavioral effects, which often go unrecognized by the affected individual. The negative neurobehavioral impact extends from simple measures of cognition (attention and reaction time) to far more complex errors in judgment and decision making. Performance effects of sleep loss include the following:

- Involuntary microsleeps occur (momentary lapse in concentration in which the eyelids will either partially or fully close for 1 to 15 seconds)
- Attention to intensive performance is unstable, with increased errors of omission
- Cognitive slowing occurs in subject paced tasks, while time pressure increases the cognitive error rate
- Response time slows
- Performance declines in short-term recall of working memory
- Performance that requires divergent thinking deteriorates
- Learning of cognitive tasks is reduced
- The likelihood of producing ineffective solutions is increased
- Compensatory efforts to remain behaviorally effective are increased [10]

The New York Times best seller entitled *Why We Sleep* by Matthew Walker, PhD describes a sleep deprivation study performed by the renowned sleep expert, David Dinges, PhD at the University of Pennsylvania. In his study, he set up a simple test to measure the concentration levels in the sleep deprived. The test measured the concentration levels of several different groups for a 14-day period that began with all the participants getting a full 8 hours of sleep the night before they were all first tested (baselined). The participants were then divided up into the following 4 different groups:

- Group 1 - 8 hours of sleep per night
- Group 2 - 6 hours of sleep per night
- Group 3 - 4 hours of sleep per night
- Group 4 - Kept awake for 72 hours straight

Here are the major findings that came out in the study:

- The group that slept 8 hours a night in a 24-hour period had near perfect concentration scores over the 14 days.
- All sleep deprived groups showed a slowing of reaction times, but something much more serious happened. All the sleep deprived groups, for brief moments, stopped responding altogether to the tests. Slowness in response was not the most serious side effect, rather entirely missed responses were. This was mostly due to involuntary microsleeps.
- The 72-hour sleep deprivation group quickly suffered catastrophic impairment. After 24 hours of no sleep, their lapse in concentration (missed responses) increased 400%. Every hour after 24 hours of no sleep, their impairment would continue to escalate in severity, with no signs of their performance flattening out at the end of 72 hours of sleeplessness.

- After 6 nights, the group that was to only get 4 hours of sleep per night displayed performance that was just as bad as being awake for 24 hours straight (400% lapse in total concentration involving micro-sleeps). By day 11 in the study, this group displayed performance that was on par with the group that had been kept awake 48 hours straight.
- The study stated that the most troublesome findings were that of the individuals in the 6 hours of sleep a night group. At the 10-day point in the study, the group's performance was on par with the performance of the group that had been kept awake 24 hours straight.
- All sleep deprived groups showed no signs of leveling out. All signs suggested that if the experiment had continued, the performance deterioration would continue to build up over weeks and months.
- Another key finding in the experiment was that when participants were asked about their subjective sense of how impaired they were, they consistently underestimated their degree of performance disability. Their personal evaluation of their performance was a miserable predictor of how bad their performance actually, objectively was.
- Something very problematic in the experiment was the baseline resetting of the sleep deprived groups after the experiment had concluded. It was originally hypothesized that the sleep deprived groups would return to normal performance after 3 nights of getting a full 8 hours of sleep. This was not the case. It actually took all the sleep deprived groups several more days on a varying scale before returning to their original baseline.
- The study concluded that an adult human requires 8 hours of sleep per night to maintain peak concentration levels throughout the day and that after 16 hours of wakefulness, concentration levels start to decline and will continue to decrease at augmented rates based on the level of sleep deprivation that is occurring.

The US Military dissertation entitled "Sleep Deprivation and Its Effect on Combat Effectiveness" by Major Clinton T. Anderson supports these conclusions with the following: "The Walter Reed Army Institute of Research (WRAIR) and the Army Research Institute (ARI) conducted joint research on the effect of continuous operations on soldier and unit performance in 1986. The analysis concluded that individuals can maintain cognitive performance indefinitely with 6 to 8 hours of sleep each night. 4 to 5 hours of sleep will maintain cognitive performance for 5 to 6 days. However, less than 4 hours of sleep leads to a rapid decline in performance rendering the soldier ineffective in 2 to 3 days."

Major Anderson's dissertation goes on to demonstrate in several charts and graphs how higher-ranking Officers are more susceptible to the loss of their cognitive and concentration skills during sleep loss periods than the lower ranking members of their units. The dissertation states, "The squad leader must perform a greater amount of mental tasks than the soldiers in their unit and is concerned with establishing defensive positions, checking fields of fire, and integrating individual squad members into a cohesive unit. In contrast, squad members tasks are generally all physical, and while running, digging positions, and carrying burdensome loads, their performance is not affected as greatly as their squad leader's."

Managing a Fire Company Sleep Deprivation Prevention Strategies

Because we typically work at least a 24-hour shift schedule, there is absolutely no way that a crew can avoid getting their sleep periods disturbed during a 24-hour shift (sometimes this can occur several times during a night). Worst case, a crew can even not go to sleep for the full 24-hours. However, there are researched-based ways that a Company Officer can effectively manage reducing the negative effects of sleep deprivation on themselves and their crew members that include:

1. All crew members getting a good night's sleep before coming to work
2. Taking a nap during the shift
3. Company Officers understanding and recognizing that after 16 hours of being awake, you and your crew's cognitive reasoning is much lower than you think
4. After the sun goes down, slow down all deployments
5. After the sun goes down, facilitate longer and more frequent rest periods
6. Getting adequate rest after reduced sleep in a 24-hour period

1. Get a Good Night's Sleep Before Coming To Work (8+ hours)

Getting a full night's sleep of 8 hours or more before starting a 24-hour shift is the best thing a Firefighter can do to help reduce the negative effects of having their sleep possibly being disturbed throughout the final 8 to 10 hours of their 24-hour shift.

Firefighters working more than a 24-hour period who get less than 7 hours of sleep in the past 24 hours are advised to follow points #4 and #5 at all times (even in the daylight) for the remainder of their work period while experiencing any sleep deprivation.

2. Napping Improves Physical and Cognitive Abilities Before and During Periods of Sleep Deprivation

Management and treatment of sleep loss are rarely addressed by clinicians, despite the large toll it takes on society (and Firefighters). According to the textbook *Sleep Disorders and Sleep Deprivation* by the Institute of Medicine, the most effective treatment for dealing with sleep loss is to sleep longer (8 hours a night) or take a short nap lasting no more than 2 hours. [11] The textbook goes on to refer to a study done on crew members on transmeridian flights (lasting 36 hours) that showed that rotations between the crew members taking naps in 40-minute durations improved alertness during the flight. [12]

Why We Sleep by Matthew Walker presents information on a NASA study, in which it was discovered that naps as short as 26 minutes in length offered a 34% improvement in task performance and more than a 50% increase in overall alertness. Walker also details that the 100-meter superstar, Usain Bolt, has on many occasions, taken naps in the hours before breaking world records and before Olympic finals in which he has won gold. Other studies support this wisdom: daytime naps that contain a sufficient amount of sleep spindles also offer significant motor skill memory improvement and a restoring benefit on perceived energy and reduced fatigue. [13]

If permitted by the AHJ, a 30 minute to 2-hour nap should be taken by all members of a crew working a 24-hour shift starting in the afternoon (2 to 3 PM) up until 6 PM. Members should be encouraged to get as complete as possible sleep periods between calls after the crew has been on duty for over 14 to 16 hours and they have all gone to bed (from 10 PM to 7 AM).

Naps should be taken in a quiet, comfortable area with little to no lighting and with a minimum amount of background noise to help facilitate a more restful sleep (the day room strato-lounger does not meet the requirements of facilitating a restful, productive nap).

3. Understanding that After 16 Hours of Being Awake, Your Cognitive Reasoning is Much Lower Than You Think

A study similar to the David Dinges experiment was performed in which 48 healthy subjects were subjected to 4, 6, and 8-hour sleep periods for several consecutive 24-hour periods that had very similar results. As displayed in this particular study (similar to the Dinges study), one of the most striking results was that all the subjects remained largely unaware of their performance deficits, as measured by subjective sleepiness ratings. [14]

There is a significant amount of data that proves beyond a doubt that people who have been awake for over 16 hours have significantly more motor and cognitive deficits than a person with the proper rest. Data also proves that the sleep deprived believe they are all operating at efficient physical performance and concentration levels when in fact, it is just the opposite!

Knowing this data, Company Officers must operate in a different mode/mind set when sleep loss is occurring during the latter part of the shift, while also understanding that sleep deprivation universally effects all sane adults in the same, exact way. If you as the Company Officer is tired, so is the rest of your crew and everyone must act accordingly (see the next bullet points).

4. After the Sun Goes Down –Slow Down All Deployments

Most people will awaken anywhere from 90 to 60 minutes prior to arriving to their workplace. With an 8 AM start time, this would equate to a Firefighter waking up prior to work between 6:30 and 7 AM. If you do the math, the W sleep regulation process will be the dominate system for approximately 16 hours after awakening. This takes the Firefighter up to 10:30 to 11 PM before the S process becomes dominate. Unless you work in Alaska during the summer time, it is pretty much dark out at this time of day in most time zones across North America.

From about 10:30 or 11 PM to the end of the shift, all members of the crew need to slow their actions down from operating at about 90% to 100% to operating at about 70 to 80%. Slow down when it is dark out, especially if you and your crew have any sleep loss! This includes:

- Slow down all apparatus movements
- Slow down all situation evaluations
- Slow down all complex medical decisions (ask your partners to confirm before acting)
- Slow down all interpersonal interactions
- Slow down everything!

5. After the Sun Goes Down, Facilitate Longer and More Frequent Rest Periods

As presented earlier in the chapter, sleep deprivation directly reduces physical performance levels, as well as increasing the time it takes to recover from physical exertion. Knowing this, a

Company Officer must pace their crew at much slower levels during nighttime activities, as well as facilitating longer rest periods that happen more often than during daytime activities. Again, slow down when it is dark out, especially if you and your crew have any sleep loss!

6. Getting Adequate Rest After Reduced Sleep in a 24-Hour Period

The 24-hour shift is now over and it is the end of your work cycle (**HOPEFULLY!**) and you had a rough night. A rough night would be defined as having 6 or less hours of sleep since arriving to work (this includes any nap time) and/or being woken up during your nighttime sleep. If this is the case:

- You should have a nap lasting at least 2 hours the first 8 to 12 hours that you are off duty.
- Your first night off (working a 24/48 schedule), you need to facilitate getting at least 8 hours of quality sleep during the night.
- The night before going back to work, avoid alcohol (alcohol inhibits REM sleep), go to bed early, and get at least 8 hours of quality sleep.

All Company Officers need to highly encourage their crew members to get an adequate amount of rest on their days off, regardless if they had a poor sleeping shift or not!

Conclusion

Sleep deprivation has serious short term and long-term effects on all Firefighters' ability to perform their jobs at high, safe levels. Understanding this, a Company Officer can help regulate and manage sleep deprivation so that it can have the least amount of negative impact as possible on service deliver outcomes and crew safety.

References:

1. https://www.cdc.gov/sleep/data_statistics.html

2. Sleep Disorders and Sleep Deprivation – An Unmet Public Health Problem, Institute of Medicine of the National Academies – 2006 – ISBN 0-309-10111-5; Carskadon and Dement, 2005

3. Sleep Disorders and Sleep Deprivation – An Unmet Public Health Problem, Institute of Medicine of the National Academies – 2006 – ISBN 0-309-10111-5; NHLBI (2003), Somers et al. (1993), Madsen et al. (1991b)

4. Sleep Disorders and Sleep Deprivation – An Unmet Public Health Problem, Institute of Medicine of the National Academies – 2006 – ISBN 0-309-10111-5; Gillette and Abbott 2005

5. Sleep Disorders and Sleep Deprivation – An Unmet Public Health Problem, Institute of Medicine of the National Academies – 2006 – ISBN 0-309-10111-5; Dunlap et al 2004

6. Sleep Disorders and Sleep Deprivation – An Unmet Public Health Problem, Institute of Medicine of the National Academies – 2006 – ISBN 0-309-10111-5; Bunning, 1964

7. Sleep Disorders and Sleep Deprivation – An Unmet Public Health Problem, Institute of Medicine of the National Academies – 2006 – ISBN 0-309-10111-5: 3 – Extent and health consequences of chronic sleep loss and sleep disorders

8. Sleep Disorders and Sleep Deprivation – An Unmet Public Health Problem, Institute of Medicine of the National Academies – 2006 – ISBN 0-309-10111-5; Ayas et al, 2003

9. Why We Sleep – Matthew Walker, PhD – 2017 - ISB 978-1-5011

10. Sleep Disorders and Sleep Deprivation – An Unmet Public Health Problem, Institute of Medicine of the National Academies – 2006 – ISBN 0-309-10111-5; Durmer and Dinges, 2005

11. Sleep Disorders and Sleep Deprivation – An Unmet Public Health Problem, Institute of Medicine of the National Academies – 2006 – ISBN 0-309-10111-5; Veasey et al., 2002

12. Sleep Disorders and Sleep Deprivation – An Unmet Public Health Problem, Institute of Medicine of the National Academies – 2006 – ISBN 0-309-10111-5; Graeber et al, 1986a, b

13. Why We Sleep – Matthew Walker, PhD – 2017 - ISB 978-1-5011

14. Sleep Disorders and Sleep Deprivation – An Unmet Public Health Problem, Institute of Medicine of the National Academies – 2006 – ISBN 0-309-10111-5; Van Dongen et al 2003

Section 3
Managing
Service Delivery

Chapter 14

Customer Service

Service is the only product a fire department provides to its community. All activity on the company level needs to be directed towards this service delivery. This has to be the starting and ending point with everything a fire company and their fire department does as an organization. Everyone's main goal in the organization must be the delivery of the highest level of customer service possible.

My father wrote a book on this subject entitled *Essentials of Fire Department Customer Service*. While it is a must read for any Firefighter delivering service, my father's book is directed more towards the middle and upper management levels (the leaders of the department) in order for them to create a department wide culture and atmosphere of delivering excellent customer service. *Managing a Fire Company's* customer service focus is more on the nuts and bolts of a Company Officer managing the safest and best service delivery possible on the company level.

One of the main themes in my father's customer service book is: **the way employee's treat their customers will be a direct reflection on how their organization treats its employees**. I totally agree with this philosophy. When the upper levels of an organization have the right outlook and support systems in place, it makes it a lot easier for Company Officers to continue to pass these concepts forward. But what if the department has not created or does not support this kind of culture? Does that mean the Company Officer does not have to either? Absolutely not!

A Company Officer is the single person who controls the station and service delivery environment that their crew members work in. Even if a Company Officer works for an "evil empire," they still have the ability to control their workplace culture. In line with dad's book *Essentials of Fire Department Customer Service* and on point with what will be focused on throughout *Managing a Fire Company*: **The fire station workplace atmosphere and service delivery culture is built upon how the Company Officer manages and treats their crew members. The Company Officer and their subordinates are one of the most important elements of a Fire Department.** To fulfill the mission statement of the department, Company Officers must make sure that that their Firefighters are taken care of and feel safe so that they are at their best when they come to work and are totally focused on providing quality customer service, as opposed to worrying about their workplace environment.

Overview of Section 3 – Service Delivery

Background – My Father had the shortest mission statement for any fire department I have ever seen. It simply read: "Survive, Prevent Harm, Be Nice."

As short as it was, it actually says a great deal. Having "Survive" as the first word in the mission statement puts Firefighters first. In order to deliver effective service on the next call, you have to survive the last call you went on. That is why Dad put the most important element of the fire service first in the statement and it is also the reason Managing a Fire Company starts out the Service Delivery section of the book on how to maintain Firefighter mental wellness and resilience while delivering service in conjunction with performing one of the most stressful jobs in the country.

This is the section of the book that Tim W. Dietz comes in. Tim writes and helps co-write chapters of this book that address mental wellness, maintaining resilience, and reducing stressors when interacting with both the public and co-workers. I have briefly introduced Tim in the Acknowledgements of the book. As you will read in his biography (below), Tim is infinitely more qualified than I am to present the information needed for you to be the most successful in managing your crew's mental wellness and resilience. Without further ado, here is Tim Dietz...

Tim W. Dietz, LPC
Captain, Paramedic, retired
Founder/CEO of Behavioral Wellness Resources

Tim retired after 30 years in the fire service and is the Founder/CEO of Behavioral Wellness Resources, a consulting/counseling firm catering to the behavioral wellness needs of emergency response organizations and individuals. He is an internationally known speaker on human emotional crisis, grief, and staying happy and healthy in the emergency services professions. He is author of the book *Scenes of Compassion - A Responder's Guide for Dealing with Emergency Scene Emotional Crisis* and has written several published articles addressing behavioral health issues in the emergency services field. Tim is the Clinical Director for the Oregon Satellite of the West Coast Post-Trauma Retreat and was the clinical advisor to the US Coast Guard's mental health response following hurricanes Katrina and Rita and to the stress management team at the Oso, Washington mud slide. In 2017, Tim received the International Critical Incident Stress Foundation's Pioneering Spirit Award as an Industry Pioneer for his programs on emergency scene control and compassion. Tim travels the continent setting up behavioral health programs in first response organizations, teaching employees how to better take care of themselves and each other and then developing resources to assist those impacted by the job's stressors. He is a Licensed Professional Counselor and has a small, private practice in Oregon's beautiful Willamette Valley where he treats stress related injuries in First Responders.

Chapter 15

Enhancing Crew Wellness & Resilience - Tim W. Dietz

"We are effective to the extent that our employees are effective." - Alan Brunacini

What You Need to Know as a Company Officer

Being a Firefighter is one of the most stressful occupations in the US. Typically, firefighter falls a close second behind Enlisted Soldiers. Why? Because aside from hostile fires, technical rescues, hazardous materials, civil disobedience, and pandemics threatening our personal life, Firefighters respond and interact with serious injury or death to all ages - sometimes by genetic or health issues, sometimes by suicide, sometimes by tragic accidents, sometimes by violence inflicted by others, and sometimes these events also occur to our friends, family members, or co-workers. Whether our life saving efforts are successful or not, we then get to interact with the spouse or witness who are in crisis or the grieving parent or friend. We see malnourished children, spousal abuse, child abuse, drug abuse, pet abuse, the mentally ill, the parents more concerned about the chirping smoke detector interrupting their movie than their hypothermic children huddled in the corner, the lonely, the homeless, the frightened, the angry etc. Sometimes our lifesaving efforts are toward the "bad guy," or the person that disgusts us. We do all of this while staying operational and maintaining composure and control.

Aside from being able to maintain composure and control in the field, the job does take its toll if we are not paying attention. In recent years, more Firefighters have taken their own life than have died in hostile fire/work conditions. According to the IAFF, 20% of Firefighters will have PTSD, a diagnosable stress related injury by the time they retire!

Let's talk about stress in the fire service. The following is what the Company Officer needs to understand to effectively manage their crew and keep them ready:

1. Where Stress Comes From
2. We See Things Differently
3. Firefighter Personality (what makes us good can also set us up)
4. Human Response to Stress (discussed in a later chapter)

Once we know these things, we can then discuss what we can do about it!

1. Where does stress come from? (Not all of it comes from responding to calls.)

- **Environmental (work) stressors include:**
    - Politics/Budgets: Tax shortfalls leading to short staffing, fear of layoff, antiquated equipment, Brown outs, etc.
    - With tax limitations, it is common to have to do more with the same or less. Fire stations running 5 to 10 alarms per 24-hour shift in the 80's are now responding to 10 to 30 alarms per shift with the same or less staffing.
    - People making decisions not in the best interest of us or our customers

- Inequitable promotional exams, transfers, etc.
  - o Over activity – Firefighters who work in busier stations tend to report higher stress levels

- **Poor relationship with co-workers/supervisors:**
  - o Working a 24 to 48-hour period with someone who you do not see eye to eye with can make a long day even longer.
  - o Change:
    - Most Firefighters like predictability and will resist change they did not help create. "I'm going to work on this day, in this house, with this apparatus, with this activity schedule. Don't be changing that on me!" We do not deal well with change – ANY CHANGE! Even positive change!

- **Environmental (personal) stressors include:**
  - o Finances
  - o Family injury/illness
  - o Personal injury/illness
  - o Relationship troubles
  - o In-laws
  - o Kids in trouble
  - o Change
  - o Other things we have just learned to live with
  - o Etc.

- **Response/Service delivery:**
  - o Line of duty death
  - o Traumatic injuries
  - o Injury/death to kids
  - o Death in general
  - o Emotionally upsetting scenes
  - o Threat of personal injury or death
  - o Any call we may personalize (hits close to home)
  - o Etc.

2. We see things differently. What may impact one Firefighter, may not impact the next. The following are factors that influence the interpretation of stress (Nature versus Nurture):

- Genetic influences – Family history of psychological conditions – Temperament
- Past experiences – Learned coping patterns – Previous exposure to stress
- Existing conditions – Closeness of the situation to your own life – The event itself – Your health status – Your resources and support system

Background: The phone rang in my behavioral health office at the 7 AM shift change. It was a Company Officer who had just come to work. He asked, "Do you remember that horrible call we ran a couple of shifts ago?" I stated that I did. He went on to explain how that call had impacted him and how the last couple of days off he was not himself, was having trouble sleeping, and was very irritable. He said, "Whatever my wife said to me, I would argue - sometimes to the point of yelling. This is not like me and I feel terrible about it."

Then he shared that, "Last night I yelled at my kid for grabbing a comic book at bedtime. I mean, I lost it with him over a stupid comic book! I feel like I am a horrible husband and dad." He went on to say that this morning on his drive to work, for the first time in 15 years, "I didn't want to be here." He then went on to say, "What is wrong with me? Am I going crazy?" I went on to explain that what he was explaining to me was pretty normal after what he had experienced a few shifts ago, I reminded him of his tools for self-care, and offered a few more (explained later in this book). I told him I would stop by his station later on in the day to check in and see how things were going.

That very same morning at 7:30, the phone rang again. It was a Firefighter who worked for that Company Officer. He did not know the Officer had called me earlier. He asked if I remembered that horrible call they went on a few shifts ago. I stated that I did and he replied, "I'm listening to my Officer and driver talk about how that call has impacted their lives." He stated he was not feeling those things. He asked, "What is wrong with me? Am I not human?" I explained that lack of stress symptoms is also "normal" and reminded him to continue his self-care. I also told him I would be dropping by his station later to see how things were going.

This was the same call, but these were very different responses! This is why we check in with everyone!

3. Firefighter Personality

The way we are wired may create unrealistic expectations. The following are some examples:

- We need to be in control
- We need to be perfect or near perfect
- We can solve others' problems
- Things get better when we arrive
- We can make organization out of chaos
- Bad things do not bother us
- People are better off because we came to work

We need to believe these things to do our jobs. Not only do we place these high expectations on ourselves, but our customers do, as well. They call us to save them and their loved ones and put their fire out. The fact is, that even with our best efforts, buildings burn and/or people die.

What We Can Do – Tools for the Company Officer to Enhance Resiliency (Lead by Example)

"If you want to make changes in the workers' behavior, change the behavior of the bosses." - Alan Brunacini

Actually, Firefighters are very resilient to these stressors. However, as good as we are at controlling human emotions in the field, eventually these experiences can impact us physically and emotionally. Let's take a look at the stuff you just read about and use it for enhancing our resilience to stress (resilience is how quickly we can bounce back from adversity) and for your role as the Company Officer to make sure the crew is healthy and ready.

1. Create the culture

2. Know your crew
3. Exercise
4. Eat Right
5. Talk
6. Know your Resources
7. Know your Policies (regarding crew wellness)
8. Life Away from the fire station

1. Create the Culture

Creating the culture makes it okay to support and take care of each other. We cannot help and support each other if we do not know things are impacting each other. Someone on the crew stating that a call bothered them IS NOT a sign of weakness, brokenness, or that they chose the wrong career. It is a sign that we are humans and sometimes things bother us. The culture on your crew should elicit the following responses if someone is having a difficult time: "You look like this call has impacted you," "What is it that bothered you?" "Do you want to talk about it?" "How can I support you?" or even "That sounds difficult," or "I don't even know what to say," etc.

A great example of creating this culture is displayed nightly at a fire department in the North Bay area of San Francisco. Every shift after dinner, the crew goes around the table and each person states their "High" of the day and their "Low" of the day thus far (they call it "High-Low"). It causes a discussion of each crew members' experiences (good and bad) during the shift and facilitates not only laughter, but support. Remember that we all see things differently.

It is also okay to address a crew member if you see them struggling (an example of this conversation can be found in a later section of this book). "See something, say something." A good rule of thumb is: if there is any change in a person's normal behavior, something is up – whether they admit to it or not.

Common changes to watch for:

- Isolating from crew
- Not engaging like usual or seems distant
- Quick to irritate
- Unusual chronic complaining
- Skipping meals
- Changes in arrival time at work/tardiness
- Etc.

If you see one or more of these behaviors, something is going on. If it is not a work thing, then something has happened in their personal life. Approaching them lets them know they are not hiding it very well. It also demonstrates that you may be concerned about them and/or their readiness at work. If they do not want to chat about it, remind them of your organization's resources (#7 on this list).

2. Know Your Crew

The better you know your crew, the better you can figure out if something is up!

If we respond on a SIDS call, I want to know who on my crew has a baby at home. Likewise, responding to an elderly gentleman who died peacefully in his sleep may warrant a check-in with a crew member who recently lost their dad or grandpa. We cannot have these conversations if we do not know who we are working with. In addition, this is quid quo pro! We would expect a crew member to say to us "Hey Captain/Lieutenant, that call may have hit close to home to you. How are you doing?"

The Company Officer should be able to identify things that may cause stress to the crew or an individual – the calls that may be "red flags" for a check-in. They can include: kid calls, unusual or difficult rescues, fires or medical calls, unnatural fatalities, victims known by a crew member, etc. Again, Firefighters can personalize a call – hence the importance of knowing a bit about each crew member and their personal life.

Is there organizational change going on - budget concerns, negotiations not going well, and/or a change in administration or the operations of the organization? Are there changes going on at home - a sick child, partner, parent or grandparent, a new mortgage or financial change, and/or relatives in trouble or relationship problems? We know Firefighters like predictability and really are not fond of change. In most cases, a Firefighter will resist any change they did not help create. As a Company Officer, we may need to have a discussion on available resources to the crew members we see impacted.

3. Exercise

It is a no-brainer that to maintain adequate company readiness, the individual members of the crew need to maintain both physical and mental readiness. As a Company Officer, you are ultimately responsible for this.

Exercise not only makes us fit for duty physically, but numerous studies have shown that people stay healthier and perform better when they are physically fit. Additionally, physical fitness maintains psychological balance. **There is no greater reducer to the stress of your job than physical exercise!** Vigorous exercise produces endorphins. California's Loma Linda University School of Medicine found that "when you strengthen muscles and improve your level of fitness, you also condition the pituitary glands that produce endorphins and other calming chemicals," causing conditioned people to deal better with stress.

The problem in the fire service is that every time you respond to an incident, your brain's reaction causes the release of stress hormones and not every alarm calls your muscles into action to burn these hormones off - recalled alarms, smoke detector checks, smoke in the area, invalid assists (when you are not the one bending over to pick the person up). Calls where you are running a clip board, a radio, or turning knobs on a pump panel are all calls that you are not burning the hormones off. As stated earlier, these hormones, particularly cortisol, damage bodily systems and can cause premature death.

Stress hormones are designed to be used to survive in the moment – not sit idle in our blood stream. This short-term survival response can have a long-term impact on us. Here is what chronically released cortisol can do to your body during your career:

- Damage the cardiovascular system
- Damage the immune system
- Damage the neurological system
- Cause thinning of bones
- Cause ulcers
- Accelerate aging
- Deposit fat around the waste

Physical exercise is important in the fire service for the following reasons:

- Exercise consumes residual stress hormones. That is why the hormones are there - to fuel your body to run or fight.
- Exercise increases the oxygen content in red blood cells, which can help you sleep!
- Exercise lowers symptoms of mild depression.
- Exercise is a natural and effective antianxiety treatment.
- Exercise reduces the risk of heart disease and stroke.
- Exercise lowers blood pressure.
- Exercise improves mood and helps you think clearly.
- Exercise gives you more energy and stamina.

The exercise routine should consist of a combination of both aerobic (for endurance) and anaerobic (for strength) and be at a minimum of 30 minutes in length, making total exercise time a minimum 2 ½ hours per week. There are lots of exercise routines for Firefighters available.

Knowing the health and safety benefits of a fit firefighting crew and the need of fitness for readiness, the Company Officer needs to make sure time is allotted on every shift for exercise to take place. The Company Officer needs to not only allot time, but to participate (remember to lead by example)!

Exercise is such an important factor in your and your crew's ability to do the job that there should be a policy regarding it! Does your organization have a "fit for duty" policy? If so, it should address the need for physical fitness.

4. Eat Right

Certainly, one's diet can have an impact on mental health and job readiness. John has covered this at greater length in a previous chapter of this book. There is one thing the Company Officer should be aware of. When under stress and the brain is in fight or flight survival mode, it craves survival food that gives immediate and sustained energy. This is biological and developed with early humans. Our ancestors sought out food for energy like berries and other fruits that contained sugars and higher fat foods for sustained energy like nuts, avocados, maybe even fat little animals. Today, however, those same cravings can lead us to soda pop, candy, donuts, and big greasy cheese covered hamburgers and French fries. DO NOT fall for these cravings! Continue to eat a healthy diet!

The crew should also make sure that they stay hydrated. Water regulates body temperature, delivers nutrients to cells, and helps keep our bodily systems functioning. It can also help improve sleep, our mood, and cognition. It is recommended that women drink at least 11 cups a day and that men drink at least 16 cups per day. This is average – think about how your body temperature raises in bunker gear. All crew members should take responsibility in keeping everyone hydrated.

5. Talk

Coughing up the Apple Analogy

When I encounter an event that impacts me (maybe an un-helmeted child who fell off their bicycle and received a permanent brain injury) it feels like I have just swallowed an apple whole and it gets stuck in my throat. This, by the way, is very uncomfortable! Now, I am resilient just like you are and for the majority of us, as long as we continue to take care of ourselves, our body will work away at this apple and it will eventually drop into our stomach and process. This however may take a few weeks, so during that time, I am not sleeping very well, I am a bit irritated, and I am isolating because I am tired of people asking me if I am okay. Plus, every time something reminds me of this incident, it reminds me of this uncomfortable apple in my throat.

Another option instead of waiting for the apple to process is to talk about it. When I say, "that call hit close to home," or "that call sucked," I have just coughed up the apple. Your job is to ask me, "Why?"

- *I've got a kid the same age at home.*
- *I caught him twice last week not wearing a helmet.*
- *That bike laying in the street is the exact same bike my son has.*
- *I'm worried he's at home riding without a helmet now because he knows I'm at work and can't catch him.*

When I tell you the parts of the incident that impacted me, I am now biting the pieces off the apple and it is dropping into my stomach and processing! This is not psychotherapy, but simply helping speed up the processing of a troubling event.

We basically have a couple choices after a stressful event:

1. Shove it in our backpack (which works – until it does not) or
2. Talk about it. If you hear a co-worker say, "well that call sucked," or "that one hit close to home," or a similar statement, your job is to ask, "What was it?" or "What hit close to home?"

When the person impacted tells you the pieces of what bothered them, they are leaving it in the cab or at the kitchen table and not carrying it home. In my experience, most stressful calls/events at work can be handled in the cab of the apparatus or around the kitchen table if we allow ourselves to talk about it! As the Company Officer, you may have to initially model this.

In the cab, returning from their 5th pediatric death this week, a conversation may go like this:

Captain:	*"How are you all doing? If we catch a call between now and the station are you all good to go?"*
Driver:	*"I'm okay."*
Firefighters:	*"I'm okay."*
Captain:	*"I'm glad you are okay, but here's what I don't like about these calls: I hate the look in a mom's eyes when you tell her that her baby is dead. Did you hear the sound of her trying to catch her breath? We've done this five times this week and if I never saw that look or heard that sound again for the rest of my life, I would be fine!"*

That Company Officer has just:

1. Modeled that to have a conversation about an uncomfortable event is going to be expected,
2. Shown their crew that it is okay to be human, and
3. Began the processing of the event so it does not go into their backpack. If one of the crew members does state that the call "hit close to home", "sucked," or "got to me," the response needs to be, "What was it that impacted you?" This facilitates coughing up the apple!

Remember that the Company Officer is the role model for how the crew behaves and responds to various activities. Make it the routine to discuss things that are uncomfortable without judgement. Talk about it! The "High-Low" described earlier is an excellent way to get people talking!

6. Know your Policies – Regarding Crew Wellness

Does your organization have policies that address the following?

- Behavioral Health
- Critical incident or traumatic stress - situations that may call for a stress management response
- Peer Team response
- Chaplain response
- Administrative leave regarding overwhelmed employees
- Fit for Duty as it pertains to Behavioral Health

As the Company Officer, you need to be familiar with these to help guide you and your crew if there is a need.

7. Know Your Resources

Sometimes we may recognize that a stressful event is bigger than the apparatus cab or kitchen table. As a Company Officer, you should know the answers to the following questions regarding resources.

- Does your organization have a Peer Support Team or Chaplain trained in CISM and do you know how to activate them or consult with them?
- Does your organization have SOPs regarding critical incidents?
- Can an apparatus in your organization go out of service for a period of time while the crew has a chance to process a powerful event?
- Does your organization have a policy if a Firefighter requests to go home after a significant incident? If not, what are that Firefighter's options?
- Does your organization have an EAP and do you and your crew know how to contact them?
- Has your Peer Team or Organization identified "culturally competent" mental health professionals in your community that know how to treat stress related injures with the intent of getting a Firefighter back to work healthy and in a timely fashion? Or identified treatment programs specific to first responders dealing with stress such as the West Coast Post-Trauma Retreat or the IAFF Center of Excellence?

8. Life Away from the Fire Station

If anyone knows how quickly things change, it's us! We get a paycheck because people's lives change! Most of them have no idea of this change until they or someone else calls 911. We are not immune from this! My next question is: What are you going to do with the knowledge that it's not "if" things will change, but "when" and that at some point in time, either you or a loved one is going to need emergency care? This means we need to live life to the fullest.

There should always be a "carrot" on your calendar - something to look forward to for both you and your loved ones. Take every opportunity while you and your loved ones are healthy and able to do stuff you all enjoy.

Here is an example:

A Firefighter encounters a stressful event while on shift and contacts their mental health therapist requesting an appointment when they get off work. The next morning after getting off shift, they go to their appointment. The therapist ask about what happened yesterday. The Firefighter states, "I'm really agitated right now, not because of the incident at work, but about what happened this morning." The Firefighter goes on to explain that he stopped by his house prior to coming into the counseling office. At home, his two little boys, who have not seen him the last 48 hours, jumped on him yelling, "Daddy's home!" He states he yelled at his wife to get the kids off of him, tells her he is tired, and needs a break. He goes on to explain that this only "ramped" the kids up to the point that he became very irritated at them and his wife yelling, "get these damn kids out of here." He then looks to his therapist for advice on how to deal with his kids. The therapist states, "If you're looking for advice on how to handle your children because they miss their dad, I'll give you some: get on the floor and play with your boys! Your boys need their dad. They don't care how tired you are." The therapist then went on to explain that sometimes you have to "fake it till you make it" and mentioned that they guarantee that after 10 minutes of rolling on the floor with your kids, you will be giggling with them.

The moral of the story is to engage with life and those you love - tired or not! Be thankful you have kids who love and miss you, as you get a paycheck because people loose kids by accidents, illness, or violence. Embrace your family whenever you have an opportunity. Just a different way to think - you will reenergize and become a better Firefighter by rolling around and doing things you enjoy instead of going home and vegging out on the couch all day.

One of the challenges to accomplish this is the "transition time" between the station and home after shift. Going from Company Officer mode to parent, spouse, partner, etc. at times feels difficult. If you have had a rough shift, is it possible to catch a run/walk/workout/yoga etc., on your way home? This may help clear your mind and put things in a better perspective.

The Company Officer is the role model. Talk about your off-duty escapades and how much you enjoy them around your crew. Let them know how important life away from work is and how therapeutic it is to go to bed every night without regrets.

What to do after a Bad Call – Putting it all Together!

Tim's Five Assignment Model

I received a phone call from a Battalion Chief one day. He stated one of their crews was currently out on their 5th pediatric code of the week. He was concerned and asked if I could do a check-in with them. I called the Lieutenant at the scene and asked if they needed any assistance on site. He stated they had the scene taken care of, but asked that I meet with the crew at the station when they returned. I was sitting at the station kitchen table when the crew walked in. The Lieutenant had not told the crew I would be waiting for them. The first two crew members came into the kitchen, saw me, then quickly said "we coughed up our apples on the way back!" "Perfect! You don't need me to cough up apples," I said. After a quick conversation on how they were currently doing, it was decided to keep them out of service for an hour and have a discussion on what the rest of their shift would look like. Here was their "homework," which turned into the "5-Assignment Model."

1. Talk

I know you "coughed up your apple" on the way back to the station. That is good! However, if you feel that lump in your throat later today or tomorrow, you need to tell somebody.

2. Exercise

Plan on doing something active. If you have already worked out today, find something physically active you can do that is fun. Maybe go run around the track after school is out. Shoot baskets, throw balls, or chase each other. I do not care what it is, but you should burn off the excessive stress hormones produced from the stressful incident.

3. Eat

Plan on eating at your normal mealtime. If the crew was planning to sit down and have dinner at 6 PM, then fix a meal and eat at 6 PM, hungry or not. The slowing of the digestive system is a normal stress response, but if you are going to remain on shift, your body needs fuel! Eat!

As a side note: While I am having this conversation, inevitably a Firefighter has already raided the refrigeration or kitchen cabinets and is stuffing themselves with food. This will also be "normal," as many of us find comfort in food.

4. Write down what you are going to do when you get off work that you can look forward to.

Pull out a piece of paper and pencil and write it down. The intent behind this is knowing that today sucks (One pediatric code a year is too much for me, but 5 in a week?), but forcing yourself to look forward to something! It can be a bicycle ride, a walk in the park, a stroll with a loved one or pet. I do not care what it is, but I want to see it in print!

As a side note: If this is a busy station and I know the crew will probably be up most of the night, I will make them write down the person who is going to go with them on their activity to hold them accountable, so to speak. I know with even the best intentions to go home and get on a bike, if you have been up most the night and are tired, you will go home, plant yourself in your "magic chair" for just a few minutes, then wake up when the sun has gone down.

5. Laugh

The last thing I will have them do after dinner and after their physical activity, when hopefully things slow down is plug in a "stupid funny" movie (non-thinking stupid humor) and as a crew, sit and watch and laugh from your diaphragm. Force it if you have to. Fake it 'til you make it. Laughter has been shown to release catecholamines and endorphins. These will help take elevated vital signs (blood pressure up to 30 points higher than before going on a call) and return them to pre-incident levels.

Closing

The Company Officer is responsible for the readiness of their crew. We maintain crew readiness and wellness by taking care of ourselves and each other! The Company Officer is the role model for the crew. Create the culture that embraces curiosity about each other, that allows for difficult calls to be talked about so the crew can support each other, and where exercise is an important part of your crew's readiness when on shift. Show your crew that regardless of how busy the day has been, you will always make time to get some exercise in. Create the culture in which eating healthy is the standard, the crew knows what resources and policies drive a wellness work environment, and off-duty time is to live, laugh, and love!

Work hard. Be nice. – Tim W. Dietz

Chapter 16

General Emergency Response and Scene Safety Guidelines

Most 911 service delivery incidents require a response to the incident scene. While the entire response should be focused on solving the customers' problems who generated the 911 call, you still have to get to the scene in the safest manner possible in order to deliver the service that has been requested. While responding to, working at, and returning from the call you will also probably interact with hundreds of more customers not directly associated with incident.

This chapter will address a Company Officer managing the following when responding to and operating at 911 service delivery calls:

1. In station response readiness and getting out of the station
2. Emergency response guidelines
3. General scene safety guidelines
4. Documenting emergency activity
5. Returning back to the station

1. In-station Response Readiness and Getting out of the Station

As presented in earlier in this book, all activities that can be performed at the fire station should be performed there whenever possible. This includes performing in service PT and company drilling. Members of a fire company must understand that fire stations are located based on an overall town, city, county, or statewide strategic response plan. The people who develop these plans are well educated and they are well informed on where fire stations should be located so they provide the best possible response times and service coverage to the communities they serve. These higher-up people get to decide where the fire stations and the fire apparatus are located, not some 31-year-old Company Officer who thinks that the city is their "beat." Stay in your first due area and as close as possible to your fire station at all times. Several smart people have figured out where you need to hang out during your 24-hour shift.

Pre-Deployment

NFPA 1710 (thanks again, Dad!) sets the standard of getting out of the fire station and starting a 911 response within 60 seconds (for an EMS response) or 80 seconds (for a fire response) of the fire station being notified of the incident. If everybody is awake in the fire station and if your PPE is set up properly (discussed next), the crew should start the response by getting in the correct gear for the call around the 30 to 45 second mark of receiving the call and being out the doors within the specified time frames.

Members should avoid putting themselves into positions around the station that would delay a prompt response, but there will be times when members are engaged in a station activity that may slow their response to the apparatus. This includes activities such as performing station drills, PT, taking a shower, maintaining a piece of equipment, etc.

When performing in-station drilling or PT, the Company Officer should set up the activity so that everyone can quickly disengage from it and make a timely response out of the station. When drilling in service, only take the equipment off the truck that you are drilling with. For example, if it is ladder throwing day (behind the station), only take one ladder off the truck at a time to drill with. Once done taking turns with that ladder, place it back on the truck and then get the next ladder off to take turns with. Most 911 calls are for EMS service, so if you are drilling with ladders behind the station and an EMS call comes in (or any other call that would not require the ladder you are drilling with), leave it behind the station where it is and quickly make the response. When back at the station, put it back on the truck or keep on drilling with it.

If an individual crew member is engaged in an activity that they know is going to put them in a slower response mode (taking a shower, mowing the lawn, etc.) they should give their Company Officer a heads up.

PPE in a Ready State for Response

All crew members should situate their PPE on and around the truck in a manner that facilitates the whole crew getting into the proper PPE for the call **PRIOR** to mounting the apparatus and belting in for the response.

Background: The crew members of L-201 and LT-201 had 2 sets of PPE for each truck. One set was for EMS calls and the other set was for fire calls. The EMS bunker pants consisted of steel toed leather ladder boots, along with a pair of Nomex brush pants that had no inside thermal layering and that were dyed navy blue. Every riding position on the truck had their PPE set up in a manner so it took just a few seconds to get into the proper gear before getting on the truck.

Because my position was the right front seat, my PPE was set up in front of the first compartment behind the cab of the Captain's side of the truck. In front of the compartment on the concrete apron were my 2 sets of bunker pants. Once the call came in, I would get into the correct bunker pants and then I would place the other bunker pants inside the compartment before the response. Inside the compartment on a hook were my turnout coat and helmet.

Most responses were for EMS calls. If this was the case, I would get into my EMS bunkers, place my fire bunkers in the compartment, close it, and then I would mount the truck and belt in. If it were a fire call response, I would get all my turnouts on before mounting the truck, starting with my bunker pants. On the face shield of my helmet, I had my fire hood draped in a manner so I could pull it out and get it over my head and into position very quickly before donning my turnout coat (always put your hood on BEFORE your turnout coat). Once all my turnouts were on, I would close the compartment and take my helmet and place it under my seat in the cab to facilitate wearing a headset while enroute to the call. The first thing I did when I got off the truck at the incident scene was put on my helmet and then I would head to the SCBA compartment.

The whole "dress out" routine prior to mounting the apparatus took about 10 seconds. All other members on the truck had their PPE laid out the same way and they did the same, exact thing before mounting the apparatus. They were all in the proper response gear and belted in before the truck turned a wheel. This type of response produces the following:

- *Starts the incident out in a well-defined, standard manner*
- *Gets all responders in the proper PPE prior to the response*
- *Ensures that all members are belted in prior to the truck moving*
- *Ensures that all members STAY belted in during the entire response (it is really easy when you are wearing the right gear before mounting the apparatus)*
- *Now, instead of focusing on getting dressed on the way to incident, the entire crew can focus on the road, the radio, their upcoming responsibilities, the visible conditions they are responding to, etc.*

2. Emergency Response Guidelines

Dispatch and Pertinent Incident Information

The incident size-up and scene safety process all starts with the initial dispatch information. Most fire departments today use a standard dispatch process when a 911 dispatch is sent out to a fire station that includes:

- Light and tones – Multi-company station - what units are assigned
- Nature of the incident (EMS, fire, hazmat, etc.)
- Address of the incident
- Tactical radio channel the call will be assigned to

All members need to pay close attention to the original dispatch information. Along with the standard dispatch process, most departments will also have an MDC/MDT mounted on the apparatus (in the Company Officer position) that is used to provide pertinent incident information that can include the following:

- Maps that provide a digital aerial view/photo of the incident's location, the building type, and the arrangement of the buildings at the address – this is a big deal if the incident is located in complex geography
- Identify any other units assigned to the incident
- Any other PII not included in the original dispatch that was/is being collected by the dispatcher who received the 911 call. This can include:
  o EMS - Patient age, gender, medical history, etc.
  o More specific details on the nature of the call
  o More specific details on the location of the incident and/or the incident's environment

Driving with Lights and Sirens

All members on an apparatus MUST be seated and belted in prior to the truck moving. When the apparatus is moving, AT NO TIME shall a member unbuckle (remove) their seat belt. Firefighters who need to be told to wear their seat belt should not be Firefighters. To me, this is a very simple intelligence test.

Driving with lights and sirens on is considered a high frequency, high risk activity. As stated earlier, apparatus accidents are the most common legal liability a department has aside from

HR issues. Company Officers must realize that even though they are not the person driving the apparatus, they are still completely responsible for the operation of the vehicle. If something bad happens, you own it.

Background: My father became the Operations Chief of the Phoenix Fire Department in 1972, the Fire Chief in 1978, and he retired in 2006. During his 34-year career of overseeing the fire department, the most common bad thing that he had to deal with in the field (consistently) were fire companies getting into serious vehicle collisions. He knew better than anyone else that there is a certain amount of risk involved when driving a 25-ton truck with the lights and sirens on. He also knew better than anybody else that it is extremely rude to kill customers in vehicle accidents while responding to 911 calls. One of his lifelong missions as a Fire Chief was to eliminate these events from ever happening on his fire department.

In 1985 (about a year before I took the Engineer promotional exam), a Paramedic engine company was making a 911 response when they were involved in a near fatal collision in an intersection. A car turned left in front of them not knowing that the fire truck was in the opposite, oncoming lanes (coming up from behind them and to their left side). The driver was struck directly on their door by the front end of the fire truck when they were making their left turn.

The driver's family sued the fire department. The case never made it to court, but my father went to every deposition that was held until the case was settled. At the end of the case, the driver's lawyer stated that if it was not a Paramedic engine company that had struck his client's car, his client would not have survived the accident (the entire crew was treating the driver's injuries less than 30 seconds after the collision occurred). He ended by telling everyone in the room that his client "was 50% less than the person they were before the accident." This statement stuck in my Dad's heart and mind for the rest of his career.

Knowing my father, I am certain that after hearing the lawyer's final statement, he went home and authored what would be the new emergency driving policy for his fire department (written below). At the time, there was a complex system to create and implement a new SOP that usually took at least a year to get through the process. Dad's new SOP was posted into the books the next day. He told everybody that he was very flexible with most things, but this one was not up for debate.

What he drafted were the driving policies I operated under as a newly promoted Engineer for 7 years and as a Company Officer for the rest of my career. As a Company Officer, I was held more accountable to Dad's driving policies than the driver was. If my father (or any other Chief Officer) saw anyone violating the driving policy, the Company Officer got 2 shifts off without pay and the driver got 1 shift off. If it happened to either person again, there was a very high probability of them getting demoted. Dad took driving very seriously and so should everyone else.

I absolutely agreed with my father on how a fire department should drive while on emergency responses and because this is such an important service delivery activity, I am including Dad's emergency response driving policy in this book. Before going over his emergency response and driving SOP, let's look at some of the driving terminology that will be referred to in the SOP. Maricopa County fire departments use the same response codes as law enforcement. They are:

- Code 1 – Vehicle driving while not assigned to an incident. All traffic laws are followed.
- Code 2 – Vehicle is assigned to an incident that is non-emergency in nature. No lights or sirens are used and all traffic laws are followed.

- Code 3 – Vehicle is assigned to an incident that is emergency in nature. Lights and sirens are used.
- Code 4 – Mostly used by law enforcement. Emergency scene hazards have been stabilized and the scene is declared safe.

Alan Brunacini's Driving SOP

Standard emergency response procedure:

- All personnel shall be mounted on board, properly attired for the call, and seated with seat belts securely fastened before the truck moves
- All radios set to the assigned channel
- Station doors fully open
- Know where you are going
- Drive defensively and professionally at all times
- All responding apparatus should have 2 members in the front seats of the apparatus whenever possible
- The driver is responsible for operating the vehicle safely
- The co-driver is responsible for being a second set of eyes and ears anytime a unit is responding to or returning from a response

The use of sirens and warning lights does not automatically give the right-of-way to the emergency vehicle. These devices simply request the right-of-way from other drivers based on their awareness of the emergency vehicle's presence. Emergency vehicle drivers must make every possible effort to make their presence and intended actions known to other drivers, they must drive defensively, and be prepared for the unexpected, inappropriate actions of others.

Code-3 Emergency Driving Procedure

- Code 3 response is authorized only in conjunction with emergency incidents.
- Unnecessary Code-3 responses shall be avoided.
- The Company Officer in charge of the vehicle is responsible for the safety of all vehicle operations and managing the compliance of this procedure.
- The Company Officer of the vehicle will confirm that all personnel and riders are on-board, properly attired, with seat belts on, before the vehicle is permitted to move.
- Fire department vehicles are authorized to exceed posted speed limits only when responding Code 3 under favorable conditions. This applies only with light traffic, good roads, good visibility, and dry pavement. Under these conditions a maximum of 10 MPH over the posted speed limit is authorized.
- Under less than favorable conditions, the posted speed limit is the absolute maximum speed permissible.
- When emergency vehicles must travel into center or oncoming traffic lanes, the maximum permissible speed shall be 20 MPH.

- Intersections present the greatest potential danger to emergency vehicles. Driver and co-drivers must be focused on intersection management any time their response vehicle nears or enters into an intersection.
- When approaching and entering into an intersection with the right-of-way (green light or no stop sign), drivers shall not exceed the posted speed limit.
- When emergency vehicles must use the center (left turn lane) or oncoming traffic lanes to approach controlled intersections (traffic light or stop sign), they must come to a **complete stop** before proceeding into and through the intersection, including occasions when the emergency vehicle has a green traffic light.
- **STOP ON ALL REDS!** When approaching a negative right-of-way intersection (red light, stop sign), the vehicle shall come to a **complete stop** before entering into an intersection and may only proceed through it when the driver can visually account that all traffic in all lanes are yielding the right-of-way to the response vehicle.
- Units responding to incidents using a freeway for response access only will precede Code-2 while driving on the freeway.
- For incidents that are located directly on a freeway, Company Officers must use their best judgment on the proper response (Code 2 or 3) based on the traffic conditions and the critical factors present.
- When the first unit reports on the scene with "nothing showing" or an equivalent report, any additional units assigned to the incident should continue into the scene using a Code 2 response.

Code-3 driving accidents were greatly reduced on the Phoenix Fire Department soon after Dad's new driving SOP was implemented. Along with this reduction, the severity and injury rate of response accidents was also greatly reduced. During the rest of Dad's career on the department (1987 forward), in well over half of the "significant" apparatus accidents that did occur on the department, the Company Officer was not enforcing the SOP, the SOP was violated, and something really bad happened. Back to Dad's old saying: "you better be doing everything right when something goes wrong." Take driving seriously and follow the SOP every time.

3. General Scene Safety Guidelines

The size up process will continue while enroute to the incident scene. The information analyzed comes in the forms of:

- Subsequent information gathered from the person generating the 911 response
- Preplan information provided by the MDC/MDT, hydrant locations, etc.
- Every Engine company responding to a fire should take note of hydrant locations while responding
- Previous experiences at the same address
- Visual information gained from the cab of the truck when approaching (smoke column on the horizon, traffic backed up behind an auto accident, etc.)

The Company Officer needs to share all PII with their crew as soon as possible while responding into the incident scene. Crew members should be sizing up the incident, as well and the more information and direction (orders) they have from their Company Officer before arriving on scene will go a long way in putting the whole crew on the same page when the truck finally stops. This will also reduce crew communications once the unit is on scene and the whole crew has dismounted the apparatus because everyone will know what is going on and what their responsibilities are before dismounting. After dismounting the apparatus on dynamic, fast paced incidents, it is difficult giving verbal orders while you and the rest of your crew members are on the "fly" and they are directly engaged in high risk activities and/or when the Company Officer is wearing an SCBA.

Most EMS scenes located in a static residential setting will usually have a standard crew deployment off the apparatus, in which the Company Officer does not have to say too much to their crew members when arriving to the scene to get them into (standard) action.

On Scene

When you can visibly see the incident scene from the cab of the truck, you are generally considered on scene, but most of the time, the apparatus has not yet stopped moving and the Company Officer and the Engineer will need to coordinate "spotting" the apparatus. General guidelines when approaching a scene and spotting your apparatus include:

- The unique hazards of driving in or near emergency scenes requires the driver and co-driver to use extreme caution and to be alert and prepared to react to the unexpected.
- Drivers must consider the dangers their moving vehicle poses to emergency personnel and spectators who may be preoccupied and/or focused on the emergency scene (GO SLOW when driving in or near emergency scenes).
- When parking at the scene of an incident, apparatus should be spotted in a manner that protects personnel who will be working on or near a roadway and scene illumination and warning lights should be properly used to divert approaching traffic around and/or away from the emergency scene (fuses/flares can also greatly assist with scene safety).
- If used, turn off the Opticom after spotting the apparatus.
- This book will not cover in detail the spotting of apparatus on freeways or busy roadways. If this is the environment you are operating in, please refer to and use your local department's freeway response SOP.
- No personnel may un-belt and exit the apparatus until it comes to a complete stop (with the parking brake set).
- Personnel dismounting the apparatus must look both ways and verify their outside surroundings are safe before dismounting the apparatus.
- All personnel working in or near traffic lanes shall wear high visibility vests (or full turnouts).

EMS Scene Safety

Because the majority of the 911 calls a department responds to are for medical services, this portion of the book will be primarily dedicated to EMS scene safety and service delivery. Since the chances are very low of responding to an EMS related active shooter incident, this book will not address scene safety at such an event and if you are dispatched to any incident in which any type of violence is occurring, you will need to refer to and follow your local department's violent incident SOP. This book will cover normal EMS service delivery in which the responders are not in any physical danger of being assaulted or shot.

Okay, you have made it to the 911 call safely and now it is time to size up the actual incident scene. Let's start with this: **All safety starts with situational awareness** (the more competent you are, the more aware you are). The Company Officer, along with all the other crew members, will need to perform a size-up of the incident scene before engaging in any control measures. Much of this initial size-up is done inside the cab of the truck before dismounting the apparatus.

Before dismounting the apparatus and engaging in any control measures, an EMS scene size-up should include:

- What environment is the patient (and any bystanders) located in and do they need to be extricated from their current environment? This could include being inside of a house or a vehicle (maybe trapped) or being outside in an open-air environment. What are the current weather conditions and how it will that affect customer and responder safety?
- Where does the apparatus need to be parked to provide the most protection for the crew and the public that has to get around it? The crew wins every time! Never be afraid/shy about shutting down a roadway when it comes to protecting first responders.
- Based on the visual observation of the scene and the amount of other resources responding, the first Company Officer to arrive to the scene may need to activate the formal command system along with upgrading the incident with more resources and/or request a higher level of patient care (ALS, Ambulance, Helicopter, etc.). Static EMS calls that require just one or two units to mitigate generally do not require the activation of the formal command system (Blue Card).
- Based on the call information and visual observation of the scene, what type of PPE does the crew need to be in?
- Based on the call information and visual observation of the scene, what type of equipment will be needed to control the problem?
- Is the patient environment in a crime scene or is there a potential for any violence?

Situational awareness equates to paying close attention to all aspects of the surrounding environment, assessing potential threats, continuously monitoring the situation for changes, and making good decisions in response to what is observed or what gut feelings and previous experiences are telling you. Company Officers must make the EMS scene size-up process the first step in patient assessment and care, as well as continuously size up the incident scene throughout the patient encounter.

Once the crew is off the truck, the crew members situational awareness on the overall scope of the incident scene will be significantly reduced as they turn their focus and attention to performing the tasks required to stabilize the incident. While your crew members are focusing on treating and stabilizing the patient, it is the Company Officer's responsibility to step back and manage the overall scene, becoming the eyes, ears, and voice of the company. When engaged in controlling an incident scene, the Company Officer will need to:

- Continuously size up the scene
- Direct the standard of care
- Document the standard of care
- Interact with the other units, agencies, and customers directly related to the incident to the degree it is necessary to stabilize the incident scene (treat and transport the patient)

A great majority of EMS incidents will occur in a static environment (not much is going on), in which the most critical factors on the incident scene are the patient's symptoms and the highest risks to the responders are blood borne pathogens and other bio-exposures. On these types of incidents, the Company Officer will most likely only interact with other EMS agencies and the management of the scene will not escalate past 1 or 2 units.

Prevention Strategies

The 3 biggest threats to personnel working at a static EMS incident are:

1. Sprain and strain injuries
2. Direct exposure to an infectious disease
3. Violence associated with an incident

1. Sprain and Strain Injuries

This level of risk is due to moving or lifting a patient (a lot of lower back injuries). Company Officers must manage all crew members working together and staying in good, safe, ergonomic positions when moving, lifting, and transporting patients.

2. Direct Exposure to an Infectious Disease

The sheer variety of patients and situations fire department personnel respond to contributes to a very high potential for having exposures to infectious diseases. Company Officers must facilitate their crew members being informed of and following all of the suggested PPE guidelines and personal protection strategies found in OSHA's Bloodborne Pathogens Standard (which safeguards workers who have the potential for on-the-job exposure to infectious diseases).

Background: My father always talked about the 2 different ways a Firefighter could die in the line of duty, both being absolute tragedies. The first way to die he called "dead right there" (like dying in a burning building, getting hit by a vehicle, etc.). The second way to die in the line of duty was to die 2, 5, 10, or maybe even 20 years later because of what happened on a specific incident. A great portion of these slow and painful deaths are caused by EMS exposures. It is a Company Officer's job to prevent both types of Firefighter fatalities (acute and chronic). Set the example and follow all the EMS PPE SOPs every time!

3. Violence Associated with an Incident and Interacting with Law Enforcement

The third biggest threat to personnel working at an EMS incident is violent behavior being acted out with someone associated with the incident (this does not include guns – please refer to your local AHJ's active shooter policy). In some cases, even a routine EMS call can suddenly become violent. As covered previously, all crew members must be alert for the threat of violence at all times, but it is the primary responsibility of the Company Officer of the unit to continually size up the crew's general work area for any possible threats while crew members are focused on patient care. Routine EMS incidents that may become violent include:

- Incidents that involve mentally unstable patients
- Patients or bystanders that are under the influence of drugs or alcohol
- Environments with highly stressed and/or grieving people (one of the first steps to go through in the grieving process is anger)
- Any one of several medical conditions that can cause aggressive/violent behaviors

When entering into and managing a high stress EMS scene, Company Officers will need to continuously size up the body language and tone of voice of all the customers involved with the incident scene. Always looking for potential signs of possible violence or combative behaviors.

The best way to handle a violent situation is with situational awareness and a proper assessment of the incident scene, along with not placing your crew members in a situation that has a likelihood of violence occurring. Fire department personnel should not enter into EMS scenes where there is a significant potential for violence to occur until law enforcement has arrived on scene and the scene has been rendered safe of hosting any potential future violence (Code-4 status). Again, always refer to your local fire department's SOPs when responding to violent incidents.

A high level of caution must be used when arriving to a scene where law enforcement has been dispatched but are not yet on the scene. On some incidents, fire department units can enter the scene and begin control measures (like on an auto accident). On other incidents (suicides, assaults, etc.) fire department units will need to let law enforcement units arrive first to the scene and achieve a Code-4 status on the incident site before EMS units can enter the scene and start treating the customer(s). Again, please refer to your local fire department SOPs on responding to violent incidents.

Some other higher risk EMS incidents will also involve the response of law enforcement. These higher risk EMS incidents can include:

- Scenes located on or near a roadway (auto accidents)
- Overdoses
- Suicides
- A deceased person

These types of incidents will require a higher level of management and interaction with responding law enforcement agencies. Generally speaking, when law enforcement is involved in an incident, they are overall in command/control of the incident scene, while fire department personnel and other EMS agencies are primarily responsible for patient treatment and transportation. It should be a priority for the first Company Officer that arrives on scene for these types of incidents to establish some sort of liaison with law enforcement. This is usually performed face-to-face with a focus on the current conditions and what fire units need to do to support law enforcement's efforts.

Law Enforcement Body Cameras

Company Officers must be aware that most law enforcement agencies have all their police officers wearing and using body cameras. While working on incidents involving law enforcement, all public actions and interactions must always be highly professional in nature.

Hazard Zone Scene Safety

When responding to incident's that have a potential of having an IDLH environment (fires, hazmat, confined space, etc.) that could possibly require the use of an SCBA, there are 2 possible scenarios that a Company Officer will face:

1. The Company Officer arrives to the scene first and they must assume Command and control of the incident
2. The Company Officer is a subsequent arriver to the incident scene, and they must fit into the current Incident Commander's IAP.

To detail the requirements of a Company Officer managing (or fitting into) these types of incidents would require at least another separate textbook on the subject of Hazard Zone Management. This textbook has already been written by Alan Brunacini. It is titled *Fire Command – 2nd Edition*. Along with *Fire Command*, my father and I co-founded the Incident Commander Hazard Zone Training and Certification program titled "Blue Card" (completely based on Fire Command and the 8 Functions of Command). This book highly recommends that any person that has the potential to manage an IDLH hazard zone or any other local NIMS Type 4 or 5 multi-unit response incident get Blue Card certified today!

4. Documenting Emergency Fire Activities

Most Company Officers are not trained as a fire or arson investigator, nor are they trained to estimate fire damages, so their fire department should not put them in a position to perform these activities when they are not qualified to do so. Some guidelines for documenting these types of incidents:

- Any significant fire or fire damage should be investigated and documented by a certified fire investigator
- Any fire incident suspected of being caused by arson should have a qualified Arson Investigator investigate and document the scene
- A typical Company Officer is no expert in estimating fire damage and the requirements and/or costs required to rebuild a structure after it has hosted a fire. A fire investigator should be used to document these types of incidents.
- Any fire incident that involves a significant injury or death
- Any fire incident that occurs at a public school
- Most fire responses that only require a single company to control and that do not involve any significant fire damage should be documented by the Company Officer into whatever fire RMS the department is currently using.

5. Returning Back to the Station

A lot of Firefighters are in the fire service today because when they were much younger they had a personal experience with a fire truck (or the Firefighters on it) that absolutely mesmerized them to the point that in that instant, they wanted to be a Firefighter when they grew up (as was Alan Brunacini's case when he was 9 years old). This event could be as simple as a Firefighter on big red smiling and waving to a kid while stopped at a traffic light. Please, never drive or act in a manner that would screw this up for anyone - us or them.

I will use this section of this book to detail the guidelines that should be used whenever performing any Code-1 driving. Typically, most of the mileage put on a fire apparatus is done under Code-1 driving conditions. During the lifetime of the apparatus (about 150,000 miles), it will literally interact with thousands of other vehicles (and the customers inside and operating them), along with the countless other bystanders watching you deliver service.

Driving Code-1 means not being assigned to a call and following all the same traffic rules that all of the other citizens have to follow. Speaking of the citizens, that is not your fire truck you are driving - it is theirs. When driving Code-1, you had better drive it in the manner that the citizens expect you to drive it in - always remembering that they were the ones who bought and paid for it. This includes:

- Following all traffic laws
- Being courteous and obliging to all other drivers on the road
- Not ever driving like "you own the road." The citizens also own all the roads, as well as the fire trucks!
- Smile, wave, and do not be in a hurry
- Slower and safer always has a better outcome than faster, faster, faster…
- You are being videotaped at all times - drive and act like it!

Background: As an Engineer from 1988 to 1992, I was assigned to E-201 B-Shift (I know! I could not get away from that station!). Station 201 was located on a major half street on the Phoenix grid system. Most of the half streets are 4 lane roads divided by a double yellow line with a 35 MPH speed limit (with no center, left hand turn lane). This was the case for Station 201 for a half a mile in both directions in front of the station.

Later on in my E-201 driving career, and for whatever reasons, my Engine Captain and I had both moved over to L-201 for the shift. In the early evening, we were driving LT-201 Code-1 back to the fire station. We were about a quarter mile away from making the left turn back into the station, we were in the left lane going below 35 MPH, and there were 2 other cars following close behind us, one in each lane. In about 100 yards, I would activate my left turn signal indicating that we were going to turn left into the fire station.

In the oncoming lanes in front of LT-201 were two cars, one in each of the oncoming lanes. I noticed that the car in the right oncoming lane was going the speed limit, but the other car in the left oncoming lane was speeding and was quickly passing the car in the right lane. The left lane, oncoming driver was driving a 1978 2 door coup. Something was not right - the oncoming car in the left lane was continuing to go faster (over 50 MPH) and he was now starting to cross over the center, double yellow line less than 100 yards in front of LT-201. He veered back a little into his lane for a split second, but not completely. Then, a split second later, he veered again sharply and almost completely into LT-201's lane. He was now accelerating and coming right at us.

I was highly trained and experienced as an Engineer on the Phoenix Fire Department and in this situation, I had about 1 second to consider my options before I had to act decisively. I had already begun slowing down for my turn into the station before I noticed the other driver's erratic behavior and these were the thoughts going through my mind from the time I noticed Mr. 78's driving to the time his car impacted on LT-201's front bumper (it seemed like an eternity):

- If there we no other cars on the road, the first best option to avoid Mr. 78 would be to veer hard left and use the opposite, oncoming lanes to go around him while he was in our lane. This was not an option because it would mean getting into a head-on collision with the other oncoming car in the right oncoming lane, who was minding their own business.
- The next best option would have been to veer sharply to the right to avoid Mr. 78, but this was not a good option either because if LT-201 could have indeed avoided him going to the right, that would mean Mr. 78 would have a head on collision with one (or both) of the passenger vehicles traveling directly behind us. The people behind us would not do a fraction as well as LT-201 would do in a head on collision (LT-201 weighed over 20+ tons) and these people were also minding their own business.
- My 3rd and last option – it is a small car and we are really big - take the car head on while not letting Mr. 78 (or LT-201) kill or injure anyone else. Based on this, I squared up on Mr. 78 and I quickly engaged the automatic braking system (I can still feel the brake pedal pumping under my foot) in order to slow the truck down as much as possible before the impact. In my mind, we were nearly stopped before Mr. 78 collided with our front bumper going over 60 MPH.

It was a white vehicle with a red interior with 2 front seat passengers: a 40+ year old male driver (Mr. 78) and a young teenager in the right front passenger seat (he was directly in front of me and Mr. 78 was directly in front of my Captain on impact). As the car impacted on the front end of LT-201 almost head-on, the truck's nose was pointed down with its rear end tilting up due to the heavy breaking done before the impact. This put the truck in the best position to absorb the impact of the collision. The front bumper of Mr. 78's car initially hit the lower portion of LT-201's bumper, absorbing major impact while simultaneously pushing the front end of Mr. 78's car below our front bumper and into LT-201's wheel and front axle assemblies (very large pieces of metal and rubber that absorbed significant amounts of energy while protecting all crew members on board). The mechanics of all of this sheared the hood off of Mr. 78's car, sending it through both A pillars and the front windshield of the white car with the red interior. At the same time, Mr. 78 had the steering wheel of his car crush deep into his chest, past his spine, and into the back of his driver's seat.

All members riding on LT-201 were belted in, along with all equipment being properly stowed in the cab and in all of the compartments of the truck (all of this equipment was working properly and was used on the very vehicle that collided with LT-201). Immediately after the collision, my Captain verified if everybody on the truck was okay. Everyone sounded off that we were all okay (no one on the truck was physically injured). From there, my Captain looked directly at me and before he could say another word, LT-201 was rear-ended by another vehicle traveling behind us just below the speed limit (this car did not expect LT-201 to come to an almost complete stop in under 2 seconds). BOOM! Thank God LT-201 weighed over 20 tons and had 2 very large bumpers!

The driver who rear-ended us only suffered minor injuries when plowing into our back end (better than being involved in a head on collision with Mr. 78) and he gave my Captain the perfect excuse to tell me to go check on the driver who rear-ended us while the rest of the crew addressed all the other mayhem that had just occurred on our front bumper.

In the aftermath that followed this incident, the young teenaged passenger of the 1978 sedan had serious, but stable injuries and he survived the collision relatively physically intact and was able to live a normal life. The final police report that I read about 6 weeks after the event stated that Mr. 78 was 4 times over the legal alcohol limit and that he died within minutes of the collision. The report also had all the eyewitness statements, along with all of the diagrams containing the math and angles of the other cars involved in the collision. The report concluded that the driver of LT-201 "had taken the best, most appropriate actions that were possible under the circumstances presented, while preventing and limiting damage and injury that could have possibly occurred to other persons, vehicles, and properties that had the potential to be impacted by the other driver's actions."

I knew as soon as LT-201 came to rest after the collision that I had no other options. I was also extremely grateful after the collision that the other person in Mr. 78's car (an innocent customer) also survived and that no other person was seriously injured in the event. LT-201 was struck by a drunk driver and everyone, except the person completely responsible for the event, survived the incident intact.

It was also very reassuring to finally read the police report and be able to say to the Fire Chief that "LT-201 was doing everything right when something went seriously wrong."

Chapter 17

The Customer's Perspective – Tim W. Dietz

Most of our customers awoke this morning in "the steady state" (described by Mitchell and Resnick in the book *Emergency Response to Crisis*). At its most basic, this is the balance between the two operational systems in the brain of survival (emotions) and cognitions (thinking). As a customer goes through the day, this balance is much like a teeter-totter – as one side goes up, it pushes the other side down. If a person is focused on a task like driving to the store, they are operating more in the cognitive brain, pushing emotions down as they watch the speedometer and pay attention to staying in their lane and the other drivers and pedestrians around them. These tasks require thinking. Suddenly a dog runs out in front of them. Their survival brain kicks into gear with emotions and stress hormones. What does that look like? Their survival brain reacts quickly and they slam on the brakes and experience some fear and shakiness, as this is not what they were expecting. When they realize the threat is gone – they did not hit the dog - their brain eventually goes back to the steady state.

The characteristic of a crisis that you most likely will deal with in the field are:

1. They are sudden - the person probably could not have predicted the event when they awoke this morning.
2. Because of the event's suddenness, the person is not adequately prepared to handle it.

When a customer interprets an event as a "crisis" - maybe something happened they did not expect (like hitting the dog), or their home is on fire, or loved one has fallen and injured themselves and now has a medical emergency, or they just witnessed something horrible, or they heard horrible news:

1. **Their "steady state" is disrupted (emotional brain engages suppressing cognitive brain).**
2. **Their usual coping mechanisms of returning to a steady state have failed.**
3. **Their brain gets stuck in survival mode, which may produce impairment.**

These are most likely the times when we as Firefighters/Medics are in their life. There will be lots of emotions. Any event that has emotions attached will be imprinted, so what we do during this time has a lasting impact on the customer for the rest of their life.

Phases of Crisis

Research in the field of crisis supports the concept that most people pass through somewhat predictable phases when they encounter a sudden emotional event. The following stages represent the usual pattern we will see in the field of this emotional reaction to a crisis event:

1. **High Anxiety or Emotional Shock -** This is the initial reaction or response to an overwhelming event or news. People will deal with their crisis in very different ways. It is important to note that people in this initial phase can either be bouncing off the wall and in your face or sitting "frozen" in the corner. Remember that the survival response is

172

"fight or flight" or sometimes freeze. They have no time to prepare emotionally for their sudden crisis and so much is happening so fast that the brain is unable to comprehend.

2. **Denial -** This is the brain's way of protecting us from too much bad information coming in too fast. It is not uncommon to hear family members who are present telling each other "he will be okay" while we are still working on their loved one, regardless of the seriousness of the situation.

3. **Anger -** This is nothing more than a normal human response to fear and/or frustration. When denial can no longer buffer the stressful situation, anger may replace it.

The experience of a customer in these first three phases of the emotional reaction to crisis (typically followed by remorse, grief, and reconciliation) creates a vulnerability. If they experience complications, chances are they will have problems in the later phases and grief process. They are, however, also vulnerable to help!

When a human being is in these first three phases of a crisis, everything they see, hear, taste, touch, and smell can be imprinted in their mind for the rest of their life! What you do in these first three phases of a crisis can be more important in that person's recovery of the event than the mental health care they may get in the months or years after the event!

Things to Know

- A crisis is always real to the person experiencing it! What may seem benign to us may be quite stressful to someone else.
- People in crisis are in their survival brain. Everything gets imprinted. The brain is taking high resolution photographs/video of everything going on. These folks will remember the words you use, if you smiled, frowned, or seemed disengaged. If they look out their window at you, they will remember if you were in a hurry to help them or not. Most importantly, they will remember if you cared!
- Research evidence in the field of loss, grief, and emotional crisis indicates that virtually everyone over the age of reason and of sound mind will remember exactly how they were informed of the death of a loved one and/or how they were treated during their crisis event.

8 Acceptable (Fire Company) Behaviors in the Field (explained in greater detail in the next chapter):

1. Be truthful
2. "Dose Out" the bad news
3. Convey caring
4. Allow significant others to spend time with their loved one
5. Allow grief
6. Offer continued support
7. Respect the deceased
8. Know your resources

Understanding our customers who are in crisis, then treating them with compassion and tact is important for everyone involved. What we do as responders during this critical time can not only set the stage for this person's eventual recovery from the event, but it can also set the stage for healthier first responders (more on this later).

Work hard. Be nice. – Tim W. Dietz

Firefighters Perspective – John Brunacini

On the other side of the customer's brain is the Firefighter's brain. Hopefully, Firefighters have all trained their brains throughout their careers to work in the cognitive mode when mitigating 911 calls. These calls are events that we have trained for and perform routinely, but are a true crisis for the customer (the worst day of their life). Firefighters MUST NOT discount what is going on in the customer's brain based on our qualifications and calmness when dealing with the situation. They are in crisis! What is routine for us (like working a full code) is not routine for the customer. They have never seen CPR performed on a loved one before.

As Tim has covered, the customer's brain is taking high speed, high definition pictures, along with mixing a digital soundtrack of their crisis event. Their emotional brain is being so overwhelmed that they will not immediately remember all parts of what is happening in the event, while other parts of the events will be crystal clear in their mind for the rest of their life. Everything we say and do is being recorded at a high level in their brain. Even though it is a tragedy you are mitigating, produce the best high definition movie of the event possible for the customers that are having to suffer through it. They will remember your actions vividly for the rest of their lives.

In the next chapter, Tim will help cover some of the details in doing just that.

- Typically, only 1 fire department unit will be necessary to mitigate an incident when no patients are transported to the hospital.
- Typically, at least 2 units are necessary to mitigate an incident when the patient is transported to the hospital. This includes the fire department unit, along with an Ambulance/Medic unit.
- Calls that are originally dispatched as BLS, but are determined to be ALS when sizing up the scene will require the additional response of an ALS unit (or the BLS unit is first due to the incident while the closest ALS unit is also dispatched). This could be in the form of a Paramedic Ambulance (Medic unit) or another ALS fire department unit.
- If a BLS unit is on scene first for an ALS call, the Company Officer of the first arriving unit has overall responsibility of managing the incident scene. The subsequent arriving higher medical authority will assume responsibility for the patient when they arrive on scene.
- If an ALS patient is stable and no additional assistance is needed, the BLS unit can be put back into service while the ALS unit assumes full responsibility for both the scene and patient management.
- If working with 3rd party EMS providers (transport agencies) with higher medical qualifications, the Company Officer of the first arriving unit has overall responsibility of managing the incident scene. The subsequent arriving 3rd party, higher medical authority will assume responsibility for the patient when they arrive on scene.

3. Customer Service Interaction with the Other Civilians Involved with the Patient and/or the Incident Scene

If the Company Officer is not engaged in direct patient care, let the crew members who are treating the patient directly interview and interact with them. They are usually communicating on the patient's level and it is very distracting for a customer who is under stress to talk to several people at once. Listen to their conversation and document accordingly.

While your crew is treating the patient, try to identify the person in charge of the social structure of the incident scene. This can include:

- Matriarch (female figure in charge)
- Patriarch (male figure in charge)
- Spouse, significant other, or close friend
- If in a business: the patient's co-worker, supervisor, or owner of the business
- Law enforcement
- 3rd party EMS services

Once identified, introduce yourself to this person, inform them that your crew is doing everything possible for the patient, and ask them if there is any additional information they can provide that will assist with patient care. This includes the patient's:

- Information needed to complete the EMS form (full name, DOB, Insurance info, etc.)
- Mechanism of their injury
- History of current illness

Chapter 18

"Fire Departments are the agency of first and last resort." – *Alan Brunacini*

EMS Customer Service

Background: Firefighters live and dream about saving people who are exposed to fire conditions. I also dreamed about making that "save." I went to a lot of fires in the residential setting, but I was never in a position to make a save. There were very few other Firefighters that I had worked with, or knew of, who had made a save on the fireground. It just does not happen very often and it happens to very few Firefighters.

However, while working on thousands of EMS incidents throughout my career, I witnessed my crew, fire station 201 personnel, and the other units on my fire department save hundreds of lives. Hundreds! People that were "biologically" deceased when we arrived on scene would bring our station chocolate chip cookies 3 weeks later! EMS is where it's at! It makes the fire department one of the most vital parts of the community and it is the biggest service delivery activity that we provide.

EMS service saves lives. It also changes people's lives - not only the patient's life, but also the lives of all the other people connected to the patient and all the other people who are witnessing the incident scene. Your actions make a HUGE impact on your community!

This chapter of the book will have both Tim and me presenting on the subject matter. I will start with the typical EMS service that we provide the majority of the time. From there, I will discuss managing high stress EMS incidents and Tim will discuss how to deal and interact with customers associated with these high stress EMS calls. After Tim's portion, I will come in again at the end of the chapter with the Company Officer's "end of call" customer service options.

EMS Service Delivery and Emotional Intelligence

This book would like touch on emotional intelligence to start out the EMS delivery section because it is so important when dealing with all the different people and agencies associated with an EMS incident scene. Out of the main traits of emotional awareness, the most important characteristic when delivering EMS service to your customers is SOCIAL AWARENESS.

Social Awareness

Social awareness equates to possessing the ability to look at and understand the perspective of the other people you are interacting with (empathy). This includes gaining an understanding of other people's diverse backgrounds and cultures along with displaying the proper behaviors and communication skills in order to effectively achieve the best outcomes. These behaviors include:

- Being aware of and informed about all of the different cultures that you routinely respond on
- The ability to identify other people's emotional states (cognitive versus emotional)
- Paying close attention to the interactions of other people
- Being a good listener

- Highly considering what you say before you say it
- Speaking in a manner so the other person you are talking to understands what you are trying to communicate (simple and to the point)

Using these skill sets when delivering EMS will go a long way in making the people you are interacting with feel like you CARE about them. When people feel this way, it equates to EXCELLENT CUSTOMER SERVICE!

From the Apparatus to the Customer's Front Door

Before getting off the truck and engaging with the customer, you should be aware of the behaviors that need to be exhibited while delivering service. Our behaviors are primarily acted out in the way that we **communicate,** both non-verbally and verbally, with the customer and any other people associated with the incident scene.

Extensive research has documented that the highest and most powerful form of human communication is based on body language (over 60%). The next highest form of communication is based on the tone of voice that is used when addressing an individual or a group of people (30%). Less than 10% of communication is based on the actual words that you say. Body language and tone of voice provide important signals and clues about the intentions, emotions, and motivations of other people.

During a scene size-up, Company Officers need to pick up on and process what other people are thinking and feeling through their body posture, mannerisms, gestures, and how their voices are used. When responding to high stress incidents, it is imperative that the Company Officer read the room in a fashion that pertains to Firefighter safety. If there is a possibility of some sort of violence to occur, please refer to Chapter 17 - General Emergency Response and Scene Safety Guidelines along with your local fire department's violent incident policy.

Just a few examples of the emotions that can be expressed with just body language alone include:

- Happiness
- Excitement
- Surprise
- Sadness
- Pain
- Anger
- Contempt

Most of how the customers are perceiving you and your crew is also based on your body language and the tone of voice you are using when communicating and interacting with them. Knowing this, let's look at your body parts and how to use them (and how NOT to use them) to properly communicate with those around you while working on an incident scene. I will start from the top of the body and work my way down.

Face

Do: Always look at someone directly when addressing them and sustain eye contact with the other person while they are speaking. Smiles are always good, but if smiles are not used (or appropriate), always try to keep your mouth (and the rest of your face) "turned up."

Do NOT: Look in other directions, blink too much, gaze or stare at people, frown, purse your lips, or keep your facial features "turned down" when communicating with other people.

Arms

Do: Have arms that are relaxed and are at your sides or gently resting on your hips. This conveys that you are ready, in control, concerned, and listening.

Do NOT: Have arms that are crossed, clasped behind your back, or are being fidgety and restless. These jesters convey that you are defensive, closed off, or aggressive.

Hands

Do: Keep your hands open. Open hands convey no hidden agendas. Also, use common hand jesters to convey your good intent (greeting wave, peace sign, thumbs up, etc.).

Do NOT: Present closed hands. Closed hands express anger or resentment. Do not use hand jesters such as closed fists, repeated opening and closing of fists, clasping your hands together, or playing with your fingers. These actions all can convey boredom, frustration, or hostility.

Legs

Do: Use your legs to get down to the level of the person you are communicating with. This includes kneeling or sitting.

Do NOT: Stand directly in front of a person and hover over them (especially when combined with other negative body language). These actions express intimidation, anger, and/or hostility. Also, do not cross your legs when you are sitting on a call when communicating with a customer. This conveys boredom, lack of interest, and/or lack of intent to act.

Overall posture

Do: Keep an open posture, with which the trunk of your body is open and exposed. Also, stand and sit up straight. This conveys professionalism, friendliness, openness, and a willingness to listen.

Do NOT: Keep a closed posture, with which you are hunching forward, keeping your arms and legs crossed, and your head down. This conveys hostility, unfriendliness, and/or boredom and frustration.

Your Voice (Not your Words)

This includes factors such as tone of voice, volume, inflection, and pitch. Your voice (and the strength of it) is the second biggest element in communicating with others and it is also the most **CONTAGIOUS** form of communication.

Background: Let me use this background to illustrate real life examples of how contagious other people's voices are - not the words they are actually saying, but in the body language, pitch, volume and speed they are using.

We will start with Chief Screamer. His voice would raise according to the level of stress in his current environment. This is not a good thing because Firefighter's routinely respond to highly stressful situations. Typically, Chief Screamer would arrive on the scene of a working incident after the 3rd or 4th unit was already on the scene and working. It was his job to transfer command of the incident to his vehicle and then to continue running the incident from his vehicle's command post. If things were not stabilized when he arrived on scene, he would immediately start screaming into the radio, mostly in an incomprehensible voice. His voice alone would raise everyone else's stress level and it would often cause other people on the incident scene to start screaming into the radio, as well. If he was assigned forward in the incident as a Division Boss, he would immediately start screaming when he arrived at his assigned work location, creating even more confusion than had already existed before he got there. Chief Screamer escalated stress, he was ineffective, and often times his screaming was contagious in places where it was the last thing anyone wanted or needed.

The opposite of Chief Screamer was Captain Calm. Captain Calm was also very contagious, but in a very good way. He always had a smile on his face and nothing ever seemed to stress him, or his voice, out. Captain Calm's station was directly adjacent to the southeast of Station 201 and L-201 was their primary ladder response vehicle on most of their runs that needed a Ladder company. During my career as the Company Officer on L-201, we routinely ran with Captain Calm and his crew at least 2 or 3 times a shift. When he was first on scene and in command of any incident, he sounded like he was calmly telling a story at the dinner table. He projected his voice in such a low, calm, and well-spoken manner that it naturally (and contagiously) slowed down the entire incident scene. His radio voice made all the other responders more calm, slower, and safer. Kudos to you Captain Calm for running such a good ship for all those years!

One of my all-time favorites was Captain Ignorant. His defining communication trait was that he would start talking louder than anyone else (not screaming, more like yelling) when other people disagreed with him, when he was not getting his way, or if he did not like the current circumstances he was in (like an EMS call that was "below" him). This was in combination with projecting very hostile, aggressive body language. He thought if he just yelled louder and hovered over everyone else like a bull, it would make him right and everyone else wrong. Yelling at other people who have Type-A personalities is a very bad thing. Aggression is CONTAGIOUS with Firefighters. Yelling at someone is a very aggressive behavior and Firefighters do not like aggression directed towards them - to the point that many times Firefighters will meet aggression with an equal amount of aggression, while maybe adding a little bit more to it on their end. Mr. Ignorant's communication skill set caused many confrontations with his co-workers, his superiors, and the customers he served during his career. This made him a person that not very many people wanted to work with or hang out with (his poor family members!).

My Dad was the best communicator I have ever witnessed. I mean this from the standpoint of how a person uses all the different forms of communication, combined with all the different settings people can communicate in. This included running an emergency scene, public speaking, directing a meeting, talking to a person one-on-one, or while sitting around the dinner table enjoying a meal with a group of people. Dad excelled at all of it! I am not just saying this. Most people who have heard my father publicly speak or have personally talked to him would agree. People who have had one-on-ones with my father often say that they never had a conversation with such a "big wig" in which that person was totally interested and engaged with every word they were saying. One thing that made my Dad a great communicator was the way he used his body language. He was Italian, so there were a lot of facial expressions (smiles) with big open-handed jesters and body movements. More than anyone, he knew how to use the tone of his voice. He could project it at both ends of the scale and it was always appropriate for the situation. His voice was compassionate when needed, forgiving when needed, concerned when needed, interested when needed, in total control of the situation when needed, and very loud and projected when needed. Dad used his voice to protect, guide, and inspire people more than any voice I have ever heard. His voice was contagiously MOTIVATING!

Voice

Do: Talk in soft, normal, caring tones. Relax, breathe, and use short, well-spaced sentences. Avoid using big words and slowly articulate what you are saying so the other person can understand what is being stated (remember that they are stressed).

Do NOT: Speak in loud, harsh, or sharp tones. Avoid speaking quickly and using a vocabulary that the other person does not or cannot understand (talking "down" to someone with big words that no one but us can or will understand) and avoid repeating yourself. Speaking simple is always better.

Uniforms

Our Fire Departments have given us a certain amount of organizational power and authority in the community and one of the symbols of this official authority is the uniforms we wear. We all need to have a uniform on when delivering service and everyone on the crew should be dressed in the same, recognizable, professional uniform that identifies who we are as an organization. This uniform needs to be:

- The same for each crew member (no one special)
- Professional looking with all the proper ID and insignia. Everyone needs to look the same and everyone needs to look like they are all ready to go to work.
- Clean, without holes, not frayed, not faded, and tucked in
- The appropriate PPE is worn for the situation
- Always follow your AHJ's uniform policy

Background: Myself, along with thousands of others, have heard my father tell his "uniforms and citizen complaints" story. He starts the story by telling everyone about the 250,000+ service delivery calls that the

Phoenix Fire Dept responds to on an annual basis, with the majority of those calls being for EMS services. This amount of annual activity (200,000+ EMS calls) would naturally produce a small percentage of dissatisfied customers that would either call him directly or that would write him a letter to complain about the service that was rendered (or lack thereof).

During his 28 years as Fire Chief, he never received a citizen's complaint about what a Firefighter was wearing. Never once did they complain that the crew showed up and their uniforms looked sloppy, tattered, or unprofessional. He never received a complaint that the fire trucks were old, dirty, or so out of repair that they were an embarrassment to the community. What they all complained about was poor service, lack of caring, lack of concern for their situation, not taking them seriously, or not doing what the customer needed or wanted them to do - nothing about the way the Firefighters were dressed.

I know how our overall appearance creates a first impression and looking professional is the best way to start out any human interaction, but the most important and lasting impression we create is how we treat other people.

Equipment

You are on scene, off the truck, using the correct body language, and in the proper uniform. Now it is time to gather all of the equipment necessary for patient treatment. Based on the nature of the call, this means **ALL** of the equipment that could be necessary. Getting all of the equipment off of the truck that could possibly be required to mitigate the call does the following:

- Projects to the customers that you are professional
- Projects to the customers that you are taking the call seriously
- Projects to the customers that you are prepared
- Projects to the customers that you are ready to go to work
- Greatly reduces the need to interrupt service delivery to go out and get another piece of equipment off the truck required for the call

Of course, there will be some incidents in which you cannot possibly have predicted (based on the call information) that you needed something that you did not originally carry in. But always carry in the standard set of EMS service equipment items EVERY TIME! You know all of the boxes, bags, and devises that I am talking about.

Entering into Private Property and your Authority/Right to Work

Now that you and your crew have all your equipment, but have not yet entered onto private property or into the caller's environment (home and/or private building/business), it is very important to know and understand a fire department's authority and your rights to perform and carry out your duty when entering private property.

Most states have laws that give fire departments the "right to make entry" in order to stabilize a situation that is either threatening life or property. On the fire side of things, the local fire department basically "owns" the property if there is a threat of fire to it. We own it until the situation is stabilized and then we turn it back over to the responsible party.

EMS obligations give fire departments many of the same "right to make entry" privileges that they have on a fire call, but EMS incidents also put a tremendous amount of liability on a fire department when we have a "Duty to Act." We also have the moral obligation to validate that everyone is okay at an incident scene and up until this point, no person can interfere with our obligation to do so.

However, entering into an EMS scene is a little different. The biggest difference between the two incidents are:

> 1. The house on fire cannot refuse our actions (treatment). If it is on fire (or exposed to fire), the owner of the property cannot stop us from putting the fire out and stabilizing the incident scene.
> 2. On an EMS scene, while the RP of the property cannot deny the fire department entry onto/into the property to ensure that no one is injured/ill, a conscious person that is awake and oriented (AxOx4 - knows who they are, where they are, time of day, and their current circumstances) can refuse fire department aid.

Law enforcement must respond to medical calls in which we have to validate the condition of person who has not been seen in normal time frames where we have to force entry into the residence in order to validate.

Not to make this an EMS class, but on the EMS side of things, our right to treat can even get a little trickery than that. People who are confused due to a medical condition, being mentally unstable, delirious, unconscious, etc. (not AxOx4) are legally considered to give EMS professionals the "implied consent" needed to treat and stabilize them. The only person who can stop Firefighters from treating a person who is not AxOx4 is a Physician. This will come in either two forms:

1. For whatever circumstances, the patient you are treating is in full arrest (biologically dead) and a Physician having medical authority over the incident scene (and/or through the use of medical protocols) pronounces the patient deceased (clinically dead) and all treatment and revival efforts will stop.
2. The patient on the incident has a known terminal illness, they are in severe medical distress to the point of being in a full arrest, and that person's medical authority (Physician) has issued a DNR order (DNRs and high stress incidents dealing with the deceased will be covered later in this chapter).

Customer Encounter and Patient Treatment

"I am not here for me. I am here for we and we are here for them." – Anchorage, AK Fire Department

Now you are at or inside the door and you are initially encountering the patient and/or other customers related to the incident scene. Using the proper body language and tone of voice, here are some phrases that can be used to start the call out in a positive manner:

- What can we do to help?

- We are here to help. What can we do?
- We understand that there is a medical emergency. What is the problem? We are here to help.
- Please tell us what happened.

One of the very best ways to start the call is by greeting the customers on the scene with the medical information that you have received by dispatch and on the way to the call. Something like, "We understand that someone is in respiratory distress (or whatever the dispatched emergency is) and we are here to help."

Always avoid using the word "why" as in "Why did you call us?" or "Why are we here?" These phrases covey irritation, aggression, and confrontation and should be avoided at all times.

Patient Management

Most EMS calls occur inside of a residence or on private property and they will usually involve at least 2 or more people (the patient and their family, significant other, friends, co-workers, other first responders, and/or bystanders). The Company Officer has to "treat" the whole scene. This means interacting with everyone involved in the call in some way. However, it all starts out with the patient.

The biggest check-off on evaluating performance on an EMS call should be based on patient treatment and outcome. Guidelines on patient care include:

- Before engaging in patient care, the Company Officer must size up the patient environment for any possible threats to both the patient and the Firefighters.
- Does the initial scene size-up indicate the incident needs to be upgraded with a higher level of care and/or more resources? If so, call for them immediately.
- If the patient is not in a safe environment, extricate the patient to a safe environment as soon as humanly possible while wearing the proper PPE.
- When it is safe to treat the patient, ensure that your crew members are engaging in the appropriate patient treatment protocols while wearing the correct PPE for the circumstances.
- Crew members interacting with the patient must also use good body language and tone of voice when interviewing and informing the patient of their actions.
- Always try to place the patient in the best, most comfortable position that assists with their treatment.
- Always protect a patient's privacy and dignity when they cannot. Use EMS blankets, towels, and/or sheets to cover a patient whenever the situation calls for it. Some situations will require the Company Officer to also dismiss people from the patient's view when they are not directly involved with patient care.
- The goal of all EMS is to stabilize and transport the patient to the appropriate hospital as quickly as possible.

EMS Scene Management

While crew members are managing the patient, the Company Officer needs to manage the rest of the incident scene. Main responsibilities for the Company Officer to address while managing an EMS incident include:

1. Overall Safety Officer of the incident site, always keeping eyes and ears alert on the current scene conditions
2. Directing and interacting with other agencies that may be involved with stabilizing the scene (this could include Law Enforcement and other EMS agencies related to the scene)
3. Customer service interaction with the other civilians involved with the patient and/or the incident scene
4. Documentation of the patient encounter

1. Overall Safety Officer of the Incident Site

This portion of the book is dedicated to the majority of EMS calls that are being conducted in a static, safe environment. Most of this subject matter was covered in a previous chapter. To recap, some of the biggest Firefighter safety objectives on a static EMS scene are:

- Ensuring crew members are in the proper PPE for the situation
- Ensuring that when moving or lifting a patient, it is done via a team effort and all members are in good, ergonomic lifting positions
- Monitoring other people related to the call who are stressed or under the influence
- Always keeping eyes and ears alert on the current scene conditions

Again, for violent incidents or incidents that occur on busy roadways or Interstates, please refer to your local fire department's SOPs.

There will be critical EMS incident scenes in which the Company Officer has to engage in patient care. When focusing on patient treatment, they will not be in a position to control the overall incident scene. This will occur on a more routine basis with 3-person crews or when the Company Officer is a PM. Whenever possible, Company Officers need to train and delegate the responsibilities for overall EMS scene management to the other members of their crew so that they can be the eyes and ears of the company when the Officer is engaged. Despite all of this, there will still be the occasional incident scene where this cannot happen because the situation will call for ALL hands to be on deck and working. Most of these situations will require a multi-company response - when more resources arrive, it will allow the Company Officer to either separate themselves from the action in order to manage the overall incident scene or if unable to disengage, they will need to delegate incident control away to a subsequent arriver.

2. Managing and/or Interacting with Other EMS Professionals

Single patient, static EMS incidents on average have about a 50% ambulance transportation rate to a hospital in order to continue patient care. This equates to:

- Past medical history
- Prescription medications the patient is currently taking and any allergies to medications
- Any other information that is related or pertinent to the call that will assist with patient treatment

Here are some general guidelines to follow when interacting with other civilians on an EMS incident:

- Again, always use good body language and tone of voice when interacting with others on the scene.
- When interacting with people on the scene, always reassure them that fire department members are doing everything possible for the patient.
- Explain your actions and what is going on to the relatives and significant others associated with the patient.
- Always be honest with the patient's relatives and dose out any bad news in stages (Tim Dietz will cover this in more detail later in this chapter).
- If the patient is in a compromised position, only let the significant others required for patient treatment or comfort be present in the room/area. Have all others wait somewhere else in a safe place.
- Other civilians associated with the incident scene (not directly related to the patient) like to know what is going on. Only share pertinent information about the patient with the people who are qualified to receive it, while reassuring others who are not qualified to have the information that the fire department is doing everything possible for the situation.
- On a small percentage of incidents, there will be deeply concerned people who immediately meet you when dismounting the apparatus demanding a described set of actions. Company Officers must understand that these are stressed out people that are not trained to deal with these situations. While not bursting their bubble, calmly explain to them that you deal with these situations all of the time and then tell them that "We are here to help, and WE GOT IT." If they are a significant other of the patient, give them something to do so they leave you alone (fetch medicines, call someone, gather up the patient's things for the hospital, etc.).
- There will be incidents when you arrive on scene where other non-first responder medical personnel are on scene and interacting with or even treating the patient. This includes doctors, nurses, medical techs, etc. Most of these people do NOT possess the medical qualifications and certifications necessary to deliver emergency medical services. While they are trained in some sort of medicine, most of it does not apply to the street. If they are not qualified, transfer patient care to your crew and document who the person is and what their medical qualifications are (the patient will want to know who these people are once they recover from their event in order to thank them for being a Good Samaritan).

End of Call Decontamination (Decon) and Managing Post-Incident Good Crew Behaviors

A decon process will need to occur after every EMS patient encounter. This could be as simple as properly disposing of masks and gloves, along with a thorough hand washing to having an extreme blood borne (or other bodily fluids) call and every piece of permanent EMS equipment must be cleaned and decontaminated. Most of this decon will occur close to the fire truck prior to disengaging from the scene (with more possibly occurring back at the fire station).

When these activities are occurring at an incident site, it is COMPLETELY NATURAL for Firefighters to start debriefing with each other. While still in the public eyes (and camera lenses), this debriefing process needs to be completely professional. This includes avoiding the following "unprofessional" behaviors while in the public hearing and/or seeing range:

- No high 5's
- No joking or laughing while on an incident scene
- No personal comments or judgements voiced about the call or the people involved with it (this can sometimes be very hard to do with pediatric drownings, child abuse calls, domestic violence, etc.)
- No horseplay

Again, it is COMPLETELY NATURAL for Firefighters to debrief after an incident. Just NEVER do it in front of the public. They have NO IDEA how we cope with the constant stress of these types of calls. Save it all for when you are all back on the truck or at the fire station where no other person can hear or see your fire company debriefing!

4. Documentation of the Patient Encounter

Most of the time, the crew can treat the patient without the need for the Company Officer to engage in patient care. This allows the officer to gather PPI and document the encounter, in addition to interacting with the other customers on the scene.

The other part of the time (again, this could be higher with 3-person staffing versus 4-person staffing), the officer will have to assist their crew with stabilizing the patient. These types of incidents will usually require 2 or more units to mitigate. The Company Officer can usually disengage from treatment activities and catch up on their documentation when additional units arrive on scene.

Some career advice: If you are working on a BLS unit and you arrive first to an ALS call, fill out all portions of the EMS encounter form that you can possibly fill out. Not much respect or goodwill is generated when you hand over a blank form to a higher medical authority (it is also not professional).

EMS Incidents and the Health Insurance Portability and Accountability Act (HIPAA)

The HIPAA Privacy Act, a Federal law, gives patients extreme privacy rights over their health care information. There are several sets of rules and limits on who can look at and receive a patient's medical health information. The HIPAA law applies to all forms of individuals' protected health information - whether electronic, written, or oral. The Security Rule (part of the HIPAA law) is a Federal law that regulates the security for health care information in the electronic form and it also comes with a big set of rules.

Violations of HIPAA law can have very serious repercussions. There have been several court cases upheld in which a Company Officer and/or a crew member have been terminated from the department for sharing patient information with the public. This is usually in the form of scene photos being posted on social medial accounts.

EMS Documentation Guidelines

There are new EMS documentation programs being developed daily. Every week in the US, a fire department and/or a local EMS provider switches to a different patient treatment and transfer documentation system. Wherever you are working, you are going to have to efficiently connect to whatever documentation system your local system is using.

Whatever system your department uses to document EMS responses, here are some universal guidelines to use regarding the documentation of emergency medical services in order to reduce you and your crew's liability:

- Know and follow all HIPPA rules and regulations.
- There should be no photography or digital recordings of any kind unless it used to document a mechanism of injury to facilitate proper patient care. Any documentation of this kind must be attached to the patient's medical record and must NOT be shared with anyone outside of the patient's medical providers.
- During and after patient treatment, only share direct patient information with the other people directly involved in the patient's care, as well as with any possible CQI program related to your EMS program's oversight.
- There should be no PPI transmitted over any radio channels.
- For internal EMS incident inquiries, only share general incident details with the people inside your own organization that were not directly involved in patient care (your boss wants to know what happened). DO NOT share any patient specific details. Example: "Hey Chief, we had a 3-vehicle accident with 4 patients. One patient was an "Immediate" and the other 3 were all "Delayed." All 4 patients were transported to Good Samaritan Hospital via Medic 1 and Medic 5." No specific patient details were used here.
- For external EMS incident inquiries, refer all inquiries from anyone outside of the fire department and EMS system to your local EMS director or PIO. Do not say a word about any service delivery to people outside of your organization unless you have expressed permission from your superiors (this includes talking to your own family members).
- Most EMS documentation systems will not allow an incident to be closed out until all documentation has been completed. Do it the correct way, do not waste time, get it done, close it out, and move on to the next call.

Managing Critical – High Stress EMS Calls

These incidents include:

- Any patient that is in full arrest (for a variety of reasons)
- Any patient that is trapped to the point that they physically have to be extricated from their environment
- Any patient with severe traumatic skeletal injuries, internal injuries, or burns
- Any patient that has experienced extreme violence or a sexual assault
- Any critical incident involving children
- Any call that involves a deceased person

These types of calls not only put a severe amount of stress on the customers, but they also put a severe amount of stress on the Firefighters. As Tim will describe, the way we treat the other customers associated with incidents that involve people who are either in critical condition or are deceased (in one form or another) will also go a long way in helping the Firefighters deal with the event. This comes in the form of knowing that we always acted and communicated in a manner that HELPED! Here's Tim...

High stress EMS customer service management – Tim W. Dietz

The majority of the following information comes from the book *Scenes of Compassion - A Responder's Guide for Dealing with Emergency Scene Emotional Crisis (2nd Edition)* by Tim W. Dietz.

We are very good at what we do! We take training seriously with the intent of providing the best possible service we can. We fight fire and save lives and we provide the best possible patient care to our customers who are sick and injured. However, sometimes our customer is not sick or injured, but the loved one of someone who is. This customer requires us to provide a different kind of assistance that many of us have not been trained to do. To do it right requires us to listen, be empathic, and provide emotional support, often pulling us out of our comfort zone.

When looking at Firefighter/Paramedic behavioral health questionnaires, dealing with family members at the scene consistently ranks among the top 10 most stressful situations in the field. This tends to put a lot of pressure on us to do the right thing. This chapter is NOT about shouldering other's grief, but rather about leaving an imprint that someone on scene (us) understood and cared about what our customer was going through.

Remember that our actions, our words, and the sights and sounds of the scene stay with our customers who are in crisis forever. If we encounter a patient's significant other at the scene of serious injury/illness or death, here are some helpful tools.

What We Can Do

1. Be truthful
2. "Dose Out" the bad news
3. Convey caring
4. Allow significant others to spend time with their loved one
5. Allow grief
6. Offer continued support
7. Respect the deceased
8. Know your resources

1. Be truthful. When someone is in crisis, they remember everything they have experienced. A little white lie becomes a big deal when the person has recovered and reflects on their experience. As it is easy to stereotype a single crisis experience as the "norm," if someone in uniform was less than honest, then everyone who wears that uniform is dishonest.

2. Dose out the bad news. Most of the crises we see in the field are because something unexpected happened in someone's life. Typically, something they saw or heard. Therefore, giving information in manageable, measured doses helps the person adjust by limiting the psychological impact.

Here is an example:

One afternoon, a man was driving home from work in his pickup. An oncoming car crossed the center line, striking him head on. He was pinned in his truck and while wiggling around, trying to get free, finds his cell phone and calls his wife. "Honey, I've been in a horrible crash. I'm hurt and trapped in the truck." He then gave his wife the location of the incident. Thankfully, a witness called 911 and the fire department was dispatched. During the extrication, the wife shows up and starts running toward the scene. A Firefighter in a support role stops her before she can get into the hazard zone and appropriately asks, "Excuse me, can I help you?" She stated that her husband was in the truck and she just talked to him on the phone. He said to her, "Stay right there. I'll be right back." He then went and got permission from the Incident Commander and Extrication Officer to allow her to get closer, but still a safe distance from the vehicles.

The Firefighter, upon returning to the wife has the following conversation (in doses):

    a. "Let me briefly explain what is going on."
    b. "We responded because your husband was in a car crash."
    c. "When we arrived, we found him trapped inside of his pickup."
    d. "He is still trapped in his pickup and we are working to get him out."
    e. "If you would like to get closer, we will allow that, but you have to stay with me."
    f.   "I need to tell you what you will see and hear."
    g. "We are cutting on his truck to get him out and the equipment is very noisy."
    h. "Your husband is hurt and he does not look comfortable."
    i.   "He has blood on his face."
    j.   "You have to promise to stay with me, so you do not get hurt."

Dosing out the news prepares the wife. She was told what happened, what is currently happening, and what she will see and hear. This can lessen any crisis response she may experience from something surprising her.

As the firefighter stays with this woman at the scene, a couple of things happened.

1. When her husband saw her, you could tell he found some comfort in her presence.
2. As the Firefighter described everything going on (including why they could not get closer), the wife knew her husband was getting the best possible care he could – by caring people!

Here is another example:

You respond to the report of an unconscious, not breathing person at a residence. Upon arrival, you find an elderly male unconscious in a chair at the kitchen table. The wife is present. Your crew determines the gentleman is not breathing and pulseless.

a. As the medics begin their intervention, someone should turn to the wife and state: "Your husband is not breathing and his heart is not beating."
b. Your crew begins CPR and defibrillates a fine ventricular fibrillation rhythm, causing asystole. Someone should let the wife know: "Your husbands' heart did not respond to the electricity."
c. The patient gets intubated and an I.V. started. ALS begins with cardiac medications – without change in rhythm. Again, address the wife: "Your husbands' heart is not responding to our medications."
d. As the scene progresses and the outcome does not look positive, the wife could be told: "If your husband does not begin to respond to our efforts soon, we may to start to think about if we should continue with your husband or stop."
e. If and when the time does come to stop resuscitation efforts in the field, someone should go to the wife and state: "I am so sorry. Your husband has died." Always use plain language when addressing death: "I am sorry your husband has died or is dead." Avoid vague expressions or euphemisms like "We lost your loved one." or "They passed away." Those only comfort the giver of the news - not the receiver!

Again, in this case, "dosing out" the bad news prepares the wife. She was basically told when you arrived that her husband was dead (not breathing, no heartbeat) and he was not responding to your interventions. If the death is declared in her presence, the dosing hopefully will have softened her response. She will still be sad and grieve, but she will not be getting the "high anxiety and emotional shock" slap in the face all at once.

3. Allow Significant Others to Spend Time with Their Loved One. Allowing people to spend time with their loved one conjures up all sorts of emotions. We need to put this aside and treat people like we would want to be treated. People who are allowed to spend time with their loved one do better emotionally in the long run. If the patient is conscious, the significant others will hear you explaining everything that is being done so they know their loved one is getting good care from caring people! If you are explaining what is being done to significant others, the patient may hear and be reassured. Most patients also find comfort in having loved ones nearby. At scenes of serious injury or death, a systematic approach is helpful when dealing with distraught family members. Here are some suggestions:

a. **Immediate family members and significant others need to be identified and separated from the other on-lookers.** This can be as easy as approaching someone trying to get close or enter into your scenes and asking, "Excuse me, can I help you?" These people typically will identify themselves as such, or if available, have known family members vouch for them. These people now become your VIPs and should be put in a private area where someone can explain the current situation and honestly answer questions. If and when safe to do so, they may be allowed inside the scene perimeter as long as they are chaperoned.
b. **If there is a fatality, tell the VIPs truthfully that their loved one has died and give them the choice to be with the body.** In my experience, I have never had anyone turn down the chance to be with a loved one who has just died. Have someone near for support.
c. **Explain to them what they will see.** Be honest. If there is blood, disfigurement, or other abnormal sights, tell the family and again, give them the choice. One of the things that

has worked for me is to try to keep the body covered with a blanket and let the family uncover (if they wish) a small area of the body that they choose to see. If there is disfigurement, usually the family just stands next to the blanket or may reach down and hold their loved one's hand under the blanket.

4. Convey Caring. It has been said that people do not care how much you know until they know how much you care! We cannot always change the outcome of a tragedy or ease the pain survivors may be going through, but we can leave an imprint that people on the scene cared about what they were going through.

Background: My pager went off while I was off duty on a Christmas morning. It was a request to respond to a fatal motor vehicle crash. An 18-year-old girl on her way to church in her new Christmas dress hit an icy patch on the highway and lost control. Her car hit a tree, killing her instantly. Her younger brother, also in the car, survived with minor injuries. The emergency responders on the scene recognized two things: first, that this Christmas morning tragedy had the propensity to produce stress amongst themselves and second, that the family of this girl, also on their way to church, was arriving at the scene.

Upon arrival, I found the VIPs had already been separated from the rest of the gathered crowd. A Firefighter was standing with them explaining that their daughter had died and that someone was on their way to assist them. The Incident Commander was explaining to the on-scene police agency the intent about their facilitation to allow the family into the scene. After making sure the police were okay with our intent, I met with the medics on scene and inquired about the condition of the body (I did not need to physically see it). I then went to the family, acknowledged their daughter's death, and explained the visual condition of their daughter. I offered that if they would like to be with their daughter for a few moments, we would stay with them.

The daughter had a massive head injury, but to the family she was still beautiful in her new dress. The mother gently covered her up with a blanket to keep her daughter warm.

The Firefighters at this scene recognized the situation and they understood they might not be able to deal with it properly themselves. Requesting help when you are feeling overwhelmed is very appropriate. Because of this, it is important to have a plan and know what your resources are for interacting with significant others if they show up at an emergency scene. I met this family again more than a year later. They approached me and identified themselves. They remembered what had been done at the scene and thanked the fire department for caring.

In my experience, significant others who show up at or are at a fatality scene have common concerns:

1. *They want to say goodbye where the death happened.*
2. *They want to say goodbye before the body gets cold.*
3. *They want the body to look comfortable – even in death.*
4. *They want to reconcile any differences with their loved one.*

These are the human needs of survivors. If they are unable to accomplish one or more of these, explain to them why getting closer is not allowable. Use "doses" if needed to help them understand.

As a side note, half of these survivor concerns can be remedied by fully covering the body. The perception is that the blanket keeps the body warm and comfortable. Even if the body is disfigured, the blanket will hide this (do not move the body to a position of comfort) and the survivor will not be able to tell if they "look" comfortable or not.

5. Allow Grief. Everybody expresses their grief in a different way. Allow people to express themselves in their own way without interference. The exception to this would be if there is destructive or unlawful behavior. In those circumstances, people should be warned that the behavior is unacceptable and that police will be brought in if they do not cease. Otherwise, allow the significant other to validate their loss.

6. Offer Continued Support. Assess the needs of the situation. As the Company Officer, you should know if there are local resources to assist those in crisis because of serious injury or loss of a loved one.

7. Respect the Body (Living or Not). The best rule of thumb is to treat everybody, living or not, with the same care and respect you would want your loved one to be treated with. Your beloved wife, daughter, mom, partner or grandma is seriously ill at home and 911 is called. Within minutes, you have 4 Firefighters and 2 Medics taking off your loved one's clothes. There must be a better way to achieve medical care without disregarding someone's dignity. Covering or shielding a body shows respect of privacy for the living, the deceased, and their loved ones.

8. Your Resources. This is two-fold. First, what are my resources to assist significant others who show up at the scene? Does my organization have chaplains? Is there a local TIP (Trauma Intervention Program) for civilians? If the crew is busy, can we dispatch another unit for the purpose of dealing with these folks? Second, we are human. One of the challenges Firefighters have is not allowing ourselves to have a normal human response to tragedy. Normal humans have responses to kids dying, multiple patient incidents, knowing the victim, gory/difficult sights/sounds/smells, and other tragedy. Knowing your available resources (Peer Response Teams, EAP's, other "culturally competent" therapists, etc.) who have been identified in the community and having a chat with them allows yourself to be human. This is NOT a sign you are weak, broken, or chose the wrong career, but that you are human! This will help ensure you make it through your career happy and healthy!

Be Nice! I learned this from a very wise man! When in doubt, be nice! We will never know the history of people when we are in their lives rendering care to a loved one. Just be nice! They may have lost a loved one in their past and fear losing another. They may have been the victim of someone taking advantage of them (particularly the elderly). They may have a history of abuse or violence by others and struggle trusting people. Be nice!
Kind Words & Caring Actions

"A good death notification and nothing changes…
A bad death notification and everything changes." - Parent of a murdered child

If we do everything right when someone is in crisis by portraying a caring behavior and use caring words, in the person who lost a loved one's mind, nothing has changed - they still have lost a loved one. If we do something perceived as uncaring like telling a joke to a co-worker in the front yard of the deceased's home or using a poor choice of words communicating to a family member, the person grieving not only has lost their loved one, but we have just taken away a once respected occupation that they thought they could call whenever they needed help.

In reflecting on calls that I have been on, I am embarrassed by some of the things I have said (all with the intent to provide comfort) to people when they were in emotional crisis - when they were most vulnerable and when everything said and done was permanently imprinted in them. My words were not helpful, but nobody told me what to say!

The following statements have been said and heard at emergency scenes with the intent to provide comfort, but did not:

Never Say…

- **"I know how you feel."** - It is impossible to "know how someone feels" unless you have been there. Even if you have experienced a personal loss, you cannot know what the person who just has is feeling.

- **"I understand."** - Most of the time, we do not. Again, it is impossible to know the history the loved ones had with each other.

- **"You shouldn't feel that way."** – First of all, that is all a human can do when in emotional crisis. The feelings have pushed down the thinking! People have the right to feel the way they do. Feelings cannot be changed by a directive to feel otherwise. Any way they look at the incident, their world has been turned up-side-down. Allow the survivors to express their feelings.

- **"You're so strong."** - A person in high anxiety or shock may be in a non-active state. When they begin to reconcile their grief, they will remember this statement and think you (the responder) are an idiot. What does "strong" have to do with being in emotional pain? People never feel strong when they are in a crisis.

- **"You must get on with your life."** - Who are we as emergency responders to tell anyone to get on with their life? Grief takes time. Nobody is past their grief until they have passed through their grief. That process can take months or years depending on the circumstances. Some never finish their grief process during their lifetime.

- **"You'll get over it."** - No one "gets over" a tragedy. At best, survivors learn to cope with what has happened. "Getting over it" may also imply that you want them to forget about their loved one. Again, such a comment asks people to do the impossible.

194

- **"If you only had…"** - Sometimes the circumstances leading to tragedy are so obvious that emergency responders want to lecture the survivors. The husband's acute chest pain that started 4 hours prior to the 911 call, the unrestrained driver, the guns laying around the house, the kids riding bicycles without helmets all can bring frustration and anger to those trying to save these people's lives. Believe me, the significant other will dwell on these tragic circumstances by themselves, without our help.

- **"Your anguish won't bring them back."** - This comment states the obvious and people generally resent that. Such a comment generates nothing except anger. Again, let the survivor deal with the crisis in their own way. They know their loved one will not be coming back. Why rub salt in the wound?

- **"They led a good life."** - This statement is not much of a consolation when someone has a big gaping hole in their life where a loved one used to be. Maybe they did lead a "good life," but most probably, the survivor is not ready to give them up.

- **"Don't question God's will."** - Some theologians will argue it is not God's will to have people die. There are many beliefs and various religions that understand death differently. Trying to bring divine meaning to anything tragic during an emotional crisis may only add confusion and frustration. The survivor will have plenty of time after the crisis to reflect on the purpose and put meaning to the situation.

- **"You'll find someone else."** - Looking to the future is not what survivors want to think about. You do not understand, nor are you expected to understand the history of any relationship other than your own. Many people are very much in love and satisfied with their relationships and do not want to think of life without their loved one.

- **"Be thankful you have other children."** - Sitting with an elderly woman one day, the conversation of children came up. She shared that she had raised five children. When they were young, the middle boy died. She told me a friend came to her after the death and said, "Be thankful you have other kids." She shared that she wanted five kids, not four, and that the middle boy was just as loved and important as the others. She thought this remark was insensitive and uncaring even after all those years. If you put this phrase in context, this woman could have lost 3 more kids and still be thankful!

- **"It would have been worse if…"** - Resist the urge to make things seem "not as bad." To the person undergoing emotional crisis, it does not get any worse than the situation at hand. Such comments are always viewed as insensitive.

In addition, when dealing with a person that has just lost their spouse/partner of many years, acknowledge that it must be difficult. They are not in a place yet to reflect on how lucky they were to have so much time with each other. The only thing they want when in crisis is their loved one back.

As a side note, always consider the timeliness of statements. This portion of the chapter deals solely with people in an emotional crisis when their emotions are high and cognitions are hampered. Statements made during the crisis that make no sense to the survivor may be comforting later in their grief process when they seek reconciliation of the event. "They led a good life" or "be thankful you had so many years together" said post funeral or in a grief group setting certainly take on a different meaning.

What to Say

I used to teach emergency responders things to say at difficult times. I had a whole list of phrases presumed to bring comfort to those in emotional crisis and grief and to make our job easier. However, as I took a serious look at them, they seemed forced and not genuine. Here is what generally works:

- **"I'm sorry."** - There are probably no words easier to say or more appropriate than "I'm sorry."

- **It is okay to state that the situation is difficult for you as an emergency responder.** In general, people truly respect the public safety uniformed services. Imagine the sense of respect they feel when a "hero" goes beyond the call of duty to share someone else's grief. I had finished giving a presentation on fire safety to a group of adults when an elderly gentleman approached me and took me aside. He shared that the fire department had responded to his house years ago when his wife passed away. He asked me if I knew what he remembered most about the experience. I was puzzled. He went on to tell me that when the medics stopped working on his wife, one of them came up to him and shared how difficult it was to see someone lose a loved one. He shared that it was a scene he would always remember and stated, "You guys really care about what happens don't you?"

  - Simple caring statements
    - "I am so sorry your loved one died."
    - "I can only imagine how difficult this must be for you."
    - "It is difficult to see people lose someone they loved."

- **Ask to hear about their loved one.** I am a history buff. Once, when sitting at the kitchen table with a grieving wife and trying to gather the needed information for my incident report, I noticed a railroad retirement plaque on the wall bearing the name of her just deceased husband. "I see your husband retired from the railroad," I said. This seemed to create a spark in her because someone was interested in her husband's story. I received a neat history lesson on the railroad and her husband's work and she received the feeling that someone cared about her husband's life. After a person has been declared dead at the scene (this works best in the comfort of their home), take the time to ask, "What did Bill (obviously use the name of the deceased!) do for a living?" In most cases, they will be happy to share their memories.

Sometimes Just Being There Helps

We tend to worry a great deal about what we should or should not say when dealing with the relatives and friends of a deceased person. However, often it is a wordless gesture which means the most. Simple things, such as holding a door open, offering a chair, or a respectful nod of the head can assist the bereaved.

Let Touch Convey Caring

Sometimes there are no words that can be said. A simple touch to the shoulder can say it all. There seems to be a comforting power in human touch that I cannot explain. Research suggests that touch has a dramatic impact on psychological health. Touch can help ease pain and anxiety and generally soften the blow of a difficult situation.

Are We Putting Ourselves at Risk?

I was teaching the "Scenes of Compassion" program to a large metropolitan fire department. I was discussing a case study of a fatal motor vehicle crash in which a young woman was killed by a drunk driver. Her family had shown up at the scene and I described the process of facilitating working with local authorities to allow the family into the scene. Following this case study, a Firefighter questioned whether our stress debriefings had increased because of all the "touchy-feely work we were doing out in Oregon." My response was, "Quite contrary!" As tragic as this scene was, we had left an imprint with the family that we cared. We felt good about what we had accomplished. You do not debrief feeling good! Did we go back to station and discuss the call? Sure. Did we do a stress debriefing? No.

Getting "touchy feely" is not typically in an emergency responder's toolbox. These words and actions can be accomplished without getting emotionally involved with the bereaved. You can show compassion without shouldering it and the emotional benefit you leave and receive far outweigh the fear of taking a caring action.

Work hard. Be nice. – Tim W. Dietz

End of Call Customer Service Options – John Brunacini

For incidents that involve the critically injured or ill, most (if not all) patients will be transported to the hospital. As the patient is being transported from the scene, it is important for the Company Officer to explain to any significant others on scene the next set of events that will occur for the critically injured or ill. This includes:

- Medical personnel will continue to provide the best treatment possible on the way to the hospital.
- Once at the hospital, the patient will be immediately triaged and will be taken directly into the ER or the OR.
- It could possibly take several hours before the patient is stabilized and will be able to see any family members.
- Discuss the possible option of a significant other accompanying the patient to the hospital. In most cases, any significant other accompanying a patient in the ambulance to the hospital should be an adult who can make medical decisions for the patient.
- Estimate the length of stay at the hospital (for example: they will be there at least a couple of days) and advise the family that the patient will need their necessities when

they are stabilized and in an actual hospital "bed." This includes all of the patient's medications.
- DO NOT let stressed out people drive to the hospital. Tell them that everyone is doing everything possible for their loved one and to take their time driving anywhere because it will be hours before the patient can be seen by any family members.

Patient and Customer Transportation Guidelines

- Significant others accompanying a patient to the hospital should sit in the front passenger seat of the ambulance (safest position).
- Outside incidents (such as an auto accident) with multiple related patients from one car should be transported to the same hospital whenever possible.
- Minors transported to the hospital should have one of their parents (or a legal guardian) accompanying them at all times.
- When on the scenes of outside incidents in which uninjured people are away from their homes (stranded), instead of leaving people who are related to a person being transported, make all efforts to get these other family members related to the patient to the hospital where their loved one was transported. This could be done by using the ambulance and/or on scene apparatus that are finished with the call.

Managing the Deceased

Highly Suspected Death by Trauma, Violence, or Terminal Illness

Other than a person who works in a hospital setting (doctors and nurses), a Medical Examiner's office, or a mortician's business, Firefighters probably see more deceased people than any other profession. Speaking from personal experience, seeing a lot of dead people in their different stages of death, while also witnessing what killed them, starts to wear on a Firefighter throughout their career (especially if it involves children).

To help limit this exposure, when dispatched to incidents where there is a high likelihood of having an actual deceased person on the scene (shootings, heavy machinery accidents, terminally ill patients, etc.) or if the incident takes place in a crime scene, Company Officers must limit the stress on other individuals by reducing their exposure to witnessing the dead whenever possible.

For incidents that we are called upon to confirm the condition of these people, a Company Officer should only send in the minimum number of personnel to confirm the patient's condition in an effort to reduce the exposure of scene conditions. For patients who are in a safe, static environment, this means just 1 person with the highest medical qualifications. In unstable environments, the buddy system should be used, so 2 people will enter the scene and confirm the patient's condition.

If these actions just reduce 1 person on the company from seeing a dead person, it is more than worth it in the long run of a 30-year fire service career.

The Deceased

All deceased people will require a chain of custody with their body until they are either cremated or buried. In any out of hospital or hospice death setting, law enforcement will be involved in managing the front end of the chain of custody that will get the deceased to either the Medical Examiner's office or to a morgue or a mortuary. If the fire department is the first local agency to encounter a deceased person, they start out the chain of custody and cannot leave the deceased body unattended until law enforcement has arrived on the scene to continue the chain of custody process.

DNRs

A DNR order is a legal written order made out by the patient's primary physician that indicates that the patient does not want to receive any resuscitation if they are currently in a state of biological death for their current terminal medical condition. Sometimes, it also prevents other medical interventions that will temporarily prolong the patient's life. A DNR must have:

- Doctor's signature
- Patient's signature (or a person having medical power of attorney over them)
- Some DNR's may have a date range, but most do not
- Must be physically displayed to EMS personnel in order for the DNR to be enforced

In most circumstances, people who have a DNR will not call the fire department, but there are times when you will respond to a patient who has a DNR. This is usually because the deceased patient's family will call the police department to start the process of getting the body to a Mortuary and the 911 police operator hears "dead person" and they dispatch EMS. The fire department gets there and the family members all state "we just called the police department."

This scenario puts a fire company into a very bad position because of our duty and obligation to act whenever people and/or property are threatened. A DNR must be presented to EMS personnel for revival efforts NOT to begin if the patient has any chance of being revived (this does not include a person who has been clinically dead for a while). If the family cannot produce a DNR and the patient appears viable, treatment must begin. If the DNR cannot be found/presented, sometimes EMS personnel can contact their medical authority and if approved, revival efforts can cease. In some states across the country, the DNR will be registered and available online to the medical community. In these cases, refer to these systems to ensure a legal DNR is in place to prevent a fire department intervention.

Another, opposite scenario could also happen in which there is a valid DNR in place, family members have traveled from all over the country to say their good-byes, and when the moment of death comes, they are in a highly emotional state and they insist that revival efforts take place despite the patient having a valid DNR. These are very emotionally charged situations and when they happen, the Company Officer will need to honor the family wishes and revival efforts must begin until told otherwise by your medical authority (always follow your AHJ's medical protocols for these situations).

In-Home versus Out-of-Home Deaths - Tim W. Dietz

Again, it is important you know your local and state laws regarding moving or covering a body or removing medical equipment from a body prior to a Medical Examiner's arrival. The County that I retired from would allow this only after an on-scene medic contacted the responding Medical Examiner and asked for permission to do so. In most cases, permission was granted with the statement "make sure you document what you did."

In-Home Death

If I declare a death in the field (in someone's home) and in my best professional opinion, it is of natural causes and if there are family members present, it would be my desire to facilitate family time with the deceased. Typically, a conversation may look like this after declaring a death:

- "I am sorry but your loved one has died."
- "Because the death happened outside the care of a doctor, we will need to call for a Medical Examiner to come to the scene."
- "While we are waiting, my crew is going to get our equipment off your loved one. Is there a blanket you would like your loved one covered with? A pillow? Would you like the head covered or not?" If we pulled the person out of bed to work them, I would often times put the body back into the bed.
- "While we are waiting for my crew, you and I will sit at the table. I need to get some more information on your loved one for my paperwork. When my crew is ready and I have the needed information from you, you may be with your loved one."

Out-of-Home Death

For out of home deaths (car crashes, industrial accidents, violence, etc.) it is always best to get permission from local law enforcement before you cover the body or allow significant others into the scene. I certainly would not want to mess up anyone's crime scene. If permitted, after the body is covered, think about taking a tarp or black plastic and cover the entire car or machinery. This helps keep the folks looking to catch something for social media from accomplishing their heartless task. Plus, it gives the family an insulating layer in their brief journey to their loved one if allowed. In inclement weather, the additional tarp expresses that you care about their loved one's comfort and the condition of their body. This also removed the tragic scene from our vision while on scene.

The Science behind "Being Nice"

As a reminder, these calls can take their toll on us if we are not paying attention. Self-care in the fire/EMS business is extremely important. As a Company Officer, you are the role model for self-care. Checking in with your crew after an unusual/stressful event is vital. Also remember, something not bothering you does not mean others on your rig are not impacted! Think about:

- The Five Assignment Model (explained in a previous chapter)
- High – Low check-in after dinner (explained in a previous chapter)

Expressing compassion by using kind words and caring actions when our customers need it the most will go a long way in that person's perception on you and your organization. Being nice has incredible power when a struggling human needs it the most!

Humans are innately wired to help each other. This is a natural, instinctual response that has aided in our survival! Research suggests connecting with others in a meaningful way (leaving an imprint that you cared), causes better mental and physical health. Being nice to someone when they are in need activates pleasure centers in the brain. UCLA and the University of North Carolina medical researchers Steve Cole and Barbara Fredrickson found that people who were happy because they helped others lived longer, had less stress, and were healthier than those who were happy because they lived the good life! No sure what to do? Treat others as you would want your family members treated.

Work hard. Be nice. – Tim W. Dietz

Section 4
Managing Human Resources

Chapter 19

Managing a Harassment Free Workplace

"Company officer expectation #2 - Someone who creates a happy, harassment free working environment."

Background: L-201 had a Probationary Firefighter position that rotated every 3 months. During my tenure, we hosted over 20 Probationary Firefighters on L-201. After supervising the first 2 or 3 rotations, I developed a set routine that I used with all Probationary Firefighters from that point forward.

A big part of a new person's success depends a lot on them knowing exactly what was expected of them in conjunction with filling them in with any details of their assignment that they may not be aware of. Knowing this, I would meet our newly assigned Firefighter during the morning shift change and I (and the rest of the crew) would inform them of the basic details they needed to get settled onto the truck and to get through the morning routine.

Each member of the crew had a set of information and training responsibilities with each Probationary Firefighter. They would start this process with the new member as soon as they arrived at the station and it would continue throughout the next 3 months. I would start my process with the new member on the crew by calling them into my office after lunch on their first shift at the station. Once in my office, I would cover a great majority of the new member's expectations and fill them in with the different personality details of their co-workers that they needed to know in order to be successful at the station. I would end my 30-minute overview with telling every recruit the following:

"You will be judged on the fire department by all others based on 2 major things. To me, they share a ratio of 51 to 49 in percentage of importance. The first 51% of the judgement ratio is based on your competence level as a Firefighter. The reason your competence level is the higher percentage is because if you are not competent, you should not be here in the first place. We have a very hazardous job and there is no place for incompetence. The other 49% of the judgement ratio is based on how well you get along with your fellow co-workers (this includes everybody on the fire department). Just like being competent, if you are difficult to work and interact with for a 24-hour shift, you should not be here."

I would conclude by telling them that it was my responsibility to make sure everyone got along together at the fire station. We did not have to love or like each other, but we ALL had to respect each other while doing our jobs. I would end my overview by asking them for their help in assisting me with facilitating an atmosphere at Station 201 in which everyone got along and did their jobs at a high level. I would do my part and they had to do their part.

All Management Must be Directed Towards the Service We Provide

The theme of this book is managing excellent customer service (not managing problems). As stated previously, the core of all excellent customer service starts with:

The way employees treat their customers will be a direct reflection on how their organization treats its employees.

How we treat our customers starts with how we treat each other. The way we treat each other will determine if we control our own circumstances (our future capabilities) or if the current circumstances (the way we treat each other) will control us.

The Workplace

Because a Company Officer is the person who is directly responsible for managing a harassment free, happy workplace, let's start this chapter by defining what the workplace is.

Workplace – *a person's place of employment*

Having defined what a workplace is, let's further define what a fire station is.

The fire station is a workplace!

Throughout this book, I have purposely avoided using the term "fire house." While the term "fire house" sounds all quaint and cozy, it should never be used because the word "house" connotates a personal possession – this is "mine," as in "this is my house." A fire station is a workplace and is elevated beyond most other workplaces in the community because the citizens paid for ALL OF IT and they will go to great lengths to hold the people in charge of it accountable for its care and use, as well as the behaviors being acted out inside of it.

Company Officers must behave like managers and supervisors. This starts with the understanding that the fire station is not your house. It is a workplace and it is attached to all of the legal systems that come with it.

Federal Laws and Regulations Governing Workplace Behaviors

Most of all a fire departments' liability comes from inside the organization. Of this liability, most of it comes from HR issues in which some sort of hostile workplace, discrimination, or harassment has occurred. Because of this, Company Officer's need to be very well informed on the regulations, laws, and federal acts that govern workplace behaviors. All of the federal laws and regulations about to be covered apply to ALL Fire Department workplace supervisors and subordinates. While many of these laws are very broad, this book will try to focus on the different parts of the laws that directly impact an Officer managing a fire company.

I will start with Title VII of the 1964 Civil Rights Act which prohibits discrimination on the basis of race, color, religion, national origin, or sex. The revised Civil Rights Act of 1991 reaffirms and further specifies the elements of discrimination. The new additions to the legislation permit individuals to sue for punitive damages in cases of intentional discrimination and shifts the burden of proof to the employer. The revised Act also permits the person being discriminated against or harassed to collect compensatory damages in cases in which the employer acted with "malice or reckless indifference" to the individual's civil rights.

To further reinforce this updated legislation, a 1993 Supreme Court ruling widened the test for discrimination and harassment under the revised civil rights law to whether comments or behavior in a work environment **"would reasonably be perceived as hostile or abusive by**

any other normal/reasonable person." As a result, employees do not need to demonstrate that they have been psychologically damaged to prove discrimination or harassment in the workplace - they simply must prove that they are working in a hostile work environment.

Most employers in the United States must comply with the provisions of Title VII. Compliance is required for all private employers of 15 or more persons, all educational institutions, **state and local governments (this includes all fire departments)**, public and private employment agencies, and most labor unions.

Protected Classes

Title VII also introduces and defines "protected classes." These currently include gender, race, religion, age, disability, national origin, color, family status, marital status, sexual orientation, and veteran status.

Almost all people in the workplace fall under one of these 11 categories. The workplace should be managed with the understanding that anyone can file a Title VII lawsuit against their employer and everyone is "protected under the law." Get protected classes out of your brain – everyone is protected!

The Legal Protection and Enforcement Systems

Employees who have perceived themselves to have been discriminated against and/or to have been a victim of a hostile work environment can be represented in the legal systems by the EEOC. The EEOC was established through Title VII of 1964 Civil Rights Act. The scope of authority of the EEOC has been expanded over the years and today it is the major enforcement authority for Title VII violations.

The EEOC works for/under the DOJ. There is an MOU between the EEOC and the DOJ Civil Rights Division. Paragraph 4 of this MOU states:

"...As set forth in Title VII, EEOC receives and investigates charges of discrimination against state and local governmental employers and if it finds cause to believe that a Title VII violation has occurred, attempts to conciliate those charges. **However, under the statute, the Department of Justice is the sole federal entity that has the authority to sue such employers for Title VII violations**..."

The top of the food chain for a fire department in Title VII matters is the DOJ. A fire department does NOT want the DOJ showing up at their doorstep for Title VII violations. Your fire department also does not want to experience any of the following legal situations associated with Title VII violations:

- Consent decrees
- Executive Order 11246 or 10479
- RICO Act
- Arraignment(s)
- Grand jury

- Default judgments

Fortunately, most employees that feel they have been discriminated against or work in a hostile work environment do not begin their case at the highest federal level using the EEOC to file a Title VII federal lawsuit. Most people that file a Title VII lawsuit have tried to solve their grievance/complaint on the lowest level possible and then they work their way up the legal chain to settle their dispute. The legal chain ends at the EEOC/DOJ.

Here is a list of some of the possible **LOCAL** methods/systems that are available in most organizations to file and settle discrimination and/or harassment complaints. This list represents how an employee will initially declare a hostile work environment before going to the federal level:

1. A worker simply states or discusses with a fellow co-worker or supervisor discriminatory or abusive behavior coming from another co-worker or supervisor.
2. The worker files a formal complaint with their direct supervisor.
3. The worker files the complaint to another higher-ranking member/person inside the organization above their direct supervisor.
4. The worker files the complaint through their local union representation and the complaint will be processed under the current MOU/CBA with the employer.
5. The worker files the complaint against their employer by themselves or through their local union representation using a civil service hearing (this usually happens when the method above is not successful in settling the dispute).
6. The worker files the complaint using a private attorney directly against their employer (and the different factions within it, such as the fire department).
7. A worker files a lawsuit against their employer using a local or state level EEOC department.
8. The worker files the complaint using the "whistle blower" method (Employment Rights Act 1996).

Okay, I am going to stop now and take a breath from all this legal doom and gloom. My father had a saying: "You have to know sin to fight sin." Knowing the laws that regulate a harassment free workplace and the possible consequences of what can happen when they are not enforced will hopefully help motivate Company Officers to avoid getting into these kinds of situations in the first place.

Managing to Prevent Inappropriate Behaviors

The first 3 sections of this book provide models on how to effectively lead by example. Leading by example coupled with having emotional intelligence is the best way to manage people. It will go a long way in minimizing the bad things that can happen to an Officer while managing a fire company. Let's recap some of the "leading by example" themes presented previously in this book:

- Always treat all people with dignity and respect.
- Take responsibility for your company's actions and always be a shield for your crew.
- Watch what you say!

- Listen to your crew members with an open mind.
- Share the workload with your crew (get your hands dirty).
- Respect the chain of command.
- Delegate often and then get out of the way.
- Take care of yourself.

While leading by example will drastically minimize most of the bad things that can happen to a Company Officer, it will not prevent all negative things from happening. When inappropriate behaviors do occur, a Company Officer must act like a supervisor.

Addressing Behavioral Issues

Directly above are the most important words in the entire book when it comes to managing a fire company (or anything else for that matter). Company Officers must address HR and service delivery issues as soon as they occur - both the good behaviors and the bad behaviors.

Addressing GOOD Behaviors!

This portion of the book will focus on addressing good behaviors. Addressing bad behaviors will be addressed in the last section of the book.

Because our service is organized as a para-military type of organization (the pyramid shaped organizational chart), we are much better at dealing with the negatives than the positives. As a matter of fact, most Firefighters feel very uncomfortable when they are given praise. This is because it usually does not happen often and when it does, it is way too formal.

The goal of this book is to look at specific situations (the most common ones a Company Officer encounters) and then help by giving some of the correct/appropriate actions and/or words to use for that situation. Here is a list of some high performing behaviors and some of the correct Company Officer responses to them:

- When somebody says "please" – say "no worries"
- When somebody says "thank you" – say "you are welcome"
- When somebody does something nice for you – say "thank you"
- When somebody does a good job – say "great job," "well done," "that looks great," or "I appreciate all of your hard work"
- When somebody is exceptionally nice to somebody else or goes beyond the call of duty for a co-worker or customer – say "great job," "thank you, that meant a lot to that person," "way to go above and beyond," "greatly appreciated," "thanks for helping that person," or "thanks for making the crew look good"
- When somebody demonstrates exceptional performance during a high stress incident – say "great job/great performance," "I can always count on you when it gets tough," "you're a superstar," "I'm proud to be supervising the best crew on the department," or "I don't know what I'd do without you"

As a long-time Fire Chief, my father understood that the ratio of the good things that the work force did greatly outweighed any of the bad stuff that ever happened, but there was no system in place to formally recognize exceptional behaviors or outcomes. The Phoenix Fire Department had a great system to recognize bad behavior - we wrote people up for rule infractions using a "yellow sheet." A lot of yellow in your personnel file was bad. Dad invented the "green sheet," which recognized a person's or crew's exceptional performance (most other departments probably have this same system in place and call it something else). The implementation of green sheets on the department created an atmosphere in which it was okay to recognize the good instead of just the bad.

I would get the green sheets out to "officially" recognize my crew members performance for the following circumstances:

- Exceptional performance during a department drill or MCS evaluation
- Exceptional performance (above and beyond) helping another co-worker in obtaining one of their professional goals
- Exceptional performance on the emergency scene during a high stress situation
- Exceptional performance in helping a customer

Background – As the Company Officer on L-201, I was extremely blessed with having a high performing crew. They made my life much easier as a Company Officer and I greatly appreciated their commitment to their fellow co-workers, our customers, and to excellent job performance.

Throughout every shift, I would use one of the previous list's phrases to verbally compliment them in their routine job performance. I would also officially recognize the entire crew using green sheets about every 3-4 months according to the green sheet list above. After about 2 years of doing this, I wrote a green sheet to the entire crew after an exceptional performance during our annual department wide MCS evaluations.

After filling out a green sheet, I forwarded it to the Fire Chief's office where he would review, comment on, sign, and then send it back directly to the individual receiving the recognition (a copy was also placed in their personnel file).

After my crew received their latest green sheet with the Chief's notes of thanks to them, the whole crew came to my office together (like a mutiny) and basically told me to stop writing them up for their exceptional performances. "Quit writing these, they are a pain." Message received – this was still too formal of a method to say thanks for a great job.

After this, I had to do something to officially recognize my crew's performance that was not so official. So, I would pay for their kitty and chow once a quarter for them, I would give them a gift card to one of their favorite restaurants, or once in a while, I would write on a small post-it-note, "Great job! From John" and I would stick it on their locker door.

Late one afternoon, I went into the ladder crew's dorm (I did not go back there very often) to tell one of my crew members that their family was at the station. When peaking my head into his bunk room to tell him his family was there, his locker door was open and proudly hanging on the inside of it was a framed post-it-note that I had given him 2-3 years earlier that simply said, "Great job on that call! From John." Wow! He framed it!

After seeing his locker, it really sank in how important it is (and how easy it is) to tell your people when they are exceptional. The framed note proved how important it was to my crew member. Talk about getting buy-in and ownership on the company level by just simply saying "thank you" to your crew members for doing a great job. It goes a long way.

Preventing the Bad Stuff from Happening

This portion of the chapter will be constructed around proactively preventing HR issues by creating a workplace environment that helps eliminate them from happening in the first place. This all starts with the information needed on the bad stuff that happens in a workplace in order to develop the appropriate prevention strategies.

According to the EEOC, the following are the top HR related issues that get people in the most trouble for either harassment or creating a hostile workplace in a fire station:

1. Verbal conduct
2. Physical conduct
3. Visual harassment
4. Sexual harassment

Let's look at what all 4 of these are like in real life and the steps a Company Officer can take to prevent them from happening in the workplace.

1. Verbal Conduct

Inappropriate verbal conduct includes sarcasm, epithets, derogatory or racial comments, rumors, slurs, code words, excessive foul language (you know the words you cannot use), sexual or sexist innuendoes, inappropriate terms of endearment, inappropriate jokes, etc.

Prevention strategy – Lead by example by not using any of the above verbiage. If a Company Officer displays any of the above conduct, they are giving their crew permission to do the same.

2. Physical Conduct

Inappropriate physical conduct includes impeding or blocking movement, stalking, petting, leering, touching, rubbing, pushing, shoving, assault, etc.

Prevention strategy – Lead by example by keeping your hands to yourself and not going around touching other people. If a Company Officer uses any of the above conduct, they are giving their crew permission to do the same. The only acceptable touching in a workplace is shaking hands or giving a high five (both require the other person's consent).

3. Visual Harassment

Visual harassment includes what is playing on the television and computer screens, derogatory posters, politically based material, department mail, cartoons or drawings, e-mails, faxes, computer transmissions, pornography, or anything else that would possibly offend a normal individual.

Prevention strategy – Lead by example by keeping your office and the rest of the station's walls and screens free from anything that is not "official." If the items listed above are present at the station, get rid of everything hanging on the walls of the station that is not official. If a Company Officer allows anything to be displayed in the station that is not official, they own all of it when it goes bad.

Background: About 4 months after getting the Captain spot on L-201, I came to work one morning and the Battalion Chief was parked behind the station. This was unusual and unusual occurrences are typically bad. When I went into the station, it was the A-Shift Battalion Chief that was present - not my boss, (my boss was the B-Shift Battalion Chief). That was a good thing because the A-Shift Battalion Chief could not write me up for anything (only a direct supervisor could). I could hardly wait to hear what had happened.

The A-Shift Battalion Chief and our A-Shift counterparts informed me as soon as I sat down at the dinner table that there had been a dispute between 2 of the Firefighters on different shifts - one on A-Shift and one on B-Shift. Below is the order of events:

- *Mr. B-Shift had worked at the station over 6 years.*
- *Mr. A-Shift had worked at the station for under 3 months.*
- *Mr. B-Shift and Mr. A-Shift both shared the same bunk space.*
- *Both knuckle heads were Big 10 college football fans.*
- *Mr. B-Shift rooted for the Michigan Wolverines and he had a Michigan poster hanging in his bunk area for the past 5 years.*
- *Mr. A-Shift rooted for the Ohio State Buckeyes and apparently looking at the Michigan poster since arriving at the station was causing him to have post-traumatic stress. His final response to the poster was bringing an Ohio State poster to work and hanging it over the Michigan poster.*
- *When Mr. B-Shift arrived to work the next shift, he promptly took down the Ohio State poster covering his Michigan poster, he rolled it up, and he put it on top of Mr. A-Shift's locker.*
- *Mr. A-Shift put it back up the next shift.*
- *Mr. B-Shift came to work the next morning and his poster was now rolled up on top of his locker, with the rival team poster hanging in its place.*
- *When Mr. A-Shift came back to work the next shift (the day before I ended up at the dinner table in the morning), he found his beloved Ohio State poster torn up into confetti size pieces and they were sprinkled all over their bunk room floor.*
- *Mr. A-Shift was now filing a grievance against Mr. B-Shift for the destruction of his personal property.*

I know - a lot going on. It probably took everybody longer to inform me of the events than the time it took for them to actually occur. In the long minutes that it took them to explain it all to me, I was personally thinking in my head, "You have got to be kidding me! KIDDING ME! 2 grown men acting like children over football posters and now the Battalion Chief is here for this nonsense!"

Once they were finished with all the details, I do not think anybody at the table expected what my response was. I stood up, opened up my wallet, and I gave Mr. A-Shift 20 bucks. I told him to go out and buy a brand-new Ohio State poster and to keep the change. I also told him and his Captain that if they ever have a problem with somebody on my shift again that they had better come to me first – not their Battalion Chief - and that both of them were full duty cowards.

From there, I addressed the A-Shift Battalion Chief (he was a good, competent Chief). I apologized for the incident and I assured him it would never happen again. I then got on the station intercom and requested my crew to report to the dining area. Once there, I ordered them to remove anything on the walls of the fire station that was not related to official city business - not destroy it, just remove it and put it all in a pile in the storeroom. It took my crew less than 5 minutes to accomplish this. Once completed, I got back on the station intercom and announced to all members at the station that "nothing unofficial is to ever be placed on ANY wall of the fire station from this moment forward. If you had something unofficial hanging on a wall, it is now in the storeroom. Anything unofficial hung on a station wall from this moment forward will be immediately removed and thrown in the trash at the owner's expense."

Just take all of it off the walls now to avoid what happed at Station 201 altogether.

To end, what was left on the walls (outside of the "official" fire department displays) were perfectly appropriate pictures of fire scenes and the different crews that had worked at Station 201 throughout the years. These were all left on the walls and are still hanging there today.

The only place to display personal visual material is inside your locker and it must be appropriate for all to view when your locker doors are open.

4. Sexual Harassment

Sexual harassment includes inappropriate language, unwanted sexual advances, suggestive sexual body language, suggestive touching, repeated requests for dates, displaying sexually suggestive visual materials, suggestions that evaluations are related to future sexual activity, etc. Also, be aware of the subtle behaviors that have the same intent.

Prevention strategy – Lead by example by not performing any of the above acts. If a Company Officers displays any of the above conduct, they are giving their crew permission to do the same. There is not much more to say on this one prevention wise – it is a pretty black and white thing to manage. I will cover this in a lot more in detail later on in this book.

Knowing and Preventing the Attitudes that get People in Trouble

At the fire station kitchen table, I have personally sat across from people who foolishly consider themselves "fire station lawyers." These are people who actually think they are completely protected by the US constitution while they are on-duty, getting paid to perform their employer's mission statement. These people really think that while in their employer's workplace, they can haze, harass, disrespect, and discriminate against other people with no consequences or they think that they are not legally or morally required to stop other people from doing the same things to each other in the workplace. These are the people who have the highest probability of creating a hostile work environment. Per Gordon Graham's experience, this delusional thinking and behavior usually comes with the following attitudes:

- Arrogance

- Entitlement
- Ignorance
- Complacency

Company Officers must recognize and combat these types of attitudes and behaviors because none of them align with any fire department VALUES.

Arrogance – There are many forms of arrogance, but in this case, I am talking about the "rules do not apply to me" form of arrogance. Many "fire station lawyers" believe that the fire station is their home and they cannot be held accountable for what happens in "my house." People who are arrogant about the rules not applying to them are dead wrong - they apply to everyone, especially to the supervisor of the workplace (who is directly responsible for making it a happy place).

Entitlement is defined as *the belief that one is inherently deserving of privileges or special treatment*. Most of the arrogant people inside of an organization also feel very special about themselves. This arrogance often times leads to an entitlement mentality. This combination usually comes with a "this whole job is about me and not the customer" attitude. But here is a news flash to the employees who believe this nonsense: the only person "entitled" to anything is the customer. They pay their taxes, they call 911, they get a functional crew to solve their problem, all while being nice (the mission statement). Let me repeat this: **THE CUSTOMER IS THE ONLY PERSON ENTITLED TO ANYTHING!**

Ignorance is defined as *lack of knowledge, information, or education; the state of being ignorant*. I can understand a farmer in the middle of Nebraska in 1802 being in a state of ignorance to people's social and civil rights, but in the "digital information age," it is impossible to excuse or condone inappropriate behaviors occurring in the workplace.

Complacency is defined as *self-satisfaction, especially when accompanied by unawareness of actual dangers or deficiencies*. When it comes to inappropriate workplace behaviors, a "I have been doing (or saying) it this way for a long time and I will continue to do so" attitude is going to end up as a train wreck (for you and your employer). The best way to combat complacency is to tell everybody to get on the truck and go drill for an hour (every shift!).

Ignorance and complacency are deliberate acts and are often accompanied with arrogance and entitlement. A "don't tell me what I don't want to hear" and a "I will continue to do as I always have" attitude is acting like an ostrich sticking its head in the sand. Lawyers love suing people who have their heads in the sand (because the lawyers will always win).

Closing

The Company Officer of the station is completely responsible for the workplace environment. Even if they do not manage it well or they have a "I didn't do it – they did it" attitude, the Officer in charge of the station still completely owns all of it. It is vital for an Officer's career that they understand, follow, and enforce all HR policies and procedures. And not just because…because it is the right way to manage regardless. Be nice and always set a good example!

Chapter 20

Communication: Expectations, Delegation, Accountability, and Employee Development

"Good communication applies to running a large fire department successfully just as much as it applies to a person performing a simple task successfully." – Alan Brunacini

Organizationally, most job expectations in the fire service have already been highly defined and communicated to all the riding positions on a fire company. This starts in the academy with MCS training, along with how we conduct business on most emergency scenes. It continues throughout all of the ranks as members are trained and tested in filling the roles and responsibilities of higher-ranking positions. All of these processes are performed to ensure that all members who walk through the doors every morning are already trained and preloaded on the expectations for their riding positions. Because a Firefighter's job is so regimented, I view a Company Officer "communicating expectations" more as just "communicating" with the people they directly supervise because most of the organizational expectations have already been communicated to everyone.

In his must-read book, *It's Your Ship*, as a new Captain, D. Michael Abrashoff took over as the Captain of the USS Benfold. When beginning his assignment, the USS Benfold had the lowest rating of any Destroyer in its battle group. When he finished his 2-year assignment, the USS Benfold was not only one of the highest rated ships in their battle group, they were considered one of the highest performing Destroyers in the US Navy. Captain Abrashoff oversaw the people who made up the lowest rated ship and with those same exact people, just over a year later, they became the highest rated performers in their group. The people on the USS Benfold, at all ranks, had all the same training and expectations as everyone else on the other ships in their battle group. So why the sudden turn around? It was because of 2 main things. Captain Abrashoff was both:

- An excellent communicator
- More importantly, he was an excellent listener

Listening

"The ability to listen is much more important than the ability to speak." – Alan Brunacini

We start with listening because it is most important out of the two communication forms for a Company Officer (talking versus listening). Again, most of the company's expectations have been communicated. What has not been communicated most of the time are the crew members expectations, observations, opinions, needs, wants, wishes, etc. You will never know what these things are unless you listen to your crew members.

People love other people who will listen to them. I mean people who really, sincerely listen to them. People who really listen to other people come across as caring about the person they are listening to. To put this concept on steroids: people who really listen to others and then "act" on the behalf of what the other person is communicating to them become true rock stars in others' eyes.

Communication is not simply delivering a message, as the message must also be understood by the other person as intended. The most effective communication styles must include a **feedback loop**, so that the deliverer of a communication knows that the message is received, understood, and supported. This requires the Company Officer to effectively listen to their crew's feedback. Crew members who know their feedback is heard and acted upon feel much more a part of the team and they are happier at work. This is all gained by listening - not by talking. Here are a few ways of motivating your crew members into giving you their feedback:

- Ask "how's it going?"
- Before engaging in a task, ask "what do you think?"
- Ask "how would you do this?"
- Ask "has something like this ever happen to you?"
- When understanding is necessary, ask "do you have any questions?" or "is this making sense?" or "is there anything else that you want/need to know to accomplish this?"
- Always try to include "what do you need from me?" or "what can I do to help you?" whenever the subject requires

A simple example of the above is while walking the decks, Captain Abrashoff would approach sailors performing their jobs and he would simply ask them, "How is it going?" On one particular day, Captain Abrashoff stopped to talk to a young man who was painting and replacing rusted bolts on the ship. Because the sailor had heard from his shipmates that Captain Abrashoff was a good listener, he felt comfortable enough to tell him he did not mind doing his job of ship maintenance and that he knew how important it was, but he felt that the maintenance required for the rusted bolts could be drastically reduced if they switched to stainless steel bolts instead of using the rust prone, iron bolts.

Right after **hearing** this, Captain Abrashoff talked to his supply and maintenance team about ordering the new bolts. The new bolts cost a little more than the old bolts, but the stainless steel bolts saved the entire crew literally thousands of hours per year by not having to replace and/or repaint them. The crewman who suggested the new bolts got some public kudos from the Captain and all his shipmates thanked him profusely for not having to spend hours a day replacing ship bolts and now they could all do more productive things with all that time. People who really listen can get things done. That is one of the big reasons why Captain Abrashoff's Destroyer went from last place to first place.

Traits for Good Listening

Now that you have a feedback loop going when communicating with your crew members, here are some of the basic traits required to be a good listener:

- Be present in the conversation. Do not act distracted. Maintain eye contact.
- Listen to listen. Do not listen to "respond."
- Use good body language to react appropriately to what the other person is saying (covered in a previous chapter).

- Keep an open mind with no hidden agendas.
- Be patient and do not interrupt (one of the worst things to do).
- Ask good follow-up questions related to what was said, summarize what was said, or add similar experiences to show your interest in what was said.
- Be emotionally intelligent (having empathy for what is being said)
- Always try to listen more than you speak (an old saying: God gave you 2 ears and 1 mouth for a reason - you should use your ears twice as much).

When you listen and truly hear what your crew members are saying, you will discover that people enjoy interacting with you more and that you have a greater influence on them. When your subordinates feel that you are actively listening to them, they are more likely to trust, have greater satisfaction, and to produce better results at work.

Background: My father had a pretty vertical promotional path on the fire department. He was also one of the highest educated people on the fire department. Before taking the Battalion Chief's test with 8 years on the job (1965-1966), he earned an Associate's Degree in Fire Protection from Oklahoma State University and he was about to earn his Bachelor's Degree in Political Science from Arizona State University (and he ended up earning a Master's Degree in Public Administration from Arizona State University in 1975). Most others in his era (all of the senior staff) had only high school diplomas and a great percentage of the current members on the department had also served in the military. In the mid 1960's, this put a large target on my father's back. The senior staff of the department believed my dad was a snot nosed, bookworm up-and-comer who wanted to change the way everything worked (which was true). They all made it their mission to make him fail.

During the time of his Battalion Chief promotional exam, the Phoenix Fire Department was also in the process of going from 2 shifts to 3 shifts. Over a year's time before the changeover, the department had hired about 200 new Firefighters to help facilitate this process. Along with this, the department went to the Shift Commanders of both shifts and asked each of them for about a third of all their personnel to be re-assigned to make up the new shift. They were all in paradise! They each stated that after making all their personnel "cuts" going to the new shift, they had to actually give the new shift some of their "decent" employees after first getting rid of all their dregs, malcontents, and troublemakers.

This group of re-assigned (special) people made up the brand new B-Shift. A new 5th Battalion was also added to the system and that is where Dad was assigned soon after coming out #1 on the Battalion Chief promotional exam. Dad was assigned to what the senior staff considered the worst of the worst of all the new B-Shift battalions - hand-picked, especially for him. They thought all they had to do was stand back and wait for all the malcontents to take the new guy down with the ship. They made 2 big mistakes in their thinking:

1. they underestimated my father
2. they underestimated all the malcontents they assigned to Dad's new battalion

As touched on throughout the book, my father was a great communicator. His strongest assets were his voice, listening skills, and the use of his body language. So that's just what he used. He got into his response sedan and he drove to each of his fire stations every shift and he listened to what his Captains had to say. He really listened and then he acted on what he heard. People love good listeners because they care.

In addition, my father had high performance standards. He communicated openly with his Captains that he wanted to deliver excellent service on all levels and he asked them all, "What are the best ways to improve the way we're doing things?" It has been documented in study after study that people's performance can improve over 25% when an employee feels like their boss truly cares about them and what they think. 25%! This cannot happen unless you listen!

The same thing happened in the 5th Battalion on B-Shift that happened in Captain Abrashoff's battle fleet - they went from the worst performing battalion to the highest performing battalion on the department for over a 4-year period, crushing all company evaluation times across the board and having the fewest amount of injuries, accidents, and customer service complaints.

Dad never underestimated the so-called malcontents. He just effectively listened and communicated with all of them. Along with this, most of the Captains in his new battalion went on to serve in much higher positions on the department in Dad's 28 years as Fire Chief (some of them even ended up being on his senior staff, as well as serving as Fire Chiefs on other departments). So much for the malcontents!

Looking/Watching

Looking at, observing, or watching an activity or interaction is also considered a form of listening. When watching something play out, here are some guidelines to follow:

- Only interrupt the event if safety is compromised or uncalled for meanness is occurring.
- Don't get distracted - keep your eyes on what is important.
- Use your feet to maintain a good view and/or stand close enough to hear well.
- Stay out of the way if you are not involved in the activity or interaction.

Communication Forms

There are many ways to communicate to subordinates in today's world. Modern communication methods include:

- Written on paper
- Written electronically (email)
- Written electronically (text)
- Phone
- Station intercom
- Video conference
- Face-to-face (verbal)

While a Company Officer will use most of these communication forms to communicate with the organization above and around them, the primary communication form used while managing a fire company is face-to-face. Because of this, it will be the primary form of communication this book will focus on, but let's take a quick look at the other communication forms listed above and how a Company Officer will use them to communicate with their crew members.

Written Communications

As stated earlier in this book, almost all of in-person communication is based on body language and the tone of voice that is used. All this non-verbal communication (intent) is eliminated in the written form. All written forms of communication create a situation in which the intent is completely subjective to the person receiving/reading it. Therefore, all written communications (on paper or electronic) must be professional in nature. NEVER hit the send button when you are angry.

The biggest written communication tool that I used as a Company Officer was the company activity calendar. As previously covered, the 90-day activity calendar contained all the important events and the comings and goings for all of Station 201 personnel. Each member had access to it and it greatly assisted all personnel at the station in being on time to wherever they needed to be.

The second biggest written communication tool that I used was my own Officer's personal log. This has been presented on previously and it will be referred to again later on.

E-Mail

This form of communication is not used very much by a Company Officer when communicating with their crew members. It would be counterproductive to send an email to the person sitting right next to you to remind them of something, but sometimes emailing a member of your crew an important date and time of an activity that needs to be completed will act as a reminder every time they log into their email until the task is completed.

While not used very much by the Company Officer to communicate with their crew members, email and other forms of electronic communication are vital forms of communication for connecting with the ranks of middle managers (Battalion Chiefs) and above. This is not a book on how to manage your email - you know the important ones you should open, respond to, and put into your activity calendar versus the ones that should go right in the trash.

Again, when using any electronic form of communication, never hit the send button on any electronic device when you are angry. Just do not do it. Emails and other electronic communication forms create permanent, digital, legal records for all to see (even the public).

Texting

Like all other forms of written communications, texting has its place when communicating with your co-workers, but most texting should be done off duty. This is because while on-duty, your crew members are standing or sitting right next to you and verbal communications would be the preferred method.

Also, when using text, it must stand the headline test. Co-workers who are sitting across from each other at the same dinner table that are texting secret messages about their other co-workers are considered to be rude. In the presence of others, talk to your co-workers with your in-person voice, not with your fingers typing text messages. If you cannot say it out loud in the workplace, you should not text it to anyone in the workplace either.

Phone Calls

Always answer the station phone by identifying your workplace and who you are: "Hello, Fire Station 201, this is John Brunacini speaking. How may I help you?"

Phone communication is also not used very much by a Company Officer when communicating with their crew members. Again, while at work, like texting, it would be silly to call the person sitting right next to you. I typically only used my phone to communicate with my crew members when I was off duty and it usually concerned managing an unexpected vacancy in which my crew members were giving me a heads up on their status or I was giving them a heads up on my status.

The biggest use of a phone when managing a fire company is when the bosses above you call you to discuss some sort of issue or when a Company Officer has to call their boss for some sort of scheduling issue, something that just got dented, for HR support, etc. There is a future chapter dedicated to when you should and should not call your boss.

Station Intercom

The station intercom system (a speaker phone to deliver a message to everyone at the same time) is a powerful tool and it was widely used to communicate with all Station 201 members.

Station 201 had 11 people on duty. Without the intercom, I still could have delivered the same message to everyone, but it just would have taken longer. Captain Abrashoff's Destroyer had almost 300 people on board, so it would have been impossible for him to directly communicate time sensitive information to each individual crew member in a timely manner. My favorite parts of his book were when he would describe the detailed and colorful messages he would broadcast to the entire ship using the intercom system. Captain Abrashoff effectively used the ship's intercom to keep his entire crew connected and informed. He understood that the more people knew about what was going on at the moment and where they fit into things, the more productive they would be.

While not as essential as when managing a US Destroyer, a fire station intercom should be used for the following:

- Notifying station personnel of in-station walk up or drive up medical incidents (or people banging on your door telling you that there is a fire down the street) that did not come through the regular 911 system
- General unit status announcements (truck is out of service, truck is back in service, personnel moves at a multi-unit station, etc.)
- Notify individual members of a phone call
- Notify the station that someone has a visitor (heads up for everyone to be on their best behavior)
- Make a chow time call

- Having all members assemble in one place quickly
- We always heard 5 or 6 "safety messages" throughout the day. A few came from me, but most of them came from all others at the station. Example: while doing chow prep, a member accidently cuts their finger and after putting a Band-Aid on it, they would announce "this is Firefighter Food Prep with a general safety announcement - always use extreme caution when using sharp knives to chop vegetables."
- My all-time favorite – notifying your crew members that it is drill time! I would never announce "get on the truck, it's drill time." I would always give my crew about a 15-minute heads up. The announcement would sound like: "We are going drilling in 15 minutes. Nobody be late." Then, 15 minutes later: "L-201 personnel, mount up immediately. We are out of here."
- Play pleasant, motivating music during morning work or PT workout activities

Here are a couple of good practices when using the station intercom:

- All intercom transmissions must be professional in nature
- Avoid using the intercom during nap and bedtime hours (unless it is for a really good reason)

Video Conferencing Systems

This book was primarily written during the COVID pandemic, in which video conferencing software played a huge role in connecting work forces remotely. In just the past couple years, these systems have made huge quality improvements to the point that they are becoming a normal part of doing business. While a Company Officer will not be doing much video conferencing directly with their crew members, I am sure they will be doing a lot of it with the rest of their organization as they take advantage of these systems.

When at the station using these systems to connect to all the different parts of the organization, it would be a good thing to have your crew members sitting next you for most of the meetings. The more informed they are, the more productive they will be while also learning a lot about what is going on outside of the fire station.

Because this form of communication is becoming so widely used, this book has put together a set of etiquette bullet points to follow when using this method of communication:

- Professional appearance
- Use good listening traits
- Video background is in good taste
- No backgrounds with motion
- No cell phone distractions or other noises
- Always use the mute feature when you have uncontrolled background noise
- Always shut your camera off when something distracting is on camera
- No eating while on camera
- No yawning while on camera
- No family members or pets in the background

- Do not perform other activities (like cooking) while on camera

Face-to-Face Verbal Communications

All people can develop good face-to-face communication skills, but this is something that is not usually taught to people throughout the course of their lives. Therefore, most people feel very uncomfortable communicating any official business or when dealing with a problem at work. An Interact survey conducted online by Harris Poll polled over 600 manager and the results showed that almost 70% of the managers said that they felt uncomfortable communicating with employees and almost 40% said that they were uncomfortable giving direct feedback about their employees' performance if they thought the employee might respond negatively to the feedback. Most managers also had communication issues recognizing good performance, receiving input, explaining the company line, giving clear directions, or crediting others for good ideas.

The only way that a Company Officer can manage excellence is by maintaining open channels of communication with their crew members. Good, positive, open communication channels between supervisors and employees improve both performance and job satisfaction. You must have good feedback loops in order to be successful with your crew.

Most of the non-verbal communication skills (using body language and tone of voice) were covered in a previous chapter. Company Officers need to use these same skills when communicating with their crew. In this chapter, I will focus mostly on the words for a Company Officer to use when officially communicating with their crew, along with having the correct body language and tone of voice.

Most of the official face-to-face conversations you will have with your crew members will focus on the following subjects:

1. Expectations
2. Delegation/Empowerment
3. Feedback and accountability
4. New SOPs and policies
5. Employee development
6. Off the job subjects (family, friends, hobbies, etc.)

1. Expectations

To start this category, I need to set a foundation for what expectations a Company Officer needs to communicate to their crew, along with what they should NOT need to communicate to their crew. Fire departments go to great lengths to hire people who are self-motivated. If the Company Officer must be the primary motivator of Firefighters instead of the Firefighters themselves, something is wrong. Based on this, I think the greatest expectation to communicate to your crew members is (and do it openly): "I EXPECT ALL OF US to be self-motivated, show up every morning, and do the job we were trained and are paid to do at the highest level possible. I will do whatever is necessary in **helping** the crew facilitate this."

This is the biggest crew member expectation. No Officer on the department should have to provide much motivation or long lists of expectations to subordinates to get them to do their jobs. The motivation a Company Officer provides to their crew members should come in the form of instruction and/or the encouragement for their crew to do the best job they can possibly do.

Not to sound like a broken record, but when leading by example in a manner in which you take the job seriously, you show up early for work, and you are always trying to do it the right way every time will go a long way in providing not only the motivation to the other crew members to do it the same way, but it also creates a standard (a culture) in which they all must follow. It is hard for a Firefighter to be goofing off inside the station in the morning when their Company Officer is outside working on the trucks.

To take this even further, below is a list of expectations a Company Officer who is leading by example should NOT have to communicate to their crew members:

- I expect you to respect your co-workers and our customers.
- I expect you to be nice.
- I expect you to work hard.
- I expect you to follow all the safety SOPs (like wearing your seat belt).

On the other side of this, I would be upset if first thing in the morning, I was addressed by the Company Officer and was told that I was expected to be nice or that I was expected to follow the safety rules, etc. The Captain needs to understand that I came through the doors preloaded that way by the department. That is why I am here at work. Please communicate to me if I do not do any of those things, but you must give me a chance to prove that I am self-disciplined before I require any of your discipline. My father had a perfect saying for this scenario: "Never over manage anyone." Only address the things that needs to be addressed.

If a Company Officer does in fact need to communicate any of these core fire department expectations and values with a crew member (like, you *really do* NEED to be nice) something is out of balance and that person is now in a disciplinary process where a later section of this book on addressing issues will apply.

When dealing with a person you have never worked with (or supervised), there are some expectations (more like covering the daily routine) that should be delivered as soon as possible to the person so they can know how the shift will roll out and where they fit in. This is usually done during the morning briefing at shift change and/or during morning fellowship and it should include:

- Riding position and the equipment they are responsible for
- General layout of the station and where their dorm room/locker is
- Chow and kitty routine
- PT routine for the day
- Any scheduled activities (drills, meetings, inspections, etc.)
- Anything else significant that is scheduled during the shift

Shift to Shift Expectations

Most likely, the biggest expectations a Company Officer will deliver to their crew members on a shift-to-shift basis will be during the morning shift change briefing and the morning fellowship routine when covering the schedule and planned activities for the day. This is the time and place for the Company Officer to open communication loops with their crew members on their expectations, everyone's individual responsibilities (including themselves), and where/how everyone fits in to getting the day's scheduled duties accomplished.

2. Delegation

Delegation is one of the most misused words on the company level in the fire service. Managers and supervisors do not delegate - they manage and supervise. The upper, executive levels of the organization delegate responsibilities (authority) away. It is a top-down thing. Company Officers do not do much delegating, but they get a lot delegated to them from the ranks that are much higher than theirs.

Lots of other books written about managing a fire company go to great lengths in describing how a Company Officer should delegate higher responsibilities to their crew members. A portion of the delegations described in these books are sometimes the actual authority of the Company Officer. A Company Officer cannot delegate any of their authority or responsibilities to another member of their crew. It is impossible. If you are having one of your crew members act up into your position while you sit in the back seat and anything goes wrong, you still own all of it. The only people who should "act" up in a Company Officer's seat are those that are completely trained and qualified to fill that role. A Company Officer cannot delegate it randomly away to an unqualified member on their company in an attempt to develop a crew member. It is not what our customers are paying for – they are paying for a fully qualified member to be in the right front seat when we show up.

Another misuse of the word delegation is when a Company Officer assigns a chore to a member of their crew while calling it delegation. For example: "Firefighter Smith, I am going to delegate you the duty of cleaning the shed today. This will go a long way in your employee development." What was just described is a chore/task. This is just like my dad saying to me when I was 12 years old, "I'm delegating to you the duty of taking out the trash every day. It will make you a better person when you are older." Ha! He told me take out the trash (and to do a number of other chores) because he did not want to do them, he had better things to do with his time, and that was the job my current seniority level was given. Chores are assigned - not delegated.

I believe true delegation happens on the leadership (executive) level of an organization and it actually involves the delegation of true authority for a major project or some sort of higher end department responsibility. As an example: a fire department's SCBAs are over 20 years old and the department has been awarded a federal grant to replace their entire inventory. Before replacing the old units, the Fire Chief wants a comparison study performed on the top 3 rated SCBAs currently on the market to decide what is the best model to choose for their fire department. When the decision is made to pull the trigger on the project, the Fire Chief and/or his senior staff will perform the basic "delegation" routine found in all the executive level leadership textbooks. This includes:

1. **Make sure the person they are delegating something to is capable of adequately completing the task. This should be based on current qualifications, past performance, and/or current potential of the individual.** In the case of the SCBA study, this project could be delegated to the Training Chief, a Battalion Chief, and/or a Senior Company Officer. Whoever the person is, they need to have a solid, working knowledge of an SCBA and some higher end management skills.

2. **Adequately explain to the person, using all of the different communication forms, what the end result needs to look like when the task is completed.** In this example, the end result would be a written report that compared all 3 units using a number of agreed upon evaluation points and who the overall winner is. It is very important that the processes that produces the end report are thoroughly explained and understood by all parties before starting the project.

3. **Time frame for completion required.** The completion times for this project would be centered around the time restrictions of using/spending the grant money.

4. **Detail any other people involved in the task, their roles, and the pecking order in managing the completion of the task.** This type of project will require several people to be involved. All pecking orders need to be well defined. There can only be 1 person in charge of any project.

5. **Explain the resources available for the completion of the task.** This would include the manufactures, fire department employees, facilities, and the funding involved for the project.

6. **What kind of support the senior staff can/will provide for the task.** Top down support is the best kind of support.

7. **Setting up of the communication feedback loop schedule needed to complete the task.** A project like this would take several different meetings with several different factions of the department being involved. The Fire Chief probably would not attend most of these meetings (that is why they delegated it to someone else), but they will probably want consistent feedback on how the project is progressing.

8. **Is the project ever completed or is it ongoing? If completed, what are the project completion considerations?** In this case, the winning SCBA would be purchased and then the project would be completed.

What is described above does not happen often on the company level. Again, most of what a Company Officer does is assign minor jobs or tasks, but let's look at the previous mentioned assignment of cleaning the shed and compare it to the above executive delegation list of to-dos. While not a major project or set of responsibilities, there still could be the need for some communication between the Company Officer and the crew member on what it needs to look like when it is finished so that both parties are not surprised with the end result.

- The shed was an appropriate assignment for the lowest person on the totem pole.
- The shed was not that dirty. The Company Officer told the Firefighter to "spruce it up and sweep the floor."
- All normal thinking humans on the planet would assume this job would take about 30 minutes to complete. The Company Officer does not mention a time frame - they just expect it to get done in a timely manner.
- The fact that they are getting no help is also not mentioned, but it is understood.

- When the Company Officer sees the Firefighter doing something else, they will assume that they are done cleaning the shed. They will also assume the Firefighter did a good job and that they will not need to inspect the shed until the next time they have to go into it for some reason.
- The shed will need to be cleaned once a week as long as it sits behind the station and the job will always fall to the lowest person on the totem pole.

The above is nothing nearly as earth shattering as delegating and managing an SCBA comparison study, but following the same basic routine of explaining the details of a task so that both parties are on the same page does 2 major things:

1. It greatly assists the crew member in performing/completing the task in a satisfactory manner.
2. It greatly assists the Company Officer in holding the member performing/completing the task accountable for the task assigned (it is very hard to hold people accountable to "vague" instructions).

Empowerment

I think on the company level, delegation needs to be replaced with empowerment. The definition of empowerment is - *the authority or power given to someone to do something.* The main thing a Company Officer should delegate (or empower) to their crew members is complete responsibility for their crew to do their own jobs without the Company Officer having to say much to them in order for them to do it successfully. To me, this is what every Firefighter wants – full rights and authority to do their job without having a supervisor hovering over them all shift long about doing their job the right way. Back to Dad's old saying: "Never over manage anyone."

This responsibility is fulfilled when a Company Officer evaluates and trains (or maintains) their crew members' competence level to no less than a Level 2 on the competency scale. Level 2 competent Firefighters are on autopilot and they should require very little supervision from their Company Officer while performing their jobs.

Background: We had more out of town fire service related riders at Station 201 than any other fire station in Phoenix. This was because my Father would send many of the Firefighters from out of town that were visiting him and/or his department to Station 201 if they wanted to have a ride along while in the city. Station 201 was busy and the old man knew we did it the right way.

I would always sit down with the out of town Firefighters while they were riding along with us and I (and sometimes my whole crew) would interrogate them on how their department was set up and how they operated. I felt myself and my crew learned just as much from them as they did from us and hopefully, they all received a good ride while at the station.

My Dad asked to meet me for lunch a couple days after we had 2 riders from a Pennsylvania fire department over a weekend shift (no big deal, my Dad and I had lunch together all the time). About halfway through this particular lunch, Dad told me that he had hung out with the Pennsylvania guys who rode at our station and that they had some" interesting things to say" about their ride along at Station 201. RED ALERT! Invited to lunch and this comes up? Think, think, how did it go that night? I do not remember anything bad happening.

What's he going to say next?! My last thoughts before Dad continued on with his story were "don't say a word to incriminate yourself!"

He started again by saying the riders had a busy night the 8 hours while they were there at the station, which included making runs for a heroin overdose, a serious vehicle accident on a freeway that required L-201 to extricate 2 patients from 2 different vehicles, a working house fire, and a shooting (and let's not forget the excellent station meal and all of the good conversation/fellowship we had!). I cautiously nodded and stated, "sounds like a typical weekend night at Station 201. I guess that's why you send them to us." I'm thinking "okay, here it comes." Dad's next statement started with "Both of the riders were highly impressed by everything they witnessed during their brief ride along." Yea! Pressure's off! They were impressed!

Dad continued with the fact that both riders were volunteer Chiefs in a not so busy department and what they saw in 8 hours at Station 201 does not happen in a 2-year period back home at their fire department. He went on to tell me that the thing that impressed both of them the most was that when on an incident scene, the crew of L-201 did not say 2 words to each other when delivering service and that we were absolutely calm and focused when chaos was going on around us. When we all got off the truck, we were all on autopilot.

All my crew members (minus the Probationary Firefighter) were all at Level 2 or higher on the competency scale and the last thing they needed was me getting in their way while they did their jobs at an exceedingly high level. They knew exactly what to do and they were all empowered to do just that. All authority and responsibility for their riding position was completely delegated (empowered) to them.

Plus, it is always good to get kudos from the Fire Chief!

3. Feedback and Accountability

Firefighter accountability is another process on the company level that has already been highly defined by most fire departments. Every riding position on a fire company should have a department provided list of what each position is accountable for. Coupled with Firefighters using self-discipline, a Company Officer should not waste a lot of their time explaining the things that have already been institutionalized, described, and trained on during our entire careers.

When you look at accountability when managing a fire company, there are 3 basic levels:

1. It all starts out with the Firefighter. Firefighters are accountable for their actions, decisions, performance, and behavior at the workplace. Firefighter accountability is all about being self-disciplined, taking initiative, and ownership of their work.
2. Company Officers are accountable for creating and maintaining an environment where their crew members are completely empowered to successfully do their jobs at a high level while following and properly enforcing all of the rules. This includes the Officer setting a good example, along with performing lots and lots of drilling on the company level (keeping all crew members sharp and focused on what we are here to do).
3. The upper levels of the department should be held accountable for having up to date SOPs and policies for all members to follow. This takes the mysteries out of supervising and it also eliminates a work force being subjected to a set of supervisors that have to make up their own rules when the department does not have any. I have never been a big fan of pet

peeves. Pet peeves happen when there are no set rules and it creates a "this is the way we do it at my station on my shift" organization. Pet peeves are eliminated with good SOPs and these SOPs make it much easier for Company Officers to hold their crew members accountable.

The term "holding someone accountable" has a negative connotation to me. Something has gone wrong and now I must hold you accountable for it. Sometimes, this is what a Company Officer has to do with a crew member and addressing issues will be discussed in the next section of this book. However, what I will focus on in this chapter is creating the communication feedback loops a Company Officer should use for managing accountability positively and proactively.

Because most of the what a fire company does has already been explained (the expectations have been delivered to everyone), a Company Officer needs to communicate to their crew members how **WELL** they want something done. When creating performance communication loops, it is vital that high performing Company Officers use some of the following phrases with their crew members, while also holding them accountable for delivering high level performances:

- "What are the biggest areas our company needs to improve on?"
- "This does not look safe to me. We need to figure out a better/safer way of doing this."
- "That took way too long. How can we do it faster the next time while still being safe?"
- "That did not go well. How should we fix it and/or do it better?"
- "That went okay, but we need to do it better the next time."
- "I think we should try doing it this way next time. What do you think?"
- "What went wrong there?"
- "Why do you think that just happened?"
- "How did that that go?"
- "What do you think it should look like when we are done?"
- "Has anyone ever done this before? What was the outcome?"
- "Any opinions on how we can do this better would be greatly appreciated right now."
- "What do you want to work/drill on today?"

All these phrases project the need to be excellent/better at doing our jobs, they engage the crew's opinions on how to get there (communication feedback loops), and they hold the crew members accountable for the outcome that they actively participate in. Once they are engaged and talking, do not be surprised on how much they can contribute to the cause, especially if the Company Officer is actually acting on what they are **hearing** from their crew members (that's rock star status).

Also, (and this is a big deal) do not ask your crew members for their opinions and not follow through with what they are telling you. Shaking your head yes and smiling while getting input from your crew and then turning around and not acting on it (or worse, doing the opposite) will do nothing but turn your crew off, which will also shut down all communication loops on the subject (future ones, as well). If it is a good idea or comment, act on it. If it is a bad idea or comment, you have the communication loop open and you can tell them why you think it is not so good of an idea and talk your way through it so that your crew member understands where you are coming from and they do not walk away upset (they might also change your mind in the process).

Background: About halfway through my tenure on L-201, our station received a glorious, brand new, American LaFrance, mid-mount, 87-foot bucket ladder with double master streams (double death from above). Our former ladder truck was a tillered stick ladder and our new bucket ladder was going to seriously change the way we were going to do business on the fireground (for the better). For working commercial building fires, it was imperative that we quickly and safely got to the roof of these buildings, but none of us had ever worked on a ladder with a bucket before, so it became DRILL TIME!

My overall stated goal to the crew members with the new truck was that myself and the other 2 Firefighters needed to be on the roof and headed to our work location in no less than 90 seconds after the parking brake was set. I told my crew that I had no idea if this time was achievable with the new truck, but that was going to be the starting point. It took about 30 shifts to get there. During that time, several of the phrases that were previously highlighted were used extensively by me and all the other crew members. This also included:" "it will not work if we don't do this first," "if we add this piece of equipment, it will shave 10 seconds off," etc. It became more about all of us working together trying to figure out the capabilities of the new truck and how we could use it to our best advantage than it was about the time we were trying to achieve to get to a roof.

There was no way that I could have figured out even half of what we needed to do to reach our goal time of 90 seconds without the help of my crew. They all had lots of experience and they were great at their jobs. I would have failed terribly at achieving the goal time without their most excellent feedback and help and they were all just as happy and as pleased as I was when we hit our goal time on a very consistent basis after we all figured it out together.

As the company members deliver good input, performance, and customer service outcomes, do not forget to address all this good stuff. The following phrases will help:

- "Thanks! That was a great suggestion. Everything went so much smoother on this one."
- "That was so much better than the last time we did it."
- "That was a huge improvement from the last time we did it."
- "Your idea worked great."
- "Way to hustle and get it done."
- "That went really well!"
- "Keep up the excellent work."

Company Officer Accountability

To recap a previous chapter: **Take responsibility for your company's actions and always be a shield for your crew.** Poor performance is almost always a direct result of poor management and supervision. A good supervisor does not throw their crew under the bus when something goes wrong. When something does not go well, a good supervisor will own it as their responsibility. Here are some phases a Company Officer can use to take ownership of the crew's and company's performances when things do not go well:

- "My bad. I screwed that up."
- "I apologize. I should have listened better."
- "I should have seen that one coming sooner."
- "This one's all on me. I should have facilitated a few more drills on that."
- "What do I need to do to help make this go better the next time it happens?"
- "Chief, I take full responsibility for what happened. It's all on me. Please leave my crew out of this."
- "Chief, I will take care of it and you can trust me to address it."

While owning it with these phrases, you are still putting a lot of the responsibility back onto your crew members, as well as keeping positive communication loops open with your crew when things are not going so well. Also, when the Company Officer openly admits their mistakes, previous failures, and shortcomings, it makes it easier for their crew members to do same thing when something goes bad. It all proves that there is absolutely NO WAY to become excellent without experiencing several failures, screw ups, and setbacks along the way. Do not get upset when they happen - just manage through them.

4. Communicating New SOPs and Policies to Subordinates

It is vital that all Company Officers communicate new SOPs, policies, or any other departmental change to their subordinates in a manner that:

- Supports them
- States that we will all follow them
- The Company Officer will enforce them

Anything less than this is unacceptable from a front-line supervisor because it gives your crew members permission to follow any negative example that is presented.

Your department's leadership and upper management will always write, change, adopt, and implement new SOPs, policies, systems, equipment, etc., because it is their job to continually improve service delivery capability and Firefighter safety. These actions will continually cause changes in the way we operate. Company Officer expectation #4 states: "Someone that the organization put into a position to understand, follow, and enforce all of the department's SOPs, policies, rules, and regulations". The chain of command implements orders from the top down and most of them stop at the Company Officer level. Subordinates do not hear the new orders being introduced from the Brass - they hear it from their Company Officer. When communicating these "changes" it MUST be done in positive manner.

If you have any complaints or serious objections about a new policy, system, or piece of equipment, etc., take it to the Brass - NOT to your crew members. Your crew members should never hear a negative word about it.

5. Employee Development

The 2 major areas of responsibility a Company Officer has in developing their crew members are:

1. Attaining and maintaining Level 2 competency at their current riding position/rank
2. Attaining and maintaining Level 3 competency and beyond

1. Ensure All Members are at Level 2 on the Competency Scale

Before spending any employee development time on a crew member, a Company Officer needs to ensure that all members of their crew can perform their current jobs at no less than a Level 2 on the competency scale. Training or developing someone on how to do the job of the rank above theirs when they have not yet mastered all the tasks of their current position is performing a dis-service to the member and the community they serve. For their safety, your crew members need to be trained to no less than a Level 2 on the competency scale (the auto-pilot mode) before moving forward with any other training.

As presented throughout this book, Level 2 competency is achieved by constant drilling and repetition of the high risk tasks that we perform. When joining a new crew as an Officer or when a new member joins the apparatus, a Company Officer must use the drilling process to first determine what competency level their crew members currently maintain. This could vary from a Level 1 to a Level 3 on the scale. Once the crew's competency levels are determined, the Company Officer must then tailor their company's drill sessions in a way that gets all members of the crew to increase or maintain their competencies to a minimum of Level 2.

2. Level 3 Competency and Beyond

Once all crew members are at least at Level 2 in competency, it is now the Company Officer's responsibility to get them to a Level 3 in competency, as well as help all crew members promote into higher ranking positions. Level 3 competence is also achieved by the constant drilling and repetition of the high risk tasks that we perform.

I firmly believe that one of the things a good Company Officer is judged on is how well they mentor their crew members into new positions/ranks. A good Company Officer who works over 10 years in the position should have 2 or 3 members trained and/or promoted up to the Engineer rank as well as having 1 or 2 members trained and/or promoted up to the Company Officer rank.

Task Books

Many fire departments have produced a set of task books that provide the critical behaviors, activities, competencies, and the associated performance requirements necessary to become certified and/or promote into all of the different ranks and other disciplines offered in the department. Task books provide both the members and the supervisors on the department the how to's on preparing for higher ranking positions and they should become an essential part of the process a Company Officer uses to assist their subordinates in promoting up the chain.

Crew Goals and Expectations

Helping a member of the company achieve their career goals and to develop them beyond their current position/rank requires the skill of **LISTENING.**

When it comes to a Company Officer addressing department goals and expectations, the focus for the Officer should be on understanding what their crew member's expectations and goals are, rather than just repeating what has already been pounded into everyone in terms of what the overall expectations and values of the fire department are. Again, this requires a Company Officer to **listen** to their crew members! Ask them all:

- What are their expectations working on your company?
- What are their thoughts and ideas on making something run or operate better on the company?
- What are their career goals?
- What, as a Company Officer, can you do to help them to achieve their goals?

Crew Responses

All the responses to these questions will help a Company Officer know the type of personal and organizational support they need to provide to each member of their crew. From crew to crew and from member to member, all responses will be different. Some will want to be shooting up the company ladder, some will be very happy at their current rank and have no plans of moving up the ladder, and some are just worried about getting up to a Level 2 on the competency scale.

Here are some examples of the responses you may **HEAR** and some different types of support you can provide to each member:

Example 1 - Your driver states that they love their current job, they have absolutely no plans to ever promote past their current rank, and they are going to retire as an Engineer. As long as this person is at least a Level 2 on the competency scale (while always working towards and/or maintaining a Level 3 competency), they will not require any grooming time for other ranks, but there still may be some areas on the department that the Company Officer can suggest they participate in so that they can contribute some of their knowledge and skill while making them even better at their own position.

Example 2 - One of your Firefighters wants to become a Company Officer and they plan on taking the promotional exam coming up in the next 18 months. Again, if they are not at a Level 3 competence level, they need to worry about a lot more other stuff before promoting (Company Officers should be at Level 3 competence for most activities performed on the company level). If they are at Level 3 on the competence scale, the Officer should devote a set amount of time of each shift to helping their Firefighter navigate and succeed through all the phases of the testing process. If a task book is available for the position, the Company Officer and the member wanting to promote will need to refer to the material to insure that all requirements are fulfilled in order to participate in the promotion process.

Here are some suggestions to pass along to the promotional exam takers:

- All promotional tests start with a written exam. The written exam separates the winners from the losers. This has been proven over and over. The top 10 written scores make up at least 85% of the people who end up in the top 10 of the final list. Based on this, know what the written test contains and HIGHLY ENCOURAGE your crew member to memorize this material. Help them by quizzing them on the material every shift before the exam.

- Heavy assistance will also be required to help the member get through the oral interview process. Help in this area should start well before the written exam is taken. The amount of attention/time given to this area should be based on how good of a communicator your crew member is and how much study time they need for the written exam material.

Example 3 – You have a 4-year Firefighter on your crew who is at Level 3 competence and they want to promote to the Engineer's position. If a task book is available for the position, the Company Officer and the member wanting to promote will need to refer to the material to insure that all requirements are fulfilled in order to participate in the promotion process. Unless the Company Officer is highly proficient at the Engineer's position, they will probably need to elicit the help of their current Engineer in the process. Much of their help will be given on the drill grounds in the actual training and mentoring of driving and pumping of the apparatus.

Example 4 - Your Firefighter says they are happy being a Firefighter for the next 5 or so years, but they do not like the way the company is setting up the vehicle extrication equipment on incident scenes and they want to drill on a new deployment method for those calls. For this person, a Company Officer's main goal would be to ensure that their competence Level was at Level 3 (you have 5 years to get it there), while also facilitating a bunch of future drills with the hydraulic tools!

Example 5 – There will always be a person on your crew or working at your fire station who has a great potential and a high competency level, but they are really happy being a Firefighter or Engineer with no other high or lofty goals of promoting. It is the Company Officer's job to recognize these people and encourage them to get passed living the good life and start nudging them to use their informal authority and talents to move up the company ladder to contribute more to the department. But as Dad said, "Never over manage someone."

Move-Ups

All crew members who are at a Level 2 on the competency scale should be trained and certified for the next higher rank. The more your crew knows about doing the higher-ranking jobs above them, the more they will know where they fit into the grand scheme of things, making them even better and more competent at their current rank. With competency and enough time in rank:

- Firefighters should be trained and certified as Engineers
- Senior Firefighters and Engineers should be trained and certified as Company Officers

As originally covered in a previous chapter, move-ups become a powerful tool for Company Officers (and the department) in helping to manage vacancies on the company. Having all of your permanently assigned members competently trained and qualified to fill in for the next rank gives Company Officers and the rest of the department more options for the personnel moves necessary to continually deliver quality service.

All of the activities (hard work and drilling) that go into mentoring your crew members into being able to fill higher ranking positions provide Company Officers with the best opportunities to communicate expectations, to delegate real authority, and to give your crew members the employee development needed not only to help them, but the entire department, as well.

6. Communications Centered Around Off the Job Activities

Throughout this book, there have been several examples on how and when to engage your crew members regarding their personal lives off the job. As presented in a previous chapter, preparing and eating meals together are the "social" times in a fire station when a great portion of the conversations should be directed and centered around all the off the job people and activities associated with your crew members. Tim Dietz also presented the importance of engaging your crew members in doing something fun with their family and friends after having a rough shift. The more you know about your crew members, the easier it is to facilitate this.

Good ways to communicate this message to your crew members include:

- Know your crew members' birthdays and always wish them a happy birthday, even if belated.
- Know the names and relationships of your crew members' significant others. This includes their kids and the relatives that are their biggest loves and pains. Always try to use their first names when asking how things are going with them (record them in your cell phone as memory joggers).
- Know what their favorite activities are off the job. You may also enjoy some of these same activities and this could create opportunities of doing these things off the job together (hunting, fishing, bicycling, hiking, etc.).
- Always try to be aware of the social situation of your crew members' significant others, such as the school and work schedules of their spouse and kids, graduations, weddings, what their parents are all about, where they came from growing up, what they do during the holidays with their family and friends, etc.
- Always try to be aware of any of the bad things going on off-duty with your crew members, such as family health issues, bad relationship, kids in trouble, significant life changes, etc.

The more you know about your crew members' lives and their support systems away from the fire station, the easier it is for a Company Officer to connect with them. Listening to your crew members about what they do outside of the workplace projects that you actually care about them and what is going on in their lives. Always remembering that people love good **listeners** because they care.

Chapter 21

Managing Probationary/Inexperienced Firefighters

"Always treat your employees exactly as you want them to treat your best customers." - Stephen R. Covey

One of the worst things that I occasionally see in the fire service is the poor way that the younger people are treated on some fire departments. And honestly, when I see and/or hear of it, it really disappointments me in our service. People who are at Level 0 or Level 1 on the competence scale need to be helped a lot more than they need to be hazed. One of the reasons that this hazing happens is because the current hazers were probably also hazed when they were young going through the same process, so they believe it is okay to pass it forward, like a tradition. Well, it is NOT okay!

Another thing that I am sick of hearing is how the youth of our service are so very different than "my generation" of Firefighters. What a joke! The oldest artifacts of mankind that have been discovered date back to about 45,000 years ago. It has been documented that in this time period (the last 45,000 years) mankind's brain has not changed at all. That's right - zero percent. The 19-year-old your fire department just hired has the same exact brain DNA that the Fire Chief has. The ONLY difference between the Fire Chief's brain and the recruit's brain is that the Fire Chief has spent about 30 years longer than the recruit has filling their brain with knowledge and experience. All of this should lead to the logical conclusion that it should be the entire department's responsibility to fill the brains of their young people with as much knowledge and experience as they can possibly adsorb in the shortest time frames possible.

The experiences we fill our young Firefighters' brains with should be positive, helpful experiences that go a long way in getting these people up to speed and on the autopilot level (lots of drilling). The experiences of hazing, harassment, and purposeful non-helping SHOULD NEVER fill the brains of the youth. Anyone on a fire department who thinks this is okay, should not be on the fire department. I am dead serious - if you cannot help the youth (the department's FUTURE) become successful in a positive manner, then you should not be here.

Probationary/Inexperienced Firefighters

When a department first hires a Firefighter, they are considered to be a Recruit in their training academy. When graduating from the academy, they become a Probationary Firefighter until they have a full year on the job. Most Probationary Firefighters who graduate from an academy are at best trained to a Level 1 on the competency scale. This is combined with a new Probationary Firefighter having no real-life application of their new skill sets.

Any Company Officer who supervises a Probationary Firefighter who thinks that their 3 to 4 months in a training academy has taught them everything they need to know about the job is living in a dream world. In my opinion, Company Officers who think this way are just plain LAZY and they do not want to put in all the work it takes to help make Probationary Firefighters competent. It is also not the job of the Training Academy to train every Firefighter to a high level of competence. It is the COMPANY OFFICER'S JOB! Company Officers have an organizational and moral obligation of providing the drilling necessary for the youth to become competent (at a high level). Becoming excellent takes a LOT of hard work.

Background: As presented in previous backgrounds, L201 had Probationary Firefighters rotate on and off the truck every 3 months. We had Probationary Firefighter Neglected rotate onto L-201 at about the 5-year mark in my almost 10-year L-201 Company Officer career. As you have probably guessed, Firefighter Neglected had some performance problems. L-201 was his third and last rotation in his first year on probation and his MCS skill sets and physical conditioning had drastically eroded since graduating from the academy. All members of the crew realized this after the first shift of drilling with him. After the 3rd shift of drilling and several verbal counseling sessions, I had to sit down with Firefighter Neglected and write out an actual API with him. How to do this is all covered later in this book.

To make a long story short, Firefighter Neglected was now in the system and the training academy staff was well aware of what was going on with him. In the end, after about 20 shifts of intensive drilling, Firefighter Neglected not only passed all of his 11-month MCS evaluations, but he also had some of the best finishing times out of his fellow classmates.

This ended up being very good for both of us. Firefighter Neglected made it out of probation and he had a very productive career from then on. It became a good thing for L-201 in a different way. L-201 impressed the training academy staff by following the right procedures and providing the time commitment needed in supervising Firefighter Neglected back up to meeting all MCS benchmarks. After these events, the training academy started sending L-201 Probationary Firefighters who were also in the system. I must add, it was not always to "fix" them - it was to use the proper procedures and documentation I had just demonstrated to help in "terminating" these problem children if it ended up becoming necessary in the long run (most of them already had a long paper trail). After first hearing this, we were all upset because that is a lot of work dumped on L-201. Nonetheless, in the long run, all the "problem children" actually lightened our load.

L-201 ended up supervising about 8 problem children over the next 4 to 5 years and after just a few weeks of filling these people in and with lots of drilling, every single problem child Probationary Firefighter assigned to L-201 ended up being a very high preforming, Level-2 competent Firefighter. EVERY SINGLE ONE OF THEM!

Most of them were in their 3rd rotation and they all described the drilling they performed on their previous rotations - ZERO! Not 1 of their previous Company Officers drilled or spent any other development time with them (same thing with Firefighter Neglected). Something always bad happened with one of these inexperienced problem children while on an actual incident scene and the reaction of the Company Officer was to put them into the system INSTEAD OF HELPING THEM! As stated earlier, if you cannot help the youth (the department's FUTURE) become successful in a positive manner, you should not be here in the first place.

The major considerations in managing probationary or inexperienced firefighters include:

1. Initial contact
2. Overview of responsibilities
3. Creating defined feedback loops
4. Drilling

5. Other crew member's responsibilities
6. Providing constant feedback on performance

1. Initial Contact

A good beginning provides the best chance for a good ending. Based on this, it is very important to start out in a positive manner with all new Probationary Firefighters you will be supervising. This all starts with the initial contact made with the new member. The initial contact can be done in a couple of different ways:

- The Probationary Firefighter calls their new Company Officer a shift or 2 in advance and they introduce themselves.
- The Company Officer calls the new Probationary Firefighter a shift or 2 in advance and they introduce themselves.
- The Probationary Firefighter simply shows up at the station on their first day. This is what usually happens on a Probationary Firefighter's first fire station rotation because they just found out the night before (graduation night) where their new work assignment is.

If phone contact is made with a Probationary Firefighter prior to them showing up at the station for their first shift, the following should be discussed with them:

- Welcome them to the crew and tell them, "We're all looking forward to working with you."
- The fire station location and directions to get there
- The time they should show-up (should be before everyone else on the crew)
- Their riding position and who they are relieving in the morning (give them the name of the person)
- The names and ranks of their fellow crew members
- Short run-down on the morning routine
- Anything significant that is planned during their first shift (e.g., we have battalion training at 10 AM)
- Chow costs and kitty fees – cash only

When making in-person contact with the new Probationary Firefighter for the first time (on their first shift), the Company Officer and the rest of the crew should:

- Make introductions, shake hands, and welcome them aboard
- Make sure they are aware of their riding position and relieving their counterpart
- Cover the areas of the truck and the equipment they are responsible for checking/maintaining
- Very brief rundown on what their responsibilities are if an EMS or fire call comes in the next 15 minutes
- Brief rundown on the station areas they are responsible for cleaning/maintaining
- As covered previously, provide them with enough information to feel comfortable (without being overwhelmed) that gets them through lunch time

2. Overview of Responsibilities

As previously presented, I would have a meeting in my office with new Probationary Firefighters on their first shift after lunch - once everything had calmed down and while most other station members were starting to take their afternoon naps. In this first meeting, I would cover the following items with the new member:

- A list (written) of the truck and the equipment they are responsible for checking/maintaining - after handing the Firefighter the list, we would go over each item in detail.
- A list (written on the same piece of paper) of the station areas they are responsible for checking/maintaining - we would go over each item in detail. Probationary Firefighters are not high paid janitors that do all the cleaning while everyone else watches TV. Station 201 Probationary Firefighters were responsible for cleaning and maintaining the bathrooms and the bays while all other members at Station 201 had their assigned areas of the station that they were also responsible for cleaning.
- Major job responsibilities on emergency scenes – this is where I would really relay the need to follow all the safety rules.
- A list of the 30-shift drill schedule - the first 10 drills were all laid out. Most of the next 20 drills performed would be based on the Firefighter's competency level and what they needed to work on.
- Details on all the people and personalities at the station and the best ways to interact with all of them
- My 51/49% speech presented previously
- Create and define feedback loops (discussed next)

3. Creating Defined Feedback Loops

The very last thing I would cover with a new member in our first meeting was informing them of the constant feedback they were going to hear from everyone at the station, but especially from me. They needed to know they were going to get feedback often during drills, after calls, and while preforming duties around the station. This feedback would be for both the positive and the not so positive and they should not be surprised to receive it. I wanted to relay that a lot of people get defensive when hearing about their performance and instead of getting defensive, they needed to have an open mind and really listen to this feedback because it would be given for the purpose of improving their overall performance. This was to help them - not to mess with them. I would also tell them to really pay attention to the interactions of the other crew members on the truck because we were all communicating things with each other all the time and my crew members had no problem telling me what I needed to improve on, as well. We all need to listen with an open mind and always be willing to make adjustments based on honest performance feedback.

4. Drilling

A Company Officer should NEVER say to a Probationary Firefighter, "Just let me know when you want to go drilling on something." LAZY! A new Firefighter will never ask their Officer to go drilling. Company Officers need to go drilling with new Probationary Firefighters shortly after they arrive to the station (first couple of shifts). The Officer should run the firefighter through the numbers (taking hydrants, stretching hose, throwing ladders, etc.) to evaluate both their fitness and competency levels. The first few drills should identify what the Probationary Member is good at, as well as what they need to work on. From this point forward, the Company Officer gets to decide what drills need to be performed in the future - not the new Firefighter.

Most of the material about drilling with Probationary Firefighters was covered previously, in which I described that L-201's drill schedule was performed around getting Probationary Firefighters up to speed and to Level 2 in competence. L-201's drill schedule was written out, it was in the company activity calendar, and a great percentage of the drills were based on getting the Firefighter through MCS (not a lot of Ladder stuff) and successfully off probation.

5. Other Crew Member's Responsibilities

A Company Officer will have the overall responsibility for a Probationary Firefighter, but a lot of the day-to-day oversite of a Probationary Firefighter can be assigned to your other crew members. A crew member's responsibilities with Probationary Firefighters will depend a lot on the staffing levels of your fire department. Here are some different scenarios based around this:

3-person company – this configuration makes the Company Officer the Probationary Firefighter's primary everything. This includes mentor, safety boss, and educator. The only person left is the Engineer. Their responsibility with Probationary Firefighters should be on the basics of how a pump works and some of the other workings of the mechanics of the truck. This should not be an area to focus on if the Probationary Firefighter is struggling in other areas because this is an advanced function.

4-person company – this configuration takes a lot off the Company Officer's plate when supervising Probationary Firefighters. Senior Firefighter's (if at a Level 2 competence) need to take the new member "under their wing" and they become the primary mentor and safety boss for the Probationary Firefighter. Instead of the Company Officer having to provide all the intricate details of their riding position, the Senior Firefighter (who is doing the same exact job) now does it. This frees the Company Officer up on an incident scene to take a step back and become the overall manager of the scene, instead of having to focus their attention on the new member.

5-person company – this configuration does not happen very often (L-201) but when it does, it takes even more of a load off the Company Officer, especially if there are 2 Senior Firefighters on the truck. Again, the more responsibility assigned to other members of the crew for the oversite of a Probationary Firefighter while working on emergency scenes will greatly free up the Company Officer to focus more on the overall management and safety of the entire incident site.

Background: After working on L-201 for about 2 years, I had our 2 Engineers take more of a formal role with educating our Probationary Firefighters. Over their 30-shift rotation, we had about 5 or 6 drills where Mr. Joker and Mr. Competent were totally in charge of the delivery of the subject matter. Because we were working on a Ladder company and we had 2 trucks of equipment to maintain, there were a lot of things for them to cover with the new member. This included breaking down and maintaining all the power tools on the truck, hydraulic rescue tool set-up, setting up the aerial ladder (the bucket), forcible entry techniques, etc.

My Engineers operated and knew this equipment better than I did and it made more sense for them to deliver the drill/information than myself.

When first discussing this with both of them, they were hesitant because they both hated having any upper-level responsibilities (that is why they were both career Engineers). However, after the first couple drills they were in charge of, they both told me, "Go inside and watch TV. We got this." Wow - I went inside and let them do their thing. After the 3rd or 4th Probationary Firefighter they helped, they started to come up with new drill sets and again, they told me to go inside and watch TV every time it was their turn to do something with the new member. I think they even looked forward to it!

6. Providing Constant Feedback On Performance

If you tell someone you are going to give them constant feedback, you had better do just that. There were certain benchmarks that happened, with which I would take the opportunity to provide feedback (covered in a previous chapter) to a Probationary Firefighter for both the positives and negatives. These opportunities included:

- Any safety related issue
- Anytime it was necessary for me to say "hey, stop, and do it this way instead"
- After any significant incident
- After all major drilling evolutions
- At the end of all drill sessions
- If no significant incidents or drills during the shift, I would try to give them feedback on their performance for the day after eating dinner
- Every Sunday that we worked, we had a formal feedback meeting and we covered the items in their monthly grading

Another part of the process of managing recruits is all the paperwork that comes with people who are on probation. This can include:

- Daily, weekly, or monthly gradings/reports
- Validating completion of check-off requirements
- Major incident performance reviews
- APIs (when necessary – covered later)

A great majority of the feedback that was given to probationary Firefighters was positive, but all feedback needs to be performance driven and nice! Even if it was critical, I always wanted to know "how I was doing" and I think if "this is how you are doing" feedback is given in a way that is meant to improve performance and not to berate the individual, it is received in a much more constructive, positive way.

Chapter 22

Annual Gradings

When I promoted to Company Officer, there was no material or any questions in my oral interviews about how to conduct an effective and productive annual employee evaluation/grading. After getting promoted, the personnel department would send me my crew members' annual performance evaluations about 30 to 45 days before they were due. If there was a merit or salary increase tied to the grading, they would put a big red sticker on it that said, "Your immediate attention is required." The personnel department did not put a 2-sided piece of paper in the package addressed to the supervisor on how to conduct a successful annual employee evaluation. Nothing - just fill it out, sign it, have the member sign it, and send it back before the date on the envelope.

To me, the process gives some Company Officers the impression they only need to give corrective (negative) feedback to a subordinate once a year in their annual performance review. This is absolutely counterproductive and it is why I believe in the shift-by-shift evaluation and grading system, in which a Company Officer is constantly providing feedback to their crew members on any performance and/or behavioral issues. This includes both positive feedback (most of all) and the corrective feedback that is necessary to address any negative performance and/or behavior issues right when they happen (covered previously).

There are a lot of other highly qualified people who also agree that the annual grading system is an ineffective way to manage people on a day-to-day basis. A 2018 People IQ survey found that 87% of managers and employees both believe that annual reviews were ineffective and not useful (while also producing high amounts of stress for both the employee and the supervisor). Public Safety Risk Manager and HR attorney, Gordon Graham, also agrees that the ineffective use of the annual grading system by supervisors sometimes creates a condition for the whole process to backfire on both the Company Officer and their department.

Gordon provides the example in which the Company Officer cares much more about how the other person they are evaluating feels about them than objectively reviewing their actual performance over the past year. This all culminates in year after year of giving high marks when they are not deserved, while also not addressing any pertinent issues with the employee during these time frames. Then all of a sudden, the employee's past issues (that were not addressed in any other previous annual gradings) have escalated to the point that the Company Officer now has to "officially" address these issues and they put the member on notice and into the "system." The part of the system defending the member who is now in trouble takes the past 5 years of the glorious evaluations/gradings given to them by their Company Officer (to avoid any conflict) and they shove them up the Officer's you know what.

The "Formal" Evaluation/Grading System

Many fire departments operate under a formalized evaluation system in which annual performance ratings are required throughout the entire organization/municipality. Describing many of the undesirable aspects of using an annual grading system to address and improve daily performance will hopefully cover most of the methods on properly conducting them if they are required by your fire department. This includes:

1. The same evaluation form is used for every employee and position throughout the entire city/organization
2. They do not happen often enough
3. Evaluators are not trained on how to properly perform formal evaluations
4. The grading scale
5. They are one sided
6. Employees are often surprised by the evaluation/grading
7. No constructive feedback is provided on how to improve/address negative performance

1. The Same Evaluation Form is Used for Every Employee and Position Throughout the Entire City/Organization

Many municipal fire departments use the same basic evaluation form that is used throughout their entire municipality for every employee (this includes all fire department, police department, water department, waste management employees, etc.). Many fire departments that are allowed to customize their annual employee evaluations will also use the same evaluation rating system and scale for all positions on the department, instead of customizing the evaluations to each individual riding position.

This creates a very vague process in which most Company Officers will have to fit square pegs into round holes when trying to effectively document their members' performance in a manner that it is related to their actual job description.

2. They Don't Happen Often Enough

Because they only happen once a year, even the best annual employee evaluations are not enough to continue to motivate, sustain, and engage the member for the next 12 months after their formal, annual sit-down. Because a lot can happen in a year and as previously presented in this book, frequent, timely, and ongoing feedback and recognition of both the positive and the negative performances and behaviors is much more important and valuable to the member and the rest of team than only providing feedback once a year in a formal evaluation.

Feedback that is given in the moment has the greatest impact for the member because it translates their latest experience into learning and/or understanding right after the event has just occurred and it is fresh in everyone's minds. Giving feedback right after the event happens translates into more deeply understanding the value there is in the feedback and learning more fully. In addition, it enables the member to not internalize the feedback as being critical, but rather view it more so as being helpful.

Bringing performance issues up 6 months after they have happened when nothing was said at the time will automatically make the member defensive, as well as make them wonder why the issue was not addressed at the time it happened (which greatly undermines the Company Officer's credibility). When you see something, say something. RIGHT THEN! Addressing an event that happened 6 months ago for the first time in a performance evaluation is unacceptable (for performances or behaviors that were either positive or negative).

3. Evaluators are not Trained on How to Properly Perform Formal Evaluations

Evaluate and grade your crew members on their actual, documented behaviors and performances - not on their feelings toward you or your need to be popular or liked by the other person. When conducting annual evaluations, here are some general guidelines:

- Let the whole crew know how they will be formally evaluated well before any formal evaluation takes place.
- At least 30 days before the formal evaluation takes place, notify the member that their evaluation is coming up. In this conversation you should lay the groundwork for the items you will need from the member to facilitate completing the evaluation/grading (goals met, new certifications attained, future goals, etc.).
- I recommend that you give a copy of the completed evaluation (a copy, not the real thing) to the member the shift before you sit down with them to conduct the formal evaluation. This will give them the time needed to process the information (and their emotions) and to properly formulate any questions or responses they may have at the final evaluation. This is especially important if it will be a negative evaluation.
- Try to make the evaluation a 2-way conversation. Have a list of questions to ask your crew member. This includes:
  o What are their career goals?
  o Discussing what work or other commitments are needed to achieve their career goals
  o Is there anything they want to be more involved in?
  o Classes and certifications coming up in the future they might be interested in
  o The good, the bad, the highs, and the lows of working on the company the past year
  o What are some of the things they think they should improve or work harder on?
  o What are some of the things that they think the company should improve or work harder on (like items the Company Officer should work on)?
- Do not sugar coat things, especially if these are issues you have addressed with the member in the past.
- Do not offer general feedback, especially if it is for anything negative. You must give very specific information about the positive and the negative behaviors that you are addressing (specific behaviors and/or performances, times, places, other people involved, etc.).
- All negative feedback must be accompanied by an objective action plan for improvement.
- Company Officers should not deliver "absolutes" in any evaluation. For example: "If this does not change, this will absolutely happen to you." Company Officers are the "sheriffs" who enforce SOPs. They are not the "judges" who get to decide the punishment for violating them.

4. The Grading Scale

Another item that completely puts the Company Officer in a very bad position when conducting a formal evaluation/grading of a crew member are the "special" items on the grading scale. It all becomes special when the grading scale has more than 3 choices for the Officer to put a checkmark next to. The only 3 choices that should be on an evaluation are:

- Performance meets standards
- Performance needs improvement
- Performance is unsatisfactory

Anything past these 3 choices are meaningless and they do nothing but create conflict and stress on both the member and the Company Officer.

Background: The Phoenix Fire Department had 2 different grading scales - one for Probationary Firefighters and one for the masses that were off probation. The Probationary Firefighter grading scale made the most sense and was paired with a formal evaluation/grading conducted monthly. The Probationary Firefighter grading scale and point system included the following 3 options:

3. Performance meets standards
2. Performance needs improvement
1. Performance is unsatisfactory

There were about 8 different categories a Probationary Firefighter was graded on, which made a total 24 points possible. Any score below a 20 would raise eyebrows. Any category with a score of a 1 would automatically put the Firefighter into the system. Very few Probationary Firefighters legitimately achieve a perfect score of 24 points on any of their first year gradings.

After getting off probation, the Firefighter would move on to getting formally evaluated only once a year and a new grading scale was used for the rest of their career:

5. Performance exceeds standards
4. Performance above standards
3. Performance meets standards
2. Performance needs improvement
1. Performance is unsatisfactory

I do not get it! Now everyone wants all 5's on their grading! When all they are really doing is just meeting the standard. Why do they all have to feel more special about themselves about doing the same exact thing that everyone else does? You are either meeting standards or you are not.

Example: The time to meet the standard of stretching a 1 ¾ inch fire hose 200 feet and start flowing water is 1 minute and 30 seconds from the time you dismount the apparatus. Let's say that 25 Firefighters perform this evolution and they all successfully complete the evolution at least 10 seconds under the time allowed. The gap between the fastest time and the slowest time is less than 10 seconds between all 25 members.

All 25 are now sitting in front of you in their annual evaluation and they all want 5's on their grading when they all did it pretty much the exact same way. Give them all 3's because they all meet the standard and explain all of this to your crew members well before you evaluate them,.

5. Annual Evaluations are Often One-Sided (Towards the Supervisor)

Company Officers need to focus annual evaluations on a member's actual performance and behaviors, rather than on their own personality and judgments. This can be very hard to do sometimes because most annual evaluations are based on a generic outdated system that produces a set of one-sided evaluation points that allow a Company Officer to become more of a judge than a legitimate evaluator. These circumstances include:

- Very broad evaluation benchmarks with little to no specific guidelines on the criteria for meeting those benchmarks leads to a Company Officer's personal interpretation "of what the benchmarks are"
- Vague feedback can be documented into the evaluation with NO specific details required for a poor or unsatisfactory rating
- Critical supervisors will only give critical feedback with little to no positive feedback
- Insecure supervisors (that want you to like them or hate conflict) will only give positive feedback with little to no critical and/or constructive feedback
- The person who is being evaluated has very little input or participation in the preparation of their formal review and/or they are not informed of the criteria being used to base their evaluation on prior to it occurring

6. Employees are Often "Surprised" by the Annual Review

An employee being surprised in an annual review is **ABSOLUTELY UNACCEPTABLE!**

Surprise performance reviews in an annual evaluation that are full of concerns and issues previously unknown to the crew member simply means that appropriate and timely feedback DID NOT take place on a shift-to-shift basis with the member being evaluated. This scenario creates a crew member who is not being coached to higher levels of performance and is not being given the opportunity to correct their performance issues. Now they are in their annual evaluation getting shocked by their boss.

As stated previously, providing feedback in the actual moment has the best, most positive impact on the member. Giving feedback or addressing an issue for the first time that happened 6 months ago in an annual performance evaluation is absolutely unacceptable. These actions drastically reduce the credibility of the Company Officer and the Company Officer is creating an indefensible position, in which the member (and/or their representative) can now call them out.

7. No Constructive Feedback is Provided on How to Improve/Address Negative Performance

The structure that is used in most annual evaluation systems does not provide a formal method of producing and applying improvement plans that are connected to performance items that are rated below standards. This, coupled with very little feedback provided by the evaluator on how to constructively improve a member's performance, can leave an employee feeling like they are on an island when it comes to figuring out how to improve their performance.

All below standard performance evaluations must come with a detailed API. APIs will be covered in detail in the next section of this book.

The GOOD Things About Annual Gradings

There are some really good things about annual gradings - none of them really touch on daily job performance matters. They include:

- Annual non-discrimination policy overview, checkoff, and signing
- Annual driver license, information, and background check
- The necessary personnel/payroll paperwork needed for any merit increases associated with an annual grading

Non-Discrimination Policy Overview

Going over and having the member sign the department's non-discrimination policy is one of the most important elements of performing an annual grading because it protects the Company Officer. When going over the non-discrimination policy with the member during their grading, the Company Officer will cover both the department's policy on the matter, as well ask the member a series of questions that verifies if the member has been discriminated or harassed against or if they have personally witnessed these behaviors from another co-worker.

If a member states that indeed yes, they have been discriminated or harassed against or they have personally witnessed these behaviors from another co-worker, then the Company Officer will need to follow the instructions laid out in the managing issues section of this book.

A member can also state that no, they have not been discriminated or harassed against and they have not personally witnessed these behaviors from another co-worker and then they sign the policy stating it has been thoroughly explained and covered. If this happens year after year, it would be very difficult for that member to go back any further than their last annual grading and claim that they worked in hostile work environment. This is why the annual review of the policy is so important - it protects both the department and the Company Officer while giving members the opportunity to inform the organization about these issues if they did exist.

Annual Driver License, Information and Background Check

These activities should be performed by your Battalion Chief or the personnel department - NOT the Company Officer. All Risk Managers suggest that all organizations use the annual grading to check up on the following for all members:

- Check that the member's driver's license is up to date and in compliance.
- Once a year during a members annual grading, the personnel department should do a brief observation of the member's personal social media accounts to insure they

are in compliance with department and/or city policies (this will be covered later in this book).

- Approximately every 5-years, the department should perform a thorough background check on all members. People change dramatically over a 20 to 30-year career. Performing just one background check on a Firefighter when they are first hired is not enough in today's modern society to manage the risks of long-term employment.

Again, all of these activities should be performed by your Battalion Chief or the personnel department - NOT by the Company Officer.

Merit Increases Associated with an Annual Grading

The very best part of an annual grading is getting any merit increases associated with them. Well over half of annual gradings have some type of merit increase or pay raise associated with them. That is why it is so important that a Company Officer completes them as soon as possible. Most merit increases or pay raises cannot be processed until the annual grading has been properly completed and turned in.

When anything is connected to a Firefighter's bank account, get it done the right way as quickly as possible. Everyone involved in the process will greatly appreciate it.

Chapter 23

Managing a Fire Company in a Multi-Company Station and the Other Shifts

I will start this chapter with a very simple statement: **as a Company Officer, the only people you are in charge of are the members of YOUR company - no one else.** Understanding this will make all Company Officers' lives much easier.

The Other Shifts

This book starts this chapter out with the other shifts because every fire company will have to interact and deal with at least their counterparts from:

- The off-going shift (the shift that you relieve)
- The on-coming shift (the shift that relieves you)

The Off-Going Shift (the Shift that You Relieve)

I will start with the off-going shift because that is how the shift will start out, as well. As covered previously in this book in the shift change chapter, the standard shift change counterpart briefings should take place between all riding positions. To recap, this standard briefing should include:

- Start out with "how was your shift?"
- Significant incident responses and equipment used during the previous shift
- Any recently used equipment that still needs to be serviced or re-stocked
- Any out of service equipment
- Anything that has been added to your daily schedule (e.g., the light bar on the truck broke last night and you have a 10 AM appointment at the shop to get it fixed)
- Any building or grounds issues that need to be addressed
- Any information on something out of balance that effects anyone's safety
- Any current vacancies with the off-going shift
- Anything else I need to know
- Inform your counterpart that "you got it"

This all sounds pretty standard. The torch is passed and everything is okay. However, many times, it is not. Most of the time, the difficulties that occur between the shifts occur with the shift you are relieving. Some of the comments I would hear in the morning from my crew members about the off-going shift we relieved included:

- The trucks are filthy.
- The station is filthy.
- There is no gas in the trucks.
- They did not restock anything.
- All the saws need to be broken down, cleaned, and re-fueled.

- The kitchen is full of their dirty dishes.
- We are missing equipment.
- This is broken and no one said anything about it.

The list goes on and on, but at the end of the day, B-Shift is stuck with what they inherited when they walked through the doors in the morning and all of the complaining about A-Shift is not going to magically fill the trucks full of gas, make the trucks clean, or make the saws look brand new again. None of it will. The only way this is going to happen is if B-Shift fixes it all in the morning in order to get ready to deliver service for the rest of the shift (note - the shift names are just an example and the same scenario can play out 3 ways). I would tell my crew members when hearing them complain about the off-going shift, "I don't care. They are all gone now and complaining about it is doing nothing to fix it, so let's go out and fix it."

Hopefully inheriting chaos at shift change does not happen very often and when it does, there is a legitimate reason for it (like they just got back to the station less than an hour ago from a working fire). However, when it does happen consistently, it can be a real pain, especially for the Company Officer inheriting it all. When it consistently happens, here are some considerations for the Company Officer:

- The bottom line at shift change is that everything that is out of order (even if it is lots of stuff) needs to be put back in order so the company can deliver safe and effective service throughout the shift.
- There will always be little things here and there that are out of balance at shift change. This is completely normal – WITH ALL SHIFTS. Put it back in balance and move on without saying anything. This is why we check things in the morning.
- You are not in charge of the off-going Company Officer or their crew.
- Trying to fix the off-going shift's Company Officer (or their crew) is impossible.
- Saying anything to the other Officer, or to their crew members, probably will not help the situation and it could possibly make it worse.
- You cannot get even with the off-going shift. The C-Shift group showed up early for work and left everything in order for A-Shift when being relieved. Leaving a dirty truck for C-Shift in protest of A-Shift's laziness is doing nothing but inconveniencing the poor C-Shifter who did nothing but leave a clean truck full of gas for their A-Shift counterpart. Also, along these lines, I am not a big fan of doing something to someone else when I did not like it being done to me (the golden rule). Do not let A-Shift make you do stupid things or turn you into a lazy person.
- If it was really, really, really bad (like arguments are now happening between the shifts at shift change), it would be much better to address the A-Shift Officer in person, rather than calling your boss in an attempt to fix things.
- Calling your boss is really not an option. Your boss is in the same position you are in - they are not in charge of A-Shift either. The most that they could do for the matter is to inform their A-Shift counterpart of what is going on and hope that they take care of it. I do not like your chances because the A-Shift Battalion Chief is probably already well aware of how A-Shift behaves at your station and nothing has been done to change their behavior so far.
- If you absolutely must talk to your counterpart, keep it professional, solution oriented, and use specific occurrences of when and what has been consistently out of balance.

Based on what is going on, it should not be too difficult to compile a detailed list of specific occurrences (a long list). After speaking with the A-Shift Officer, I still do not like your chances of resolution.

- Again, you still must get things in order in the morning to get ready to deliver safe and effective service the rest of the shift.

The On-Coming Shift (the Shift that Relieves You)

Having just covered how not to leave a station and the trucks for the on-coming shift, there is not much more to add than the following:

- How your company leaves the trucks and station for the oncoming shift is a direct reflection of how the Company Officer manages their crew and fire station.
- All members on your shift need to perform morning briefings with their counterparts.
- Have a little morning fellowship with the on-coming shift and a fun and safe 2 days off (you have earned it).

Managing a Fire Company in a Multi-Company Station

The most common multi-company stations configurations include:

1. Engine with an Ambulance or Medic Unit (ALS versus BLS combinations)
2. Engine and Tanker
3. Engine and Brush Truck
4. Engine and Ladder
5. Engine and Engine
6. Engine with a Heavy Rescue (or any other unit with a Company Officer)

1. Engine with an Ambulance or Medic Unit (ALS versus BLS)

This is probably the most common fire station apparatus configuration in the country. The different staffing and management models for this configuration can include:

BLS Engine (staffed with EMTs): This type of unit will obviously have a BLS/EMT Company Officer who is also supervising only BLS/EMT Firefighters. By rank, this makes the Company Officer the highest medical authority on the apparatus. While delivering BLS medical services, the Company Officer will be responsible for both the patient and overall scene management. On an ALS incident, the Senior Paramedic on another unit on-scene will have all decision-making authority over the patient, while the Company Officer maintains all responsibility for overall management of the scene.

ALS Engine (staffed with Paramedics): This type of unit could have many different types of personnel configurations that would depend on whether the unit was staffed by 3 or 4 people and/or if the unit is staffed with 1 or 2 Paramedics. The biggest Company Officer management considerations for how the unit is staffed are:

- If the Company Officer is a Paramedic, by rank and medical qualification, this makes the Company Officer the highest medical authority on the apparatus. While delivering any type of EMS, the Company Officer will be responsible for both patient care and overall scene management.
- If the Company Officer is a BLS/EMT, the highest medical authority on the truck will be the Senior Paramedic and they will have all decision-making authority over the patient. The Company Officer will maintain all responsibility for overall management of the scene.

BLS Ambulance (staffed with EMTs): This type of staffing would typically be paired with an ALS Engine. In most of these configurations, a Company Officer at their fire station will be the Ambulance crew members' direct supervisor. This was the scenario at Station 201 - L-201 supervised the BLS Ambulance crew. L-201 members being on my crew made it easy for me to be aware of what they were doing most of the shift, but the Ambulance was another story. This was because the majority of their runs were with E-201 or another unit outside of our first due area. Supervising people who you do not have eyes and ears on all the time, especially when they are young and inexperienced, can be very challenging at times (almost to the point of having to refer to the section of this book on addressing issues).

ALS Medic Unit (staffed with Paramedics): This type of unit could be staffed with 1 or 2 Paramedics. If housed with an Engine with a BLS Company Officer, the Senior Paramedic on the unit will have all decision-making authority over the patient while the Company Officer maintains all responsibility for the overall management of the scene. There are a couple of different direct supervision scenarios that could happen:

- The Company Officer of the Engine or Ladder is the direct supervisor of the unit (majority of fire departments)
- The Paramedic personnel are assigned to an EMS Division, which is considered to be their direct supervisor. The Company Officer at their fire station is considered to be their station supervisor.

Supervising 3rd Party EMS Providers

Many fire departments respond with 3rd party EMS providers. This usually comes in the form of either a BLS or ALS ambulance/transport company. Most of these agencies provide their own quarters, but sometimes a 3rd party ambulance/transport unit will actually be housed at and respond out of a fire station.

In these situations, the Company Officer is considered their on-site supervisor (at the station and on EMS scenes), but they are not their direct supervisor or their medical director. Around the station and on EMS calls, the Company Officer has the ability to direct these personnel as the situation requires, but if there are any serious performance or HR issues to address, the Company Officer usually has to get their boss involved, along with the 3rd party's bosses, in order to properly process any issues. There is usually an agreement in place that outlines the system to use to process any complaints (both ways). If these agreements are in place, Company Officers need to understand them and fit into the procedure when processing any issues that need to be addressed.

2. Engine and Tanker (Water Tender)

The majority of what will burn in the US does not have a fire hydrant close to it, making this a very needed and common staffing configuration. There are a couple of different methods used to staff and manage Tanker personnel:

- There is a member permanently assigned to the Tanker (best scenario). If this is the case, the member is most likely certified as an Engineer and the Company Officer will most likely be their direct supervisor.
- Another very common way to staff a Tanker when they are needed is having someone on the Engine (or Ladder) move over to drive and operate the Tanker. If this is the case, I highly recommend that the member moving over to do this be certified to drive and operate the vehicle. Never hand the keys to the Tanker over to someone who is not certified to drive and operate it. Over half of the Firefighter LODDs involving a Tanker roll-over have a young, unqualified driver behind the wheel.

3. Engine and Brush Fire Apparatus

This a very common deployment configuration in the western US and it is managed very similar to having a Tanker at your fire station. Again, the big thing to manage here is ensuring the member working on the unit is qualified to both drive and operate all the pumping equipment on it.

4. Engine and Ladder

When managing a fire company in a multi-company station with more than 1 Company Officer, I need to reiterate: as a Company Officer, the only people you are in charge of are the members of your company - no one else. Having said this, all the crews of the multi-apparatus (multi-Company Officer) stations that I worked at throughout my career all got along for the most part. There were always some personality clashes here and there, but by and large, everyone got along. On the other side of this, throughout my travels across the country, I have literally seen multi-company stations where a white stripe was painted down the middle of the station (not good). A fire station with a white stripe down the middle of it represents a bunch of Company Officers who refuse to manage their crews and who do not respect the other people they work with (I would hate to see what happens at one of their fires!).

Background: At Station 201 (ALS Engine, BLS Ladder, BLS Ambulance) the work and responsibilities throughout a shift were shared in the following ways:

- *The last year I worked at Station 201, the Engine responded on about 4,000 calls, the Ladder responded on about 3,500 calls, and the Ambulance responded on about 3,700 calls (with over 2,000 patient transports).*
- *Every permanently assigned member at the station was at Level 2 or higher on the competency scale (most were at Level 3).*
- *The Engine responded on all the ALS calls while the Ladder responded on all the BLS calls, so there was not much debate on whose call it was.*

- *The Engine responded on about 2 more calls per shift than the Ladder and their calls usually took twice as long to mitigate.*
- *All patient transports for A-201 averaged about an hour each (with an average of 6 transports a shift).*
- *If the entire station was dispatched on a fire incident all at once, the responding out of the station order was: Engine out first, Ladder second, Ambulance third. This allowed the Officer on E-201 to arrive on-scene first and start out the incident command process on working fires.*
- *If the entire station was dispatched on an EMS incident all at once (perhaps a serious vehicle accident on the freeway), the responding order out of the station was: Ladder out first, Engine second, Ambulance third. E-201 on EMS incidents needed to focus more on patient treatment than overall scene management, so the responsibility for command and running the incident would go to the Ladder to help facilitate this.*
- *For any incident the Ambulance was dispatched on with another unit from Station 201, the Ambulance responded out of the station last and followed that unit to the scene – 300 feet behind them.*
- *The Ladder drilled more than the Engine, but E-201 drilled as much or more than any other Engine company on the department and again, they were highly competent.*
- *On all incidents that we ran together, we all had our own separate responsibilities that did not really spill over into the other unit's. This created a situation in which I never really had to provide much direction to the Engine crew while working on an incident scene and visa-versa with the Engine Captain.*
- *The station and grounds were divided into equal areas where all 3 units had their assigned areas to clean and maintain.*
- *Every crew member and officer had their own, separate dorm room.*
- *All quarterly workloads were divided equally between the Engine and Ladder (hydrant testing, hose testing, fire pre-planning walk throughs, etc.).*
- *In a previous background presented, the whole station would perform together during our morning core PT routine.*
- *Chow is a big deal with 11 hungry people. Cooking duties rotated every shift (this included cooking both lunch and dinner). Whoever cooked also cleaned the kitchen. The rotation was: The Ladder would cook, the next shift was the Engine's turn, and the next shift was the Ambulance's turn (every 3rd shift it was your turn to cook).*
- *On shifts that there were activities occurring for the unit cooking that prevented them from cooking lunch, all 3 units would be on their own for lunch and the unit up in the cooking rotation would prepare the dinner meal. This counted as a cook day.*
- *Some shifts had so much going on that it was impossible for the unit whose turn it was in the rotation to cook either meal. If it was the Ladder's turn to cook on a shift like this, all units would be on their own for chow for both meals and L-201 would still be up next shift for their cooking rotation.*
- *There was always a shift that the unit cooking would get back from the store in the morning with all the groceries, they would get dispatched on a call, and you would not see them again until 5 pm. When this would happen to a unit on their cook day, the other 2 units would have to step-up and start cooking lunch and/or dinner (we are all hungry). If this happened to the Ambulance, it would count as their cook day. If it happened to either the Engine or the Ladder, it would be up for debate if it counted as a cook day.*
- *When chow time is called, do not insult the cook by showing up late for the meal.*
- *On most shifts, all official activities were taken care of by lunch time. From then on, we were all on stand-by for 911 service delivery. Over half of Station 201's calls were between 9 PM and 6 AM.*

- *Nap time (1:00 PM to 4:00 PM) was quiet time at the station. There were to be no intercoms, loud workout routines, banging of pots and pans, etc. (the reason for this at Station 201 was because we were going to be up all night delivering service).*
- *After-dinner activities that were routinely performed together as a group included behind the station fellowship, card games (pitch – a truly great card game), watching evening movies and sporting events, light PT activities, etc.*

5. Engine and Engine

This deployment configuration usually happens in very busy areas of the response system. The same general guidelines for an Engine and Ladder station configuration will apply for most things, but here are some other management considerations for this type of deployment configuration:

- If one Engine is BLS and the other is ALS, the BLS Engine would take all the BLS calls and the ALS Engine would take all of the ALS calls. Fire calls dispatched as a single unit would rotate between the 2 units.
- If both units were either ALS or BLS, both units would take turns taking all calls. This could lead to debates on whose turn it is for the next response.
- If the response is for a working fire and both units are dispatched, the direction the trucks had to turn out of the station would determine who would go first. If they turned right out of the station, E-1 would go first. If they turned left, E-2 would go first. If this was unfair, (like the majority of the working fires involved turning right out of the station), each unit should take turns responding out of the station first on working fire dispatches (from there, it would be luck of the draw).
- PT activities would vary from station to station, but I am sure there would be a lot of E-1 versus E-2 competitions that both Company Officers would need to closely manage.
- Division of chores, chow, nap time, and after dinner activities would all probably be managed the same way as they were at Station 201.

6. Engine with a Heavy Rescue or Squad (or any Other Unit at your Fire Station that has a Another Company Officer Assigned to it)

This deployment configuration usually happens in larger, well-staffed fire departments and it will follow the same basic guidelines as an Engine and Ladder configured fire station. ALS versus BLS configurations will also need to be considered when multiple Company Officers are working out of one fire station.

Chapter 24

Personal Electronics and Social Media

When managing your crew members personal electronics and the impact an employee's social media accounts can have on them, the major considerations include:

1. Fire department data connections
2. Personal data connections
3. Cell phones
4. Personal social media accounts

1. Fire Department Data Connections

Fire department data connections include:

- Any fire station computer connected to the internet, intranet, LAN, etc.
- Any wireless internet system provided by the fire department
- Any digital mobile computer terminal or phone/cellular connection on an apparatus
- Any fire department radio system
- Any multimedia cabling inside of a fire station (even if paid for by the Firefighters, it is still coming into city property and therefore, the city (and public) have all the rights to see what you are watching on TV and looking at on the internet)
- Any phone line inside of a fire station (again, even if Firefighters paid for it)

Every one of the items on the above list creates a very detailed data trail of the person using it. The fire department can access this data trail any time they wish. Along with this, all data trails are also available to the public via the Freedom of Information Act (1967). The inappropriate use of any item on the above list has led to the termination of many Firefighters across the country since the first day any of these systems were invented and installed into a fire station.

The ONLY thing any of these data systems should be used for is OFFICAL fire department business - nothing else!

2. Personal Data Connections

The internet, and all that comes with it, has become an ingrained part of our society and everyone wants to be connected (all of time). The need to be connected while on duty is not going to magically go away for 24 hours (especially for the youth). I also completely understand the need to stay connected while on duty, but there is a time and a place to do it and there are also times and places NOT to do it.

The place, as stated above, needs to be on your own connection - not the fire department's. What a Firefighter does on their own person smart device while using their own personal cellular connection cannot be viewed, audited, or subpoenaed by the fire department or the public. Knowing this and coupled with today's cellular availability, a Firefighter should never hook up to or use a fire department electronic device or connection to digitally connect to the internet for personal business or entertainment (of any kind).

3. Cell Phones

Cell phones became widely available in the early to mid-90's. This was about the time I was assigned to L-201 and I must say that I never had a problem with any of my crew members messing with a cell phone when they should not have. Not to sound like a broken record, but the way the Company Officer uses their cell phone will set the example of how the other members of the crew should use theirs (lead by example).

Since my days out in the field, cell phones have grown into an even more powerful tool that is available for Company Officers and their crew members while delivering service. The Company Officer (or their crew) can use their cell phones in the following official ways to deliver better service:

- If not available on the apparatus, a mapping function on a personal cell phone can be used to get routing information and to provide aerial photos of the incident site.
- Many HAZMAT programs can be accessed using a cell phone.
- EMS information and data can be accessed using a cell phone.
- Cell phones can be used to communicate with the dispatch center in order to reduce tactical channel radio traffic.
- Cell phones can be used to call the various SMEs of the different disciplines on the department to get advice on how to mitigate the incident you are currently on. Sometimes sending pictures or video of what is being described will greatly assist.
- Cell phones provide a streamlined way for a family member to get a hold of a Firefighter in case of an emergency.

Cell phones provide a great tool for a fire company. Lead by example by only using them for official business while delivering service and keep them in your pocket on vibrate unless they are otherwise needed on a call.

4. Personal Social Media Accounts

There is a lot of the 1st Amendment of the Constitution woven into and around this issue. This book does not want to go there.

Having said this, the following is a list of the items that are absolutely prohibited by employers for their employees to post on their social media accounts. Any violation of these could result in the immediate termination of the member. All the following social medial "no no's" have been upheld over and over again in higher courts of law (some of these items have gone as high as the Supreme Court). They include:

- Employees cannot engage with personal media accounts on their employer's connection when they are on duty - official business only.

- Employees must not represent or speak on behalf of their fire department. Members must also not give the appearance that they are speaking on behalf of the department.
- Employees cannot post anything that contains proprietary images or materials belonging to their department.
- No employee may engage in political activities involving any election that will impact their fire department (in any way) using any type of social media account.
- Employees are ABSOLUTELY prohibited from posting any photographs, video, or audio recordings taken on department property and/or in the performance of official duties onto any of their social media accounts.
- Employees CANNOT use their official roles to disparage their organization, elected officials, or fellow employees on their social media accounts.

Again, all these examples have been upheld in the higher courts and most of them ended in the termination of an employee for misusing their social media accounts. Don't do it. I would suggest that you just delete them all, so that you never have to worry about it.

Section 5
Managing Issues/Problems

Chapter 25

Addressing Issues

Background – I started studying for the Captain promotional test at the beginning of 1993. I was an Engineer at the time and had the plan of staying an Engineer. My plans exploded when my long time Captain (of 4 plus years) bid into a sweet Ladder spot and I was left to fend for myself. Engineers are the best judges of a good Company Officer and I had been working for one of the best. Then came along the roving Captains (for an endless time). This was because no one wanted a permanent spot on a rig that ran 4,000+ calls a year. None of the roving Captains were quite as good as my former boss and over a 4 to 5-month period I soon was frustrated with a few of the same roving bosses that kept showing up, again and again. During this period in my life, my dad sensed my frustrations and he told me that it was time for me to become my own boss (sort of) by taking the next Captain promotional test. I started studying for the test in February. At that time, I had over 12 years on the job.

The Captain's written test was 100 multiple choice questions based on a bibliography you could not jump over. It was given in the middle of June. Once completed, the successful candidates had about 6 weeks to prepare for the oral interview process (which by the way, was based on fantasy). During this interview preparation time, I often met with my Dad to discuss the HR issues associated with managing a fire company. The very first time that we met to start discussing the Captain's test HR interview process, he said the following 2 things to me (set in stone in my mind to this day):

"John, I am going to start out the process of HR management with you by talking about 2 (new) key principles in your life that you need to wrap your mind around. Every time that we talk about the subject of managing humans for the rest of our lives, these two key principles will be at the center of our discussions and they will prove over and over again to be the basis in managing and solving most HR issues.

The first principle is: You can ONLY manage (or supervise) a person's BEHAVIORS - not their FEELINGS!"

Wow! This was new to me. He quickly followed this up with the second new principle I had never heard of:

"The second principle is: try to manage a person's "FEELINGS" and you will quickly become their PRISONER."

He finished all of this by saying, "As you can see, these two principles go together, hand-in-hand."

I am a very independent minded person and while contemplating these two new principles, I focused on the word "prisoner" while my Dad wrote on napkins and drank his iced tea. This was his style - present a radical new concept to a person and then give them some time to think about it while acting amused and distracted. At this point in any of the critical conversations I had with my Dad in my adult life, he would not say anything else to me until I spoke first (most of the time). I knew this about him, so now I had to say something (semi-intelligent) in order to make him talk to me again and in my brain all I heard was the word "PRISONER, PRISONER, PRISONER!!!"

After about 30 seconds of contemplating this single word, I responded back to my Father with, "I am not going to be anybody's PRISONER."

He tilted his head a little while looking up at me, he got that smile on his face, and then he waited a couple of seconds before saying to me, "Then you are going to make a good Company Officer. Now, let's talk about the best ways to manage people's behaviors. This all starts out by ADDRESSING THEM and a person that does not want to be held prisoner by anybody else's feelings or behaviors needs to ADDRESS non-conforming behaviors in a corrective, positive fashion."

To recap:

You can ONLY manage (or supervise) a person's BEHAVIORS - not their FEELINGS!

Behavior is defined as *"the way in which one acts or conducts oneself, especially toward others."* You can manage this.

Feelings is defined as *"an emotional state or reaction."* You CANNOT manage this. Any attempts to do so will end in disaster.

Addressing Out of Balance Behaviors and Performances

Company Officer Expectation #7 - A supervisor that can address personnel and service delivery issues as soon as they occur, keeping them on the smallest scale possible.

The two things that will happen if you DO NOT address out of balance behaviors or performances are:

- Nothing will improve
- Things could get worse

Based on this logic, a Company Officer has absolutely nothing to lose when they address an issue if it is done in the correct manner (detailed in this chapter).

A lot of a Company Officer's success will depend on their ability to address out of balance issues. Usually, an ineffective Company Officer's downfall is that they care more about being liked and how their crew members feel about them (a prisoner), rather than putting in the effort needed to effectively train and manage them. Effective Company Officers care a lot more about managing positive and negative behaviors and performance than they do about being popular with their crew members. The ironic thing about the 2 different Officer types is that most people want to work for a Company Officer that is NOT running a popularity contest.

Major Considerations When Addressing Negative Issues Include:

1. The burden of being in charge
2. Acting decisively
3. Corrective, progressive, and lawful
4. Progressive discipline types
5. Time and place (territories)
6. Structuring a corrective conversation – by Tim W. Dietz
7. Performance issues versus attitude/behavior issues

8. Un-witnessed out of balance behavior
9. Off-duty infractions

1. The Burden of Being in Charge

"If you condone it, you own it." - Unknown

If everything and everyone acted and behaved perfectly, life would be easy. If this was the case, there would be no need to manage anything. This is never the case and being in charge of a fire company while striving for excellence takes a lot of hard work, even without having any HR issues. When they do occur (and they will), they must be addressed. As the **basis** of this chapter, an effective Company Officer must sometimes immediately address issues and they need to have the ability to say the following statements to their crew members whenever it is necessary:

- No
- Stop
- Stop it
- Slow down
- Knock it off
- Do not do that
- That is enough
- We do not do that here

If you cannot say these words whenever they are necessary, do not even sign up for the job (because you are going to have to say them). This is the burden of being in charge and it leads us into the next point.

2. Acting Decisively

Non-discretionary decision-making time problems are issues that the officer must address immediately with very little time to critically think about them. These zero-time decisions usually involve safety violations or a member being disrespectful to a co-worker or a customer.

A good way to understand this decisive reaction concept is looking at the two major ways our brains and nervous systems process information and react to it. These two neurologic brain modes are:

1. The sympathetic nervous system
2. The parasympathetic nervous system

1. The sympathetic nervous system prepares the body for intense physical activity and is often referred to as the "fight-or-flight" response. These produce what I call the most black and white decisions/reactions/responses a human can have. Very little grey area is involved in making these types of critical (sometimes life or death) decisions because they are made from the primitive "reptile" area of the brain and they are all based on our training and previous experiences.

When the situations of SOP safety violations, acting inappropriate to a customer and/or to a co-worker, or performing an act that is endangering another person in some way present themselves in the workplace or on an incident scene, the person in charge must IMMEDIATELY react to them (like a sympathetic discharge). There should be very little grey area involved when dealing with these black and white situations.

SOPs are written by the organization to provide the managers and supervisors with the authority, responsibility, and accountability to act in solving high risk problems and resolving major infractions of the rules. The person in charge MUST react decisively when these events occur in order to stabilize the situation and make it safe again for all involved.

Background – There is always a moment of enforcement truth when you become a supervisor. This moment equates to stopping something immediately that will result in bad things happening in the near future (despite what the other person is feeling or thinking about at the time). My first moment of truth happened to me soon after I became a roving Captain.

Phoenix is a hot and dry place 9 months out of the year. A few months during the year (July to the end of September), Phoenix is both hot and humid. This is the time of the year that the monsoon season comes to town. During this time, every 3 to 4 days, thunderstorms build up to the point that large amounts of wind and/or rain get dumped directly on the greater Phoenix metro area. When these storms come through the valley, the 911 dispatcher center lights up like a Christmas tree.

These were the circumstances when we rolled out as a west-side ladder company (in an old reserve unit) at 5 PM for a "power lines down" dispatch. There were power lines down all over the valley. It was raining well over an inch an hour with wind gusts of over 70 MPH. This was nothing new for a Phoenix summer monsoon storm. However, my driver treated this dispatch as a high priority call (like a person was trapped) and he started driving way too fast for both the current conditions and the situation we were responding to.

After about 5 seconds of his high-speed response, I told the driver to slow down through the company intercom system. He did not even look over at me and he kept driving even faster. I told him again through the headsets to SLOW DOWN, but with much more volume to my voice this time. I got the same reaction as I did the first time - no response by the driver, except for more speed.

Okay, here is my moment of truth, plus I am really irate at this person for responding to my order to slow down by going faster, especially because the truck is now starting to hydroplane. At this point, I reached over the engine cowling, I removed the driver's headset (I thought that maybe it was not working), and I yelled in his right ear, "SLOW DOWN! or pull over and stop the truck." At this point, I was projecting my voice in a manner that eliminated any doubt of what I was trying to convey. He finally looked over at me, eyes all wide, but he did not slow down. Okay, he has listening issues, as well. I repeated myself in the same exact manner, but with a lot more body language that involved pointing to the side of the road.

During the fourth time, I emphasized "pull over and stop" since he could not bring himself to obey my direct order of slowing down. He knew at this point I was dead serious, so he disrespectfully obeyed my order by giving me a dirty look and then he slowed the truck down to a safe and prudent speed. I could really tell he was not happy about somebody else "telling him how to do his job."

This was a sympathetic discharge. That is exactly what was going on in my body at the time. I solved the safety issue right then and there, keeping all of the crew members as safe as possible for the rest of the response (including the Engineer). Part 2 is coming next.

2. The parasympathetic nervous system has almost the exact opposite effect of the sympathetic system. This relaxes the body while inhibiting or slowing down many of the higher energy functions. This state of mind is totally geared towards supplying the brain with the most oxygen and sugar it can deliver in order to support cognitive thinking (a no stress, higher thinking mode). This nervous system is dedicated to the grey matter upstairs. This is where people process and contemplate the current systems that are in place and the future control measures needed to regulate, support, and improve critical processes.

Putting the 2 Nervous Systems Together to Address Issues

These two nervous system processes usually go together when addressing high risk issues or enforcing safety SOPs, but the immediate, corrective reaction always needs to come first. The higher thinking part should come second. This is where the supervisor uses their discretionary decision-making time (once the situation is stabilized) to follow-up with the person involved and try to develop and implement a long-term solution so the problem does not ever present itself again.

Background Part 2 – After Mr. Hydroplaner slowed the truck down, we safely arrived at the incident scene. There were powerlines downs in the middle of the road with no injuries. We took care of it by blocking the road for 20 minutes until the utility company showed up and took over the scene. While waiting for the utility company, Mr. Hydroplaner stayed on the truck, shooting me dirty looks every time I glanced his way. At this point, I really did not care about the utility poles on the ground because I was much more focused on how I was going to address Mr. Hydroplaner when we got back to the station. This was the discretionary thinking time.

I also did not care if Mr. Hydroplaner was mad or if I hurt his feelings (which I did). On the way back to the station, he told me that no one has ever told him how to drive "his" truck before. He went on to explain (over and over again) that he was the greatest Engineer that was ever born and that I should just worry about doing my job while leaving him alone to do his. I told him I was doing my job and for him to please spare me from his greatness until we got back to the station.

When back at the station, I did not say a word to him. I got off the truck and went directly to my office. In my office, I pulled out the safety SOPs that addressed emergency response driving and I highlighted all the different sections of the standard that he had just violated. On a blank piece of paper, I wrote down a brief description of the event, that I would not tolerate it again, and then I drew a long, flat line on the bottom of the page for him to sign to acknowledge his "verbal counseling."

About 20 minutes after we had gotten back from the call, I picked up the station phone and hit the pound key (which activates the stations intercom system). Once the double beeps were sounded, I announced "Engineer Hydroplaner, report to my office immediately." About 2 minutes later, Mr. Hydroplaner showed up and I closed the door.

I started by telling him that my job was to manage the overall safety of the crew and to follow and enforce the SOPs of the department. I handed him the driving SOPs and pointed out the items that he had just violated. I told him I would not tolerate another infraction like the ones that just occurred. I asked him if he could comply with this the rest of the shift, because if it happened again with me on board, I was going to relieve him of duty. He stated that he would comply and he signed the memo. He followed the SOP driving rules the rest of the shift and I never worked with Mr. Hydroplaner again throughout the rest of my career.

My non- discretionary time reaction (sympathetic) = SLOW DOWN!

My discretionary time reaction (parasympathetic) = use brain and department resources to prevent further occurrences from happening in the future

3. Corrective, Progressive, Lawful

Corrective

As presented throughout this book, "corrective" is a proactive process of communicating in a positive manner with your crew members when addressing any issue. Most counseling should come in the form of feedback that is given in the moment. As previously presented, this immediate feedback has the greatest impact for the crew member because it translates their latest experience into learning and/or understanding right after the event has just occurred and it is fresh in their mind. If the feedback is given right after the event occurs, it is much more likely that it translates into understanding and acceptance more fully and does not get internalized as being critical. Addressing issues in this manner puts everyone on the same page and it leaves no doubt on what is expected from the Company Officer. Managing in this fashion will solve most of the HR issues that occur on a fire company.

Progressive

Because the corrective phase of discipline is so effective at solving problems, hopefully a Company Officer will not have to ramp up the process much past that. If necessary, the chain of "progressive" discipline translates into the following:

- Corrective – feedback
- Career counseling
- Verbal counseling
- Written record of a verbal counseling
- Written reprimand of unsatisfactory performance or behavior
- Suspension, demotion, or termination

All of these will be covered next in the chapter, but as previously stated, a Company Officer must realize they are the "sheriffs" who enforce the rules. They are not the "judges" who get to decide the punishment for violating them.

Lawful

Company Officers must understand that any official disciplinary action taken in which they put a member into the system will be reviewed by their superiors and could be subjected to either a grievance process or an employment appeal process. A person is in the system when their supervisor has officially documented unsatisfactory performance on official fire department paper (or electronics). Any actions taken past a verbal counseling with a member that creates an official fire department paper/documentation trail must have the support of the Company Officer's boss, the personnel department, possibly the training academy, as well as making the member's Union representatives aware of the issue the member is having (to insure due process for the member).

4. Progressive Discipline Types

The formal discipline realm of a Company Officer evolves around the following 4 types of feedback and counseling. Anything past these 4 types of discipline must have the "lawful" groups involved:

- Corrective feedback
- Career counseling
- Verbal counseling
- Signed written record of a verbal counseling (kept in the Company Officer's personal log)

Corrective Feedback

As covered throughout this book, corrective feedback should be the first and main method a Company Officer uses to manage any issue when it happens. If this is done in a positive, corrective manner, it will solve most of the issues a Company Officer has to deal with.

If corrective feedback is given in the moment, there is typically no need to do any follow-up with the member and most corrective feedback given to a member does not need to be documented by the Company Officer in their personal log (unless you predict there will be future problems ahead).

Career Counseling

Because "verbal counseling" sounds so official and actually performing this can be considered in the realm of real discipline, at Station 201 we came up with the term "career counseling." Career counseling was more of an informal way of making a member aware of any adjustments they needed to make in their behavior or performance in order to have a smooth, problem free career. Whenever I gave career counseling, it was always in the best interest of the member and if the problem was corrected, they never heard about the issue again (which was usually the case).

I would also sometimes use a career counseling session to follow-up on a corrective feedback discussion that was had with a member to ensure that we were both on the same page. These centered around more serious rule infractions and they were always held in private - some of them happened in my office, but most of them usually happened on the apparatus bays after returning from a call or a company drill.

Career counseling, along with any other type of counseling past this, should happen as soon as possible after the event has occurred and **should be briefly documented by the Company Officer in their personal logbook.**

Later in this chapter, Tim Dietz will present on how to structure a corrective counseling session's communications.

Verbal Counseling

A person has a serious issue if you are to this progression in the discipline process. You are either dealing with a serious first-time offense (Mr. Hydroplaner) or the 2 or 3 corrective feedback and career counseling sessions that have occurred in the past with the member have not fixed the problem.

I would always make it very clear to a member on what type of counseling they were receiving - career or verbal. If it was a verbal counseling I would state that the issue had not been resolved and now we were now at the career counseling stage or state that what had just happened was completely unacceptable and that a verbal counseling session was needed.

At this point, the Company Officer must also build a paper trail to document the events that have occurred, as well as your actions in dealing with them. This should have all started with brief notes of any past career counseling sessions you have had with the member in your personal log including where the event happened, the time, date, specifics on the occurrence, and your and the member's reactions to it.

Signed Written Record of a Verbal Counseling

All verbal counseling sessions should be documented by the Company Officer. Most verbal counseling that occurred (this did not happen very often) with a permanently assigned member on L-201 was NOT officially documented on paper where I had the member acknowledge and sign it. I would only do a written record of a verbal counseling and have the member sign it if the following was the case:

- I had a strong feeling the issue was not going away and the problem would eventually escalate beyond my level of authority
- It was for a non-permanent member who I had no previous work history with
- If it was for a serious offense (like Mr. Hydroplaner trying to kill us all)
- Any verbal counseling session with a Probationary Firefighter

Having a member read on paper about the occurrence and the adjustments that are required to get things back in balance sends a clear message that the Company Officer is serious about fixing the issue and big changes must be made on the member's part in order for the matter NOT to go to the next level. This document would then be placed in the Company Officer's personal log.

Any issues that progress past this level of counseling will require the lawful part of the system to be involved in the process. Again, this includes your boss, the Personnel Division, and if a prerequisite, the Union.

Written Reprimand of Unsatisfactory Performance or Behavior – The System

Being officially written-up for a performance or behavior issue is a big deal and it puts the member into the system. This is the stuff that goes into the member's permanent personnel file and it can affect their merit increase, pay raises, longevity benefits, and they also do not help very much if the member ever wants to promote in the near future. Enough official paper in a personnel file could ultimately lead to the member being terminated.

It is the Company Officer's responsibility to inform their boss of a situation of this type (discussed in a future chapter). In that discussion, the Company Officer's boss will decide if the incident warrants an official letter of unsatisfactory performance/behavior and what actions should be taken next. If it is deemed necessary to write the member up, the Battalion Chief should be in the room when it happens. It is the responsibility of the Battalion Chief (and above) to dole out the discipline (punishment) required for the situation - NOT the Company Officer.

As presented previously, the Company Officer will be the person who actually writes the occurrence up, but in no way do they get to decide what type of discipline will be imposed on the member. It is way above a Company Officer's pay grade to communicate what punishment the system is going to enforce on a member. Again, Company Officers must understand they are the "Sheriffs" who enforce the rules. They are not the "Judges" who get to decide the punishment for violating them.

Most fire departments have a standard form that is used to document unsatisfactory performance or behavior. These are structured for the Company Officer to properly document the following:

- Location of where the event happened
- The time and date the event happened
- Very specific details on the occurrence - Company Officers MUST avoid using judgments and vague descriptions of events. Specific details and the facts of what actually happened will stand up in a court of law much better than "I don't like their attitude."
- Detail the specific actions that you have taken to address the situation. This includes all previous career and verbal counseling sessions that have been documented.
- The reaction of the person with the unsatisfactory performance or behavior when the issue is being addressed (accepting responsibility versus being defiant or apathetic)
- Some forms also require a written action plan for improvement to be included (discussed in a future chapter)

When officially writing someone up, the room will probably have at least 4 people in it. This could include:

- Company Officer

- Member having the issue
- Company Officer's boss (usually a Battalion Chief)
- Possibly the Personnel Chief, Training Academy Chief, Operations Chief, and/or Shift Commander
- Member's union representation (to insure due process)

In some systems it is the member's responsibility to inform their Union representative to help represent them if they so choose. In other departments that have MOU/CBA in place, this may happen automatically, and it is just part of the process.

Suspension, Demotion, or Termination

To decide these types of consequences is way above a Company Officer's pay grade. If something like this does occur to a member for on-duty performances or behaviors, the Company Officer will not be involved in the process beyond being a professional witness when needed. If this is indeed going to happen to a member, a Company Officer's compliance of following all HR SOPs and their documentation skills will be key factors in supporting the process.

5. Time and Place (Territories)

As previously presented, addressing any significant issue usually comes with 2 parts:

1. Stabilize the situation
2. Follow-up

1. Stabilize the Situation

Issues concerning safety violations or inappropriate behaviors directed toward customers or co-workers MUST be addressed immediately. **The stabilization part of addressing a serious issue is not time or place dependent. It must happen right then and there - and it does not matter who it happens in front of.** Example: While eating dinner, Firefighter Inappropriate makes a very politically incorrect comment in front of all the other station members. The Company Officer's immediate reaction should be "Knock it off! We do not say things like that here. In my office NOW!" The situation is stabilized. Next comes the follow-up conversation.

2. Follow-up

There is not much of a choice on when or where a Company Officer will need to stabilize a serious issue. However, the Company Officer does get to decide when and where the follow-up conversation with the member will take place.

Follow-up conversations should take place as quickly as possible after the event has been stabilized. The time frame could range from performing an immediate follow-up to performing it 1 or 2 hours later, but all follow-up conversations should occur by the end of the shift. Always avoid having a follow-up conversation the next shift (or longer) after the event has occurred. The impact of the follow-up conversation will be less and less effective with the more time that passes between the event and you addressing it.

Territories

All HR centered follow-up conversations must be held in private and all communications on the manner (voice and/or paper) must remain completely confidential. There are several areas at a fire station where a Company Officer can have a private meeting with a crew member. Choosing the right setting for the conversation will greatly assist a Company Officer in setting the overall tone for the conversation.

Company Officers must also understand that Firefighters are very territorial. I always looked at Station 201 as a map that was made up of a bunch of different territories. A Company Officer must be aware of the territory they pick to have a corrective conversation. The major considerations for choosing the right territory for the conversation are:

Neutral territory– the best neutral territories to have a private conversation with a member include the apparatus bays or the park bench behind the station (with no one else in hearing range). Corrective conversations in neutral territories are the most casual setting to have them in and it will produce the least amount of stress on the member. This is where I had most of my corrective feedback and verbal counseling sessions and they usually happened right after getting back to the station after a service delivery or drilling issue.

Background: Firefighter Walls was the Senior Firefighter on L-201 for the last 5 years I was assigned to the station. Firefighter Walls was one of the most dedicated and competent Firefighters I have ever worked with, but he was a little short on having much sympathy or compassion for our customers.

Occasionally (about once a year) Firefighter Walls would say something inappropriate to a customer on a call. When this happened, I would immediately address it by stating, "that's enough Firefighter Walls." After this, we would finish the call and when we got back to the station, I would follow it up with a career counseling session.

Firefighter Walls knew I would always do a follow-up with a member after addressing a serious issue, but depending on the circumstances, it could take up to an hour or 2 for the follow-up session to happen. Firefighter Walls did not like having to wait for a follow-up that he knew was coming. He told me it reminded him of being a little kid waiting for his dad to get home to give him a spanking. Whenever one of these events occurred, as soon as the parking break was set back at the station, Firefighter Walls would get out of truck, he would go stand next to my door at attention, and he would say "just give it to me now so I can get it over with." Everyone else would go inside the station and Firefighter Walls would get his career counseling as soon as possible after the event occurred while it was performed in the proper setting.

Firefighter territory – Anytime a supervisor enters into a Firefighter's territory (their dorm room), the Firefighter will immediately become defensive - even if the supervisor is not there to address an issue. NEVER have a corrective conversation in a Firefighter's personal space. Only go into to Firefighter's dorm space to tell them that you need to talk to them privately somewhere else.

Company Officer territory – The Company Officer's territory is their office. Having a corrective conversation in a Company Officer's office sets a whole new tone and elevates it to a much higher level of seriousness. I would describe the demeanor of most members called into my office as being apprehensive and/or stressed. Knowing this, I would only have a corrective discussion in my office if it was for a one-time serious occurrence (Mr. Hydroplaner), if the member was a repeat offender, or if it was for some sort of behavior problem and I wanted the entire crew (or station) to know that those behaviors were unacceptable and that the Company Officer was addressing them (Firefighter Inappropriate). Always try to avoid having a corrective conversation in your office for minor issues that you know will be resolved quickly, as it causes too much stress on the member. No one likes being called into the boss's office.

Once the territory is chosen and the member is now in front of the Company Officer, it is time for the conversation. Tim Dietz is the best person to present on how to structure that conversation so it is the most productive that it can be.

6. Structuring a Corrective Conversation – Tim W. Dietz

The following communication guideline is adapted from Team Awareness to help Firefighters and Company Officers manage difficult conversations. The model works well, as it enables people to defuse conflicts at the lowest level and before things escalate. [1]

A couple points to remember from this chapter:

- Address the behavior – NOT the feelings!
- Failure to address the behavior leaves you with two possible outcomes:
  1. The behavior does not change
  2. The behavior gets worse

The Guideline:

1. **Consider what you want to say**
2. **Make your move**
3. **Get to the point**
4. **Practice good communication skills**
5. **Make a clear request**
6. **Roll with resistance**
7. **End on a positive note**
8. **Document**

Let's dissect this guideline:

1. **Consider what you want to say**. Does the behavior affect shift goals, violate an expectation, policy, guideline or mission/value statement? Before addressing the issue, decide what you want to achieve. Think about what you know, what you suspect, and your specific concerns. Make notes. Have some idea of your desired outcome.

2. **Make your move.** Is this something that needs to be addressed now (non-discretionary) such as a safety issue, hostile act, or is it causing embarrassment to the organization etc.? If not, ask the person to meet with you at a particular time (discretionary). Consider the appropriate territory.

3. **Get to the point.** When you are anxious or nervous, you might talk around a subject. This dilutes your message.

4. **Practice good communication skills.** Use "I" messages and active listening skills. "I" messages are non-blaming, nonaggressive ways of presenting ideas, feelings, and concerns. Listening creates a supportive atmosphere.

5. **Make a clear request** about what you want to achieve. Make an explicit request that the behavior stops or that they access help to address the behavior or situation.

6. **Roll with resistance.** Your crew member may get angry or deny the problem. These are normal defensive reactions to hearing things that we do not like to hear. Listen carefully and use calm repletion to dissipate strong feelings and to ensure your clear request for action is taken seriously.

7. **End on a positive note.** Thank the person for their willingness to listen. State your belief that the crew member can and will handle the problem.

8. **Document** the conversation as necessary. It is difficult to do progressive discipline if you have not documented past infractions.

Let's put all of this to work together with the following example: Bob, a Firefighter on your crew, takes a while to find a needed piece of equipment at an emergency scene. He seems unfamiliar with where it is stored on the apparatus.

1. **Consider what you want to say**. Does this unfamiliarity with the equipment impact your goals or violate an expectation? If yes, how can you communicate this concern in a nonconfrontational way?

2. **Make your move.** Are you going to have a conversation at the scene or wait until you are back at the station? In this scenario, you can wait until you get back to the station and say something like, "Hey Bob. After you get your stuff restored from this last alarm, can I have a chat with you?"

3. **Get to the point**. If Bob is like most Firefighters, he is thinking the worst (what did I do now?), so do not spend time discussing the weather, family life, upcoming training, or any other impertinent topics. "Hey Bob, the reason I wanted to talk to you was to discuss how familiar we are with where the equipment is stored on the apparatus." Now Bob knows exactly what the conversation is going to be about, which can help lower defensiveness.

4. **Practice good communication skills**. It is going to be hard for Bob to get defensive if I make the issue about myself by using "I" statements. "When I called for the saw and heard the compartment doors slamming around the apparatus, it frustrated and concerned me that we may not be familiar with where our equipment is carried." You may even add this lack of familiarity violates expectations, mission statements, etc.

5. **Make a clear request.** "I need to have us be familiar with where the equipment is stored on the apparatus at the beginning of every shift."

6. **Roll with resistance.** Bob may have his reasons for why he did not know where the equipment was located. He might say, "Yesterday's crew failed to put the saw back where it belonged," or "This is a reserve apparatus and the maintenance guys placed it in the wrong compartment." Listen to Bob, acknowledge what he is saying, then repeat your request. "Okay, that might be the case, but here is what I need: I need us to be familiar with where the equipment is stored on the apparatus at the beginning of every shift."

7. **End on a positive note.** "Listen Bob, I enjoy working with you and I do not want to see anyone get hurt or get into trouble."

8. **Document.** When necessary, all conversations addressing unacceptable behavior need to be written down.

Here is another example: The crew is in the grocery store shopping for dinner. You, the Company Officer, has engaged with a young family whose children have seen the apparatus in the parking lot and you in your uniform. One of your crew members down the aisle drops an F-bomb causing an immediate reaction from the children who look at their parents. The parents look at you with an expression of shock and disgust. At this point, you'll need to apologize to the family, reassure them that you'll address the issue and that it won't happen again.

1. **Consider what you want to say.** Does this behavior impact your goals or violate your expectations of crew behavior in public? If yes, does it warrant a response now or later? In this instance, it does warrant getting the crew members attention and letting them know that what they just said was heard by others and to knock it off (non-discretionary).

2. **Make your move.** This situation should be best addressed in the cab of the apparatus on the way back to the station (as a lesson to all).

3. **Get to the point.** Since your goal is to address this behavior as soon after the event as possible, resist the urge to use small talk to ease your way into the subject.

4. **Use good communication skills.** Using "I" statements and listening skills, you may state the following: "When I heard that language and saw those kids' reaction and the look on their parents' faces, I was embarrassed and frustrated." You may add, "We represent our organization and I want people to think positively of us."

5. **Make a clear request.** "I do not want to hear that kind of language in public anymore."

6. **Roll with resistance.** The F-bombing Firefighter might say, "Well I have heard you say that in public," or "The Chief talks that way in public," etc. Your response should be: "After what I saw in the store today, we all need to stop that behavior. Please call me out if you hear me say something like that and I will certainly chat with the Chief if I hear them say that in public. I am going to stick with my request that we never use that type of language in public again."

7. **End on a positive note.** "I enjoy our organization's reputation in this community and I do not want to jeopardize it. I also do not want to see anyone get into trouble."

8. **Document.** Document the date/time the conversation happened and a brief synopsis of why it happened. You may hear about this event again in the future.

If the behavior that needs to be addressed violates a policy, guideline, mission/value statement or written expectation, make sure you address it and make sure the crew member reviews the document(s) violated, as well. That helps the offender understand this is not just a Company Officer being "picky," but that an organizational value has been violated. Also make sure you follow your organization's MOU/CBA regarding progressive discipline/due process steps when addressing performance or behavioral issues.

This simple communications model has worked well in fire service organizations in which crews are taught to handle things at the lowest level possible. As a side note: Handling things at the lowest level DOES NOT always imply that the Company Officer's supervisors are not kept in the loop and aware of the situation. Issues that need to be brought to the attention of your Battalion Chief will be covered in an upcoming chapter.

What Does NOT Work

When confronted with a corrective communication, avoid triangulation. This involves communicating with Person B about Person A. This can be seen as manipulative in trying to get Person B on your side and/or getting Person B to have the conversation with Person A so that you do not have to. Remember that as a Company Officer you should do the following:

- Always talk directly to the person you have a concern about or do not talk at all.
- If you need coaching on how to address an issue, that is fine as long as it is YOU that addresses the issue with the person.
- Refuse to tolerate others that come to you with complaints about others.
- Your first statement back at these folks should be: "Have you talked to them about this issue?" Then help coach them through it if needed.

Work hard. Be nice. – Tim W. Dietz

7. Performance Issues Versus Attitude/Behavior Issues - John Brunacini

Most HR issues will fall into 2 categories: performance or attitude. Out of the 2, the easiest issues to resolve are performance issues, but they usually take the most work.

Performance Issues

Because a person's level of competence is directly correlated to their level of SAFETY, a Company Officer must evaluate the competence level of all their crew members performing MCS (high risk, high stress tasks) and then take the necessary steps to either maintain or increase their crew member's competency in these areas to the highest level possible. This is done with lots and lots of drilling.

Because most fire departments do a good job hiring the right people, most performance issues are solved with a little career or verbal counseling and a lot of drilling (all the hard work) in order to get the member's performance back up to meeting department standards and there is no need to elevate the issue beyond that.

However, there could be a crew member who has significant performance issues that all the drilling in the world cannot fix. People having these types of severe performance issues will also usually have other issues associated with their poor performances such as being physically unfit, obesity, or they are injury prone to the point that the Company Officer is unable to get their performance to minimum levels in between their injury cycles. These people will all have to be put in the system and will need an official API (discussed in a future chapter).

Attitude/Behavior Issues

Let me start by going back to Dad's 2 basic HR management rules:

1. "You cannot manage a person's feelings" (or their attitude - attitude is a direct reflection of the way a person "feels"). What a Company Officer is paid to do is manage people's behaviors.

Always avoid saying to a crew member, "I do not like your attitude." Do not do it! Address the behavior the attitude is producing. Here is an example: You are working with a first time Engineer that has 15 years on the job. On the first 2 EMS calls you go on, he stands with his arms crossed and he glares at the patient whenever he is not doing something. After the 2nd call, you address it back at the station in the apparatus bays. Do not say, "I do not like your attitude on EMS calls." Instead, say, "I can tell you are not happy about being on an EMS call because of your negative body language. I need you to quit crossing your arms and glaring at people while on EMS scenes. None of us should have been surprised we were going to go on EMS calls today. Please quit crossing your arms and glaring at the customers. This is what we get paid to do."

It has been proven that if a Company Officer enforces the above career counseling session with that member over the next 30 to 60 days (whenever necessary, say, "Quit crossing your arms and glaring," or "You had great body language on that last call. Thanks!") it will become a HABIT for him to not cross his arms and glare and he will never do it again.

If you have Mario Andretti driving your apparatus and for 30 to 60 days, you continually enforce the Code-3 response policy while driving, following the driving rules will become a habit for Mario. As a matter of fact, after 6 months of doing this, driving faster than what the SOP calls for will even make Mario feel a little uncomfortable.

Manage and document behaviors, not feeling or attitudes, while trying to create and reinforce positive operational habits.

8. Un-Witnessed Out of Balance Behaviors

I know my crew probably did not like it when I asked them to talk in private in my office. What they did not know was that I disliked them saying the same thing to me even more (because it was always bad news). Most of the news they shared would concern HR infractions committed against themselves or they would disclose a known or suspected nefarious activity of another crew member to me. It is not good if something like this is dropped off at your doorstep, especially because you did not witness any of it.

This book has purposely avoided presenting any material on performing an HR "investigation," particularly any that concern Title VII violations. Investigating a Title VII violation is way above a Company Officer's pay grade. Company Officers are not paid or trained to be a private investigator that conducts interviews trying to determine who is telling the truth and what really happened in unwitnessed HR matters. Most Company Officers do not even know a lawyer and even fewer own and operate a working lie detector testing machine.

Your bosses and/or the personnel department have the authority and the qualifications to investigate all Title VII HR infractions. ALL matters concerning these types of un-witnessed issues must be passed up the chain of command, starting with your boss. A Company Officer attempting to solve problems like these on their own could make the problem worse, could significantly increase the department's liability in the matter, and the result could even threaten the Company Officer's career. Do not do it! Take all Title VII HR matters up the chain of command, starting with your boss (discussed in the next chapter).

9. Off-duty Infractions

All off-duty infractions should be handled by the Fire Chief's office and/or the personnel department. Company Officers should have no participation in the processes that takes place when a member has an infraction that occurs outside of the workplace. The only thing a Company Officer can do when this happens is to provide any possible support that is appropriate for the situation.

References:

1. Bennett, J. B., Bartholomew, N. G., Reynolds, S., & Lehman, W. E. K. *Team Awareness: Training for workplace substance abuse prevention*. Fort Worth: Texas Christian University, Institute of Behavioral Research (2002)

Chapter 26

Your Boss, the Brass, and Department Resources

There are two main points I want to make to start this chapter:

1. I never wanted my boss to address any issue at Station 201.
2. My boss never wanted to address any issue at Station 201.

1. My boss was a Battalion Chief and he worked out of another fire station that was about 5 miles away from Station 201. The position and rank of Battalion Chief represented the system when dealing with personnel issues. This was the last person I wanted involved in solving a personnel issue at my fire station because most of the time it also came with a lot of other people from the system. This would always include the Union and sometimes it could include the Shift Commander, a Training Chief (performance issues), and/or a representative from the Personnel Department. That is a lot of Brass looking down their noses at a problem at my station.

As presented previously, getting written up is a BIG DEAL and a lot things have probably had to have gone wrong for the problem to get to that point. I never wanted any issue to get to that point, so I did whatever I could do to avoid going to a higher level of discipline by using the following tools that are available to every Company Officer to prevent these problems from happening in the first place:

1. Corrective feedback
2. Career counseling
3. Verbal counseling
4. Written record of a verbal counseling

The continual use of these 4 progressive discipline types whenever needed solved most of the negative issues that happened on L-201. Any issue that cannot be solved using these 4 progressive discipline types will require notifying and getting your boss involved.

2. My boss did not want to show up to Station 201 to help solve a problem any more than I wanted them to. If my boss did need to show up, they expected me to have used the 4 progressive discipline types to keep things on the smallest scale possible to prevent needing their presence in the first place. When it comes to being involved in higher level HR and performance issues, all Battalion Chiefs also expect a well-documented paper trail and other supporting information and material from their Company Officers whenever there is an issue that requires a member to be put into the system. It would not go well for a Company Officer if the standard discipline progression had NOT been followed properly and now the Battalion Chief is involved in solving an issue at a fire station.

Background: As a roving Engineer (worst job on the department), I roved into E-247, a busy Paramedic Engine company in central Phoenix, for just one shift. The entire crew had worked together for over 3 years and the Captain Paramedic (Captain Simmer) of the truck had worked at the station for almost 10 years.

We had 4 EMS calls before noon and each one of them required a trip to the hospital to pick up the Paramedic who cared for the patient in the ambulance while enroute to the hospital. On the 3rd call, I could see Captain Simmer having brief "words" with the Firefighter Paramedic (Firefighter Care Bear) when we were at the hospital. It lasted less than 30 seconds and I was too far away to hear what was said.

On the next call of the shift, after loading the patient into the ambulance and getting ready to head to the hospital to pick up Firefighter Care Bear, Captain Simmer got on the truck and (based on his body language) he was MAD! He was so mad that his entire face was as red as the fire truck! He did not say a word on the 10-minute ride to the hospital, he did not get off the truck at the hospital, and he did not say a word on the way back to the station. It was an uncomfortable ride and I had no idea what was going on.

As soon as we got back to the station, Captain Simmer called Firefighter Care Bear into his office. At this point, I need to call attention to the fact that most Captain office doors had a return air vent in them and it was not the other Firefighters' or my fault that we were cleaning the hallway next to the Captain's office and we may have overheard some of the conversation (more like a shouting match) coming out of the air vent.

The gist of the issue was that Captain Simmer was very upset because for a "good long while" that Firefighter Care Bear was needlessly going to the hospital with BLS patients that did not require ALS care or treatment on the way, he was sick of being out of service un-necessarily, and he thought Firefighter Care Bear was doing this on purpose because he liked being at the hospital more than the fire station. All of this was needlessly wasting the fire department's time and resources. Captain Simmer ended by saying that he was going to call the EMS Division along with his Battalion Chief and that he was going to write up Firefighter Care Bear for all the times that he has witnessed these behaviors. We barely had enough time to finish our hallway cleaning duties before Firefighter Care Bear exited the Captain's office.

It was only noon and these events made for a long shift.

The Battalion Chief showed up 2 ½ hours later. In that time period, we had to respond on 2 more EMS calls and on both calls, we had to pick up Firefighter Care Bear at the hospital. That went really well... In between calls, Firefighter Care Bear was on the phone with his Union representative while Captain Simmer yelled into the phone while calling people in the EMS Division. It all ended very shortly after the Battalion Chief arrived at the station. He went directly into the Captain's office. It is funny how quickly a hallway can get dirty and since we did not want the Battalion Chief walking down a dirty hallway, we had to clean it again. It was so dirty that it took all 3 of us to clean it this time. The Battalion Chief was only in the Captain's office less than 5 minutes. Here is a summary of what was heard through the vent while cleaning the hallway:

- *The Battalion Chief gave Captain Simmer about the first minute of the meeting to further explain what was going on. He did not interrupt him while he was talking. Captain Simmer ended with "I want him written up by either me on the fire side or by the EMS Division."*
- *In a raised voice (he was not yelling, he was projecting) the Battalion Chief started with, "NO, that is not going to happen and the only person that should be worried about getting written up is YOU!"*
- *"You stated that this has been going on for over 9 months, but this is the first time you have ever addressed it with Firefighter Care Bear and this is how you approach it! Absolutely Unacceptable!"*
- *"You are the overall medical authority on your truck in both rank and Paramedic seniority. That puts all the responsibility for what happens on an EMS call on YOU!"*
- *"If you do not like what is going on at an EMS call, then address it and fix it right there! Not after tolerating something you have not approved of for 9 months!"*

- *"Do not ever get into it with someone else that has the same medical qualifications that you have if they want to "overtreat" a patient. They will win that match every time. I have talked to EMS and they agree that this is a NON-issue. Quit calling them!"*
- *He ended with, "Get it together. I had better not have to come back here and fix another issue that should have been addressed and solved 9 months ago. I like the fact that Firefighter Care Bear has worked here the past 3 years because you have not had any citizen complaints since then."*

It is amazing that the 3 of us barely made it out of the hallway after cleaning it again right before the Battalion Chief exited the Captain's office. On his way out of the station, he said over his shoulder, "Nice work on that hallway."

As you can imagine:

- *The rest of the shift was even worse (black cloud over the station) with no evening meal together.*
- *The issue was handled so badly that Firefighter Care Bear soon left E-247 to go work at another fire station.*
- *For the rest of his career, Captain Simmer believed that the department and his Battalion Chief did not support him when he was addressing an issue. Ha! What a joke!*

The 2 Major Considerations for Calling your Boss are:

1. When to call
2. When NOT to call

1. When to Call your Boss

"Bad news worsens with age." – Alan Brunacini

There are 4 major personnel issues that require you to call your boss:

1. An issue that a Company Officer has addressed that has gone through the first 4 phases of discipline and the issue has NOT been resolved, so it needs to go to the next level and into the system
2. A one-time event involving a very serious infraction
3. Any Title VII HR harassment or hostile work environment issue
4. Fit for duty issues – covered in Chapter 29

1. Addressed Issues that Need to go to the Next Level

If a fire company is managed properly, this should not happen very often. If this does happen, it will typically involve performance or fitness issues, or behavioral issue. When getting your boss involved to go to the next level with any issue, it is very important that the Company Officer has completed the proper documentation on the issue. At this stage in the progression, there should be a lot of supporting documentation that justifies writing up the member and your boss should be involved in the loop as soon as the Officer recognizes that the issue might not go away.

Example: A 10-year Firefighter bids into the open spot on your Engine company and he is now a permanent member of your crew. He has worked at slower stations the last 5 years and he is 50 pounds overweight. On his second shift at the station, you go drilling and do a set of hose stretches that he makes non-passing errors on or he finishes the evolution well over the time limit allowed. You were also planning on throwing ladders during the drill, but the new member starts vomiting, he is too exhausted to continue, and you end the drill session. Back at the station you go right to a career counseling session and you tell the new member all the areas that he needs to improve on based on the last 45 minutes of his performance. When talking to him, he is quite aware of and admits that his performance was well below standards. **IMMEDIATELY** after talking to him you should go to your office and document the following into your personal log:

- The date, time, and place of the occurrence
- The specific evolutions performed and failed
- The specifics of the errors made and the unsatisfactory completion times
- The physical conditioning witnessed. For example: "Firefighter was physically exhausted after 3 evolutions and he vomited repeatedly. The rest of the drill had to be canceled."
- The time and territory of the career counseling session and what was discussed in the conversation. For example: "When returning to station, in the apparatus bay, the unsatisfactory drill performance and the physical conditioning of the Firefighter were discussed right after returning to the station."
- What you as the Company Officer did to address the issue. For example: "The Firefighter was urged to call a department Peer-Fitness trainer to start getting him back up to meeting standards in terms of physical fitness and that his current physical condition is a huge contributing factor to his poor performances."
- The reaction of the person with the unsatisfactory performance or behavior when the issue was being addressed (accepting responsibility versus being defiant or apathetic). For example: "Firefighter Neglected took full responsibility for his performance in the counseling session."

Two shifts later, basically the same thing happens again while drilling. There is unsatisfactory drill performances and a lot of vomiting. This time the corrective conversation happens in your office and you inform the new member that the conversation that is about to happen is a verbal counseling. The most important thing to find out in the meeting is if the member has made contact with a department Peer-Fitness trainer. He replies that he has not. Again, **IMMEDIATELY** after talking to him you should document the same information and details into your personal log.

At this point, you realize that this is a "neglected" Firefighter who has not drilled in over 5 years and he will not turn into a "super" Firefighter in just a few shifts. You also have great concerns that until that happens, the member detracts from the company's effectiveness in critical situations that require extended periods of physical exertion of 10 to 12 minutes (a standard work cycle on working fires). This is about the time you give your Battalion Chief a call and give them a heads up on what is going on and where you think the issue is headed so that they are not surprised if the situation needs to officially go into the system in the future.

Over 2 more months of documenting every failed field experience and unsatisfactory drill performance, several more counseling sessions on the matter occur. All the while, your keeping your boss informed about the situation every couple shifts. There is some overall improvement, but Firefighter Neglected is still not consistently meeting standards and has also not lost any noticeable weight. In the last verbal counseling session performed with him after another unsatisfactory drill performance, he admits again that he still has not contacted a Peer-Fitness trainer. After hearing this, you make the member sign a written record of a verbal reprimand and you inform him that it is time to take the issue to the next level and for him to stand-by.

Before calling your Battalion Chief, you go over the 25 pages of notes that you have documented into your personal log the past few months and you jot down the major information points you need to convey. When talking to your Battalion Chief, you cover the following points on the issue (hopefully, they have already been informed of most of this):

- Firefighter Neglected has been here for 3 months.
- You have drilled 15 times (almost every other shift) and a total of 45 evolutions were performed.
- Firefighter Neglected had unsatisfactory performances on 19 of those evolutions.
- You have had 4 working fires that required at least 1 full work cycle (12 minutes) and Firefighter Neglected had unsatisfactory performances on 2 of those working fires.
- You have documented a total of 7 official counseling sessions (5 after drills and 2 after working fires), as well several other corrective feedback discussions with the member.
- Firefighter Neglected is out of shape to the point that it makes him vomit when under physical stress and his SCBA air consumption rates are twice than the other crew members', which greatly shortens the company's work cycles on emergency scenes.
- Firefighter Neglected has been repeatably urged to make contact with a Peer-Fitness trainer to address his fitness and nutrition issues and to date he has not made contact.
- You suggest that Firefighter Neglected be formally written up and be remanded into a Peer-Fitness training program while you continue to drill and work with him at the station.

The Battalion Chief agrees with you. The Battalion Chief has you write up the yellow sheet of unsatisfactory performance and states they will call the Union and will set up a meeting at the station in the next few hours. The Battalion Chief ends by requesting that you also start preparing an API and that it should be the central discussion point in the conversation. You respond back to the Battalion Chief that you have already prepared the yellow sheet and the API and you are ready for meeting with Firefighter Neglected.

In your office 4 hours later, Firefighter Neglected is officially written up for his performances. Also in your office is your Battalion Chief, Firefighter Neglected's Union representative, and a Peer-Fitness trainer. The meeting lasts just over 20 minutes with most of the discussion centered around the API.

In a 3-month period that started with the "official" write up, Firefighter Neglected finally connected with the Peer-Fitness trainer (because he was remanded into the program), he loses over 25 pounds, and he goes from an almost 40% fail rate on drill and field evolutions to a consistent 0%. It took the Battalion Chief and everyone else in the room to finally make him realize that some serious adjustments were needed on his part to fix his issues and that no one was picking on him. He also knew that his Company Officer was being fair, but he was serious about the performance of the Engine company and everyone on the company meeting standards.

Every yellow sheet and API should have a path to get square with the organization again. Firefighter Neglected met all requirements necessary to fix his issues and he got square again. The yellow sheet that you had written him was permanently removed from his personnel file 6 months after it was placed there. After this was done, the Battalion Chief called and thanked you for doing such a professional job of handling the situation and he added that Firefighter Neglected should be happy that you are his Company Officer.

Based on this example, you can understand how much work and effort there is for a Company Officer to do when dealing with a chronic issue like this. Sometimes, the Company Officer will have to put more time and effort into solving an issue than the member that is having it puts in. That is why there are so many Firefighter Neglected's out there - because so many Company Officers do not want to put all the work in that is required to fix issues or help people become better at doing their job. Please do not be that Officer!

2. A One-Time Event Involving a very Serious Infraction

Most serious infractions fall on the shoulders of the Company Officer since they are the one responsible for most everything that goes on during a shift. An event like blowing up a large water main while not following SOPs when checking hydrants (mentioned in a previous background) will get you in trouble every time. Most safety type of infractions (like running red lights) also fall on the Company Officer because, again, they are the ones responsible for most everything that goes on during a shift. However, some serious infractions that could warrant a crew member to be written up include:

- Serious mistreatment of a customer
- Some forms of insubordination
- Gross neglect, misuse, or purposeful destruction of department property
- Going AWOL (Away Without Relief)
- Title VII – HR infractions with coworkers (described next)

Most of these occurrences will be obvious and many of them will also require the Company Officer to first stabilize the situation before going through with the follow-up process. Like all issues that require a member to be written up, you must call your Battalion Chief first, before proceeding to the next step.

3. Title VII HR Harassment or Hostile Work Environment Issue

ALL TITLE VII VIOLATIONS (OR SUSPECTED VIOLATIONS) MUST BE TAKEN TO YOUR BOSS IMMEDIATELY!

This includes:

- Inappropriate visual conduct or harassment

- Inappropriate verbal conduct or harassment
- Inappropriate physical conduct or harassment
- Inappropriate sexual conduct or harassment
- Any other behavior directed toward another member at the workplace that any normal person would consider "hostile"

All the above items not only threaten the person's career who is acting out any of these behaviors, but they can also threaten the Company Officer's career if they do not handle the situation correctly.

Witnessed Title VII Violations

If a Company Officer witnesses any of these activities, it should create a sympathetic nervous system discharge, in which the situation must be addressed and stabilized immediately (stopped). Once stabilized, perform a brief follow-up in your office with the member so that everyone on the crew knows you are dealing with the issue (like with Firefighter Inappropriate) and that these behaviors are absolutely unacceptable in the workplace. Once in your office, convey to Firefighter Inappropriate in the follow-up meeting that their behavior is absolutely unacceptable, it also threatens your job, and you are going to call your Battalion Chief to get their advice on how to proceed further. **Dismiss Firefighter Inappropriate and then do what your Battalion Chief tells you to do after you call them.**

Your Battalion Chief's response should be based on several different things:

- What was actually said and its severity
- History of the member (previous occurrences)
- The member's overall attitude when addressing the issue (accepting responsibility versus being defiant or apathetic)

Un-Witnessed Title VII Violations

An example will follow, but as previously presented, all un-witnessed Title VII violations need to immediately go up the chain of command (a Company Officer is not paid to be a private detective).

Example: You work on a 4-person company. Your crew consists of:

- Engineer – 10 years on the job, 5 years as an Engineer, 3 years at the station
- Senior Firefighter – 8 years on the job, 4 years at the station
- Junior Firefighter – 4 years on the job, 1 year at the station

Your Senior Firefighter sustained a knee injury and he will be off duty for 4 to 6 weeks. Division has sent over a roving Firefighter that has 3 years on the job to temporarily fill his position until he returns back to duty. He has worked at the station for two weeks and he has performed well on drills and when delivering service.

After dinner you get a knock on your office door. It is your Engineer and she asks if she can talk to you for a moment in private. In your office she informs you that the temporary Firefighter has been creating a hostile work environment. She states, "Ever since he got here, he keeps calling me either the "C" word or the "B" word. He has said it 7 times. The first time and every time since he has called me that, I have told him to never call me that and I'm sick of it and him." Red Alert! Red Alert! An unwitnessed Title VII violation!

At this point, the biggest thing in your mind should be to CALL YOUR BOSS ASAP! Before doing that, you will need a little more information. Here is what you ask:

- Can you remember the specific time and place of each occurrence? She states, "Yes, I have them all written down."
- Was there any other person that witnessed any of the occurrences? She states, "No, he only lets them fly when no one else is around."
- What is his response when you tell him to knock it off? She states, "On two occasions, he called me that word again and he has not stopped. The last time was an hour before dinner on the apparatus bays. I told him after the last event that I was sick of him and I was taking the matter to you."

At this point, tell your Engineer that this type of behavior is absolutely unacceptable, that you are going to call your boss, and that you will talk to her again later after talking to your Battalion Chief. **Excuse your Engineer from the meeting, call your Battalion Chief, and then do what your Battalion Chief tells you to do after you call them.**

At this point, DO NOT:

- DO NOT ask your Engineer what she would like to happen to resolve the issue. If you do this and it is not resolved to her liking, she will be even more upset with the outcome and you. Let the Brass ask her this question.
- DO NOT interview the Firefighter being accused. If you do this, there is a high likelihood that he will deny ever saying anything and now you are stuck with figuring out who is telling the truth. Let the Brass interview him.
- DO NOT interview and ask the other Firefighter on the truck if they ever witnessed anything. Doing this could alert him to a situation that he previously knew nothing about. This act could also get you into trouble because you are sharing very sensitive HR information with a person that has no business hearing anything about the issue unless they are directly involved in the matter. Let the Brass decide if he needs to be interviewed.

Do try to keep the two crew members separated to avoid having another occurrence in the next 30 minutes (until you and your boss can address the issue with the Firefighter).

As previously presented, a Company Officer attempting to solve Title VII problems on their own could make the problem worse, it could significantly increase the department's liability in the matter, and it could even threaten the Company Officer's career. Do not do it! Take all Title VII HR matters up the chain of command starting with your boss AS SOON AS THE SITUATION HAS BEEN STABILIZED.

You call your Battalion Chief and explain the issue. They tell you the following:

- I am quietly taking you out of service.
- I will be there in less than 15 minutes.
- Document what your Engineer told you (each word if possible).
- Do not talk to anyone else about the matter and I will meet you in your office when I get there.

Once your Battalion Chief arrives at the station, go with the flow and do what you are told. Your Battalion Chief might also involve other people in the issue. This could include their boss, as well as people from the Personnel Division. At this point, a Company Officer:

- Is not trained to conduct an HR investigation
- Has NO authority to decide any of the consequences for any violations committed
- Has limited knowledge and/or experience running any of the complex HR processes that will happen way above their rank

NON-HR Related Issues that your Boss Should Know About

These issues include:

- Any time your unit will be out of service (others who may also need to be notified include the dispatch center, Shift Commander, mechanic shop, etc.)
- All vacancies and injuries that will cause time off, which is made easier with modern day staffing programs and smart phones
- Any non-department scheduled out of station drill or out of service drill
- Major station repairs and lack of emergency equipment/supplies will usually have to go through your Battalion Chief and/or the Resource Management Division
- Any time your apparatus hits anything
- Anything else you have a "gut feeling" about

2. When NOT to Call your Boss

Most of the major issues that require you to call your boss have been covered. However, I am sure there are other issues that were not covered that will come up that will require a phone call to your boss. Other than these issues, you do not need to call your boss for much else.

The daily management and communications with your crew members does not need to go up the chain of command. Just manage your company, do lots of drilling, deliver good service, and be nice.

Department HR Resources

Most issues that go up the chain of command have other contributing factors associated with them that also need to be addressed (covered in an upcoming chapter). Most career fire departments provide access to several HR resources that can greatly assist in getting members with work and/or off-duty personal issues back on track. These resources include:

Operations Division chain of command (the Brass) – A Company Officer's boss is usually a Battalion Chief, but any sworn chief above their rank represent the Brass. All the Brass on most smaller fire departments will either be involved in fixing major HR issues or at a minimum, they will be acutely aware of them. Depending on what the problem is, along with all the other different rank systems and organizational structures that are used, a Company Officer could have a lot of brass sitting in the same room when an issue is being addressed. Hopefully, they are all there to support a Company Officer who followed all the HR rules and the progressions of discipline and they are not there to put Captain Simmer in line.

Personnel Division - Larger fire departments will usually have their own Personnel Division. Smaller departments will usually hook-up with their city's Personnel Department and/or they will use contract services to deal with the more serious personnel issues (lawyers and such).

These people are the experts in Title VII HR policy, procedures, law practices, precedence, etc. Company officers are NOT TRAINED to deal with these issues. Leave it to the professionals, stay out of their way, and do not do anything to make things worse!

Employee Assistance Program (EAP) – This is usually a voluntary, confidential, work-based program that offers free assessments, short-term counseling, referrals, and follow-up services to employees who have personal and/or work-related mental wellness issues. Some Firefighters that are in the system can also be remanded into an EAP to assist in dealing with some of the personal issues related to the performance/behavior issue the member is having on the department.

Most EAPs do not specialize in treating PTSIs or addiction. Members who are having these types of issues must seek out "culturally competent" clinicians who have been identified as those who understand the fire service, the personnel who work in it, and what they are exposed to daily. They also are up to date on best practices for the treatment of PTSIs. These clinicians may be covered by your current health insurance carrier. Many Peer Support Team members know who these people are.

Peer-Support Team – This is an internal resource of co-workers with special training in CISM. Typically, their responsibility is to check on crews/individuals following a powerful emergency incident that has the potential to create a stress reaction. Their job is to evaluate the crew/individual and keep/get them operational or pulled out of service. They are also a great resource for reminding the crew of tools for resiliency and other self-care options. Many states have laws that protect conversations with a trained peer, so co-workers feel safe talking to them. They also are a great resource for referrals to qualified/competent mental health providers

Health Center – A typical fire department Health Center provides the following for their membership:

- Evaluate and treat any member who has been subjected to any work-related injury, illness, or exposure

- Provide strength training and nutrition programs
- Provide annual physicals
- Track and manage the overall work-related health records and exposure data throughout a member's career

Most fire departments are not large enough to fund their own "Health Center" and they will contract these services out to another occupational health and wellness provider. Most fire departments that use contract health services usually have a consistent place that members go to for work related health issues.

Firefighter Neglected was 30 years old and he was not so out of shape that his Company Officer thought that his health was threatened by physical exertion. He just needed to lose weight and get into better shape, but he was reluctant to do so. In this case, the Health Center provided a Peer-Fitness trainer to help get the member back on track.

Your local Health Center could also come into play if you have a Firefighter Neglected that comes through your station doors who is not just out of shape, but physically appears and behaves in a manner that their current health status not only prevents them from doing their job, but also jeopardizes their overall welfare. This type of situation will be covered in detail in the upcoming chapter on being fit for duty.

Peer-Fitness Trainer for Physical Fitness and Nutrition –To recap (presented in a previous chapter), Peer Fitness trainers are a tremendous resource for a fire company. These people are actual Firefighters who have been trained and certified as personal trainers with the single focus of the physical requirements and ergonomics of performing the routine tasks of firefighting.

Peer-Fitness trainers are a great resource to help Company Officers get all the Firefighter Neglected's out there physically back on track in the most positive and productive way possible.

Department Chaplain - Many fire departments across the country, large and small, have a dedicated Chaplain. They provide very important services to the fire department and to the community. These services can include:

- Visiting fire stations to boost morale
- Performing weddings, baptisms, funerals, etc. when requested by members
- Providing some light, confidential counseling to members when requested
- Responding to major injury incidents involving a Firefighter and being available to make or assist with family notifications when requested by the department
- Hospital visits to the membership, when requested
- Responding to high stress incidents to assist in dealing with the customer and/or their family members
- Many are members of the CISM Team
- Being available to the Brass for special projects and assignments that concern the membership's welfare

Chapter 27

Producing Written Action Plans for Improvement (APIs)

As presented in the last chapter, there is a lot of work for a Company Officer when a member is put into the system for an on-the-job performance or behavior issue. A lot of that work goes into the administrative responsibilities of the process. One of those responsibilities is producing a written API. An API will be required most of the time a member is written up and put into the system, especially when it concerns a performance issue.

The purpose of an API is to identify and define the specific issue in a member's work performance or behavior that is not meeting standards, clarifying the expectations of the standard or policies being violated, and then providing an action plan for improvement to the member so they have an opportunity to address their performance or behavioral issues with the overall goal of the member correcting their issue in order to get them back into good standing with the organization.

I will highlight the Firefighter Neglected example used in the previous chapter as the guide for preparing an API. To recap, this is a 10-year Firefighter that has not drilled in the last 5 years, he is now 50-pounds overweight, he is out of shape and failing over 40% of MCS field and drill engagements.

The major components of an API include:

1. Identify the performance/behavior that does not meet standards – In this section, all performance and/or behaviors that did not meet standards should be listed. The Phoenix Fire Department had a Manual that contained the MCS task level evolutions with accompanying check off sheets for each riding position. Each checkoff sheet contained at least 1 or 2 items that, if not performed correctly, constituted an "immediate failure" of the evolution. For example, the Firefighter did not put the hose clamp on the supply line and the supply hose bed was flooded. Even if the Firefighter did everything else correctly, they would still fail the evolution. Here, the Company Officer would reference the standard MCS evolutions that had an unsatisfactory performance or immediate failures.

In addition, the Company Officer would also detail that Firefighter Neglected's physical conditioning was not meeting standards. The best way to document not meeting physical conditioning standards is to reference the person's SCBA air consumption rates and their performance while under physical stress. Air consumption rates are a medically proven mechanism to determine the overall conditioning of a human. At NO time throughout the API should you document Firefighter Neglected's weight issues. Always tie conditioning to air consumption rates and performance - not physical appearance. Referring to a person's physical appearance is discriminatory. Only address performances and/or behaviors. I worked with several overweight Firefighters during my career who were still highly competent and performed at high levels on drills and emergency scenes. Being overweight is not a condition of employment - proper performance and behaviors are.

API documentation – Firefighter Neglected has had several documented failed MCS evolutions while riding in the Senior Firefighter position (see the documentation portion of the last chapter). Over the past 90 days, this includes unsatisfactory performances on 17 of 45 drill evolutions and on 2 field incidents that included failures in the following categories:

MCS Manual – Section 3 – Evolutions 2, 3, 5, 6, 8, 11, and 14

Firefighter Neglected's physical conditioning is a very large contributing factor to his unsatisfactory performances while doing any MCS activity under physical stress. On the last 4 working fires, Firefighter Neglected's air consumption rates were over twice the rate of his fellow crew members (including myself). This non-standard performance has drastically reduced our company's work cycle while wearing SCBAs from 10 to 12 minutes to less than 6 minutes before the crew has to exit the hazard zone due to Firefighter Neglected being low on air.

MCS Manual – Section 5 – Physical conditioning standard 2.3 – Not maintaining a minimum aerobic capacity of 42 mL/.

2. Outline expected standard – The Company Officer would outline the expectations of the standards that the member is failing to meet. It is repetitive, but it takes any vagueness out of the document and it gives the member going through this process very clear expectations of what they will have to do to get back into good standing.

API documentation – During several drills and field deployments, Firefighter Neglected has had several immediate failures and several failed completion times while performing Evolutions 2, 3, 5, 6, 8, 11, and 14 out of the MCS Manual (see supporting documentation). Firefighter Neglected must improve his performance to the point that he consistently completes all MCS evolutions under their specified time frames along with having no immediate failures during an evolution.

Firefighter Neglected's SCBA air consumption rates are well below the minimum standard set in the MCS Manual – Section 5 – Physical conditioning standard 2.3 and this plays a significant role in Firefighter Neglected's performance. Firefighter Neglected must increase his aerobic conditioning to a minimum aerobic capacity of 42 mL/ if he wants to perform to standards.

3. Provide specific examples for the need of the API – The Company Officer would go over the progressive discipline that has occurred and how Firefighter Neglected got to this point.

API documentation - The drilling ground is the place to have things go wrong while building competencies. Some failures are expected to happen, but having consistent failures on both drills and while on field deployments in live settings is unacceptable and is unsafe for everyone involved. The lack of physical conditioning is a major contributing factor to Firefighter Neglected's unsatisfactory performance and if not addressed, he will continue to have unacceptable failures not only on the drill grounds, but in the field as well. Over the past 90 days, Firefighter Neglected's performance has improved to some degree, but it is still consistently unsatisfactory and it must improve during the time frames specified in this API.

After several drills, field deployments, and counseling sessions, Firefighter Neglected states that he understands the seriousness of the issues he is facing and he has had a positive attitude in dealing with the situation, while showing some improvements.

4. Identify needed training and support – In addition to the administrative work a Company Officer must complete when writing up a member is the physical work you will need to perform when dealing with a member with a performance issue. This is where a Company Officer would detail all the drilling and PT that would be required in order for Firefighter Neglected to get back to meeting standards. Also, list any other HR support programs that are needed or mandated in the API.

This can be a double-edged sword. Firefighter Neglected probably wants to perform all this drilling so that he can quickly improve and put this entire issue behind him as soon as possible. What hinges on this is the Company Officer following through with the task list in the API. If this does not happen and Firefighter Neglected's performance does not improve, it is ALL ON THE COMPANY OFFICER because they did not follow through with their own plan (LAZY!). This creates a situation in which Firefighter Neglected cannot improve his performance and it also puts him in the driver seat if the Company Officer still wants to hold him accountable for his performances (Firefighter Neglected cannot take the truck and go out and drill by himself).

API documentation – At a minimum, Firefighter Neglected will need to perform at least 4 MSC drill evolutions over the course of every 2 shifts. These drills will all focus on MCS Manual – Section 3 – Evolutions 2, 3, 5, 6, 8, 11, and 14. This drilling schedule will continue during the time frames specified in this API.

Based on the direction of his Peer-Fitness trainer, Firefighter Neglected will follow the diet and workout routine specified every shift while on duty for the duration of the time frames specified in this API.

Based on the direction of his Peer-Fitness trainer, Firefighter Neglected will also follow all off-duty diet and exercise routines specified in his training program for the duration of the time frames specified in this API.

Firefighter Neglected must get his minimum aerobic capacity above 42 mL/ within the specified time frames of this API.

Background: As previously presented, L-201 was where the system sent their problem child Probationary Firefighters. Most of them were on their last field rotation and ALL of them were the victims of lazy Company Officers. NONE of them drilled 1 time after getting out of the academy. As previously stated, they all became rock stars in a short period of time.

Most of the problem children were in good physical condition and their biggest problem was their former Captains not drilling with them. It did not take very long for most of them to fall back into the groove once they started getting their hands dirty again. This usually happened by the end of their first month at the station (less than 10 shifts).

However, L-201 did have a couple Probationary Firefighters that had both a lack of drilling and a physical fitness issue. They were not as bad as 10-year Firefighter Neglected, but it was still a contributing factor to some of their poor performances and it took longer to get them back up to speed and meeting standards.

The point of this background is that the other crew members on L-201 were all highly competent and they did not mind going out and drilling once every 2 shifts. They also did not mind taking a problem child drilling every shift for about month straight because they saw improvements in these people every shift and they knew the other side of the rainbow was not too far away. When it came to the other 1 or 2 Probationary Firefighters who took a lot longer to get there (20 plus shifts in a row of drilling versus 8 or 9), they got tired of it - sometimes to the point that I really had to become a shield for these people.

This is a natural occurrence that happens inside of a group of people when one person is lacking and the rest have to suffer through it while having their routines changed when "they didn't do anything wrong." I understood it, but I did not care. I cared a lot more about how I would want to be treated if I was having the same kind of problem and the last thing these neglected Probationary Firefighters needed was taking grief from their fellow crew members because the system had failed them - not the other way around.

Always protect these people and do whatever you can to help them become successful.

5. Identify the need to mandate other tasks or activities –A mandate is an official order to do something that has a consequence attached to it if what is specified is not performed or successfully completed. In many cases, mandates are a condition of employment and if the member fails to meet the mandate at any time, it could lead to immediate termination. The only way to mandate a Firefighter into a department program is if that member is in the system and their Union representation also agrees to it (if applicable). One of the biggest reasons for writing up Firefighter Neglected was to be able to mandate him into an HR program that would improve his performance and help him solve the issues because he was not taking the initiative to do it himself.

Another HR program that is often mandated is the EAP to help a member solve any possible personal mental wellness issues that are contributing to their on-the-job issues.

API documentation – This API is officially mandating Firefighter Neglected into a Peer-Fitness training and nutrition program with the overall goal of getting Firefighter Neglected's aerobic conditioning to a minimum aerobic capacity of 42 mL/ within the time frame specified in this API.

Firefighter Neglected will meet and consult with his Peer-Fitness trainer based on the schedule his Peer-Fitness trainer prescribes. Failure to do so or failure to follow any suggested fitness or dieting routines recommended by his Peer-Fitness trainer will automatically jeopardize Firefighter Neglected's ability to complete this API.

6. Schedule check-ins, review points, and set finishing time frames to achieve goals–
This is one of the most important segments of an API and it is where the basic plan and all the time frames and deadlines are laid out for the member to correct their unsatisfactory performance.

API documentation - *Firefighter Neglected will have no more than 90 days to meet standards for both his MCS performances and his aerobic conditioning capacity. Firefighter Neglected will fit into the following plan and schedule for the duration of the next 90 days:*

- During the write up session, Firefighter Neglected will make initial contact with his Peer-Fitness trainer.
- Within 1 shift (3 days) of the write up session, Firefighter Neglected must meet with his Peer-Fitness trainer to be initially evaluated (baselined) and he will be given his first set of instructions from his Peer-Fitness trainer.
- Firefighter Neglected will meet or consult with his Peer-Fitness trainer whenever the Peer-Fitness trainer deems it necessary.
- Firefighter Neglected's Peer-Fitness trainer will provide a fitness progress report on Firefighter Neglected on a bi-weekly basis to all parties involved in the write-up session.
- Firefighter Neglected will perform and be evaluated on no less than 4 MCS evolutions every 2 shifts and his performance at the end of the 90-day API must fully meet MCS standards.
- At the end of 90-day period, Firefighter Neglected must consistently meet (90% +) all MCS time frames as well as performing to standards on all field deployments.
- All parties in Firefighter Neglected's write-up session will meet or consult with each other every 30 days until the 90-day compliance limit set in this API. These discussions will focus solely on Firefighter Neglected's progress in complying with this API.
- If, by any of the 30-day meetings, Firefighter Neglected's performance is not compliant (or is worsening), it could immediately cause the next steps to be taken in the disciplinary progression.

7. Sign and acknowledge – This category is self-explanatory and the more names that have signed it, the better it is for the Company Officer (more names equate to more support).

APIs are a huge part of the process of getting members that are having issues and are in the system back on track. Because they provide the road map to success or failure, they are a lot of work for everyone involved, especially for Firefighter Neglected and his Company Officer.

The amount of hard work involved when putting someone into the system is the reason there are so many Firefighter Neglected's out there. When something like this does happen (there is a lot of blame to go around, but the issue has to be fixed), these members deserve the right to admit their mistakes, get due process, and be given the opportunity to get back into good standing with the organization. It is a brother and sisterhood - all of us should act that way by continually helping each other (especially helping those that need it the most). If the whole organization acted in this manner, there would be no Firefighter Neglected's.

Chapter 28

Performance/Behavioral Issues Associated with Personal Wellness/Mental Health – Tim W. Dietz

We Hire Good People

Most organizations hire good people. When reflecting on your own hiring and academy with others, most of us have fond memories of our academy class working hard, supporting each other, and developing a bond of the brother/sisterhood in the fire service. Therefore, in most cases, when a co-worker/subordinate begins to change behaviors away from working hard, supporting each other, or severing this bond, it is most likely stress induced.

As presented throughout this book, the fire service is one of the most stressful occupations out there and it is one of the Company Officer's roles to help their crew maintain their resiliency to this stress. This chapter will not discuss how to address issues, nor dive deeply into types of corrective counseling, as these items have been thoroughly discussed in previous chapters. **What we will discuss in this chapter is when normal crew stress responses turn into behavioral health related issues that may interrupt shift dynamics, service delivery, and safety on the job.**

Knowing the personality type it takes to work in this high stress occupation, I will present the typical human symptomology of acute and delayed stress responses and the tools/resources we can use to assist those members being impacted by these symptoms.

The Backpack Analogy

We were all born with a backpack. This backpack holds experiences that we do not want to think about - things that are not supposed to happen. Because these events are not supposed to happen, the brain has a hard time processing them. Imagine in a person's lifetime the experiences they may have that really are not supposed to happen. Common things can include adverse childhood experiences (abuse, neglect, chaos in the home, etc.), unforeseen death or serious injury of loved ones by violence or accident, divorce, and/or fear of one's own serious injury or death. We shove these experiences in our backpack because we do not know what else to do with them – and in the backpack we do not have to think about them. The backpack has lots of room, so most humans can make it through a lifetime holding these events successfully. However, some of us have jobs where we see things or are involved in incidents that are not supposed to happen. Kids are not supposed to die or get seriously injured from any cause, nor are our co-workers. If one of our personality traits discussed earlier have been violated (e.g., we are in control, we can perform perfect or near perfect, we can solve others' problems, bad things do not bother us), that may go into our backpack. All this means is that a Firefighter's backpack may fill up sooner than the general population. Also, remember that we interpret things differently and we each use different tools to deal with stressors, so even folks working on the same crew can have backpacks that fill at different rates. If we are not dealing with/processing our stress effectively (past and present), our backpack will eventually fill up, start to leak, and the next thing you know, you are displaying signs and symptoms of stress like exhaustion, anxiety, trouble sleeping, irritability, and isolation (because you do not want to talk about it or let others see you struggling), etc.

The Human Response to Stressors (Fight or Flight at its Most Basic)

Stress in the fire service can be from the daily wear and tear of a combination of personal, environmental, and "typical" response incidents or a single significant event or "critical incident." For any of these situations the Firefighter deems as a threat, there is a biological action that takes place that we have no control over. We go into the survival response of "fight or flight" as a way to keep us alive.

The human response to an acute threat (as interpreted by the Firefighter) causes an immediate response of the structures in our survival brain (Limbic System). This activates a survival response, including the sympathetic nervous system (discussed in the training portion of this book), all with the intent of keeping us alive. Hormones are released – namely adrenalin (for immediate energy) and cortisol (for sustained energy). These hormones will increase your heartbeat, blood pressure, and breathing rate to aid you to fight or run. Non-essential bodily functions like digestion, immunity, and reproduction are shut down to shunt energy to muscles. Blood glucose levels go up for fuel, the spleen increases red blood cells to promote oxygen supply, the vascular system constricts to keep pressures up to get the fuel to needed areas, and cognitive areas of the brain are suppressed (quit thinking and respond). This occurs in a couple of seconds or less. Back at the fire station, a Firefighter in a "fight or flight" response may display the following normal signs/symptoms:

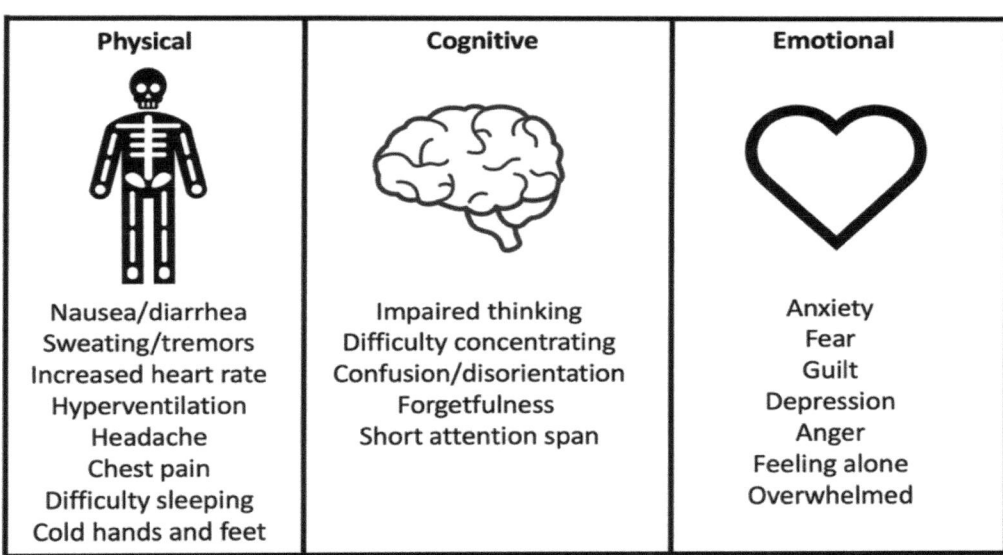

Physical	Cognitive	Emotional
Nausea/diarrhea	Impaired thinking	Anxiety
Sweating/tremors	Difficulty concentrating	Fear
Increased heart rate	Confusion/disorientation	Guilt
Hyperventilation	Forgetfulness	Depression
Headache	Short attention span	Anger
Chest pain		Feeling alone
Difficulty sleeping		Overwhelmed
Cold hands and feet		

The purpose of this "fight or flight" survival response is to keep us alive when we feel threatened. It has done its job well as humans still exist! However, there is a downside for those continually exposed to stressors. When you take an event and attach it to an emotion (fear, sadness, guilt, anger, overwhelmed, etc.), it gets imprinted in the survival brain. This happens so that if we encounter something similar in the future, we can rapidly react to survive again. Once more, the intent of this is to keep us alive! However, there can be a problem if you work in the emergency response business. The station bells that you heard before the horribly tragic fatal fire may have been imprinted with that incident and the next time you hear them your body goes into survival mode and you get sick to your stomach. Driving through the intersection where that family tragically died may cause your heart rate to increase. These are known as "triggers." Why is this a problem? Because as more and more stressful experiences pile up over a career, there are more experiences imprinted - triggering us more often. Every time we get triggered (go into survival response), adrenalin and cortisol are released. It is not such a fun career if every time the station bells ring, or the radio squelches, or you hear screeching brakes, someone yelling, a gunshot, a child cry, or you drive through "that intersection," past "that vacant lot," by "that school," near "that shopping mall," or you smell smoke (even at a BBQ) your body goes into survival mode and releases stress hormones. And while cortisol is important for short-term survival, it can have long-term negative effects on our health.

Managing Employees with the Symptoms of Stress

What we will discuss in this chapter is what happens if an employee's stress symptomology begins to impact the crew's service level, becomes a safety issue, or violates a shift expectation or organizational policies. Remember the crew expectations John gave us earlier in the book:

"I EXPECT ALL OF US to be self-motivated and to show up every morning and do the job we were trained and are paid to do at the highest level possible."

In other words, give our customers the best level of service possible! Plus, we have these implicit (unspoken but understood) expectations:

- Respect your co-workers and our customers
- Be nice
- Show up on time
- Work hard
- Follow all the safety SOPs (like wearing your seat belt)

If a company officer does need to communicate (address) a violation of any of these core shift/organizational expectations with a crew member (like, you *really do* NEED to be nice) something is out of balance with that person. The issue must be dealt with and most of time, it will need to be looked at in 2 separate ways:

1. Standard disciplinary process and progression (being accountable for your behaviors)
2. Mental wellness recognition of stress symptoms and the recommendation process

As far as managing a company, it really does not matter if the issue is performance based or behavioral health based. If a shift expectation has been violated, the issue needs to be addressed.

A couple of very important things to keep in mind when handling behavioral health issues with a crew member are:

- Your role in dealing with a behavioral health issue on your crew is as a Company Officer – **NOT as a therapist.**
- As a Company Officer, we can help guide/support an employee, but our crew members still have to be accountable for their behaviors/actions.

Dealing with Behavioral Health Issues

I will cover the following topics:

  1. Watch-outs

2. How to handle
3. Resources

1. Watch-outs

Delayed symptomology can present as:

- Fatigue
- Depression
- Irritability
- Trouble sleeping
- Non-specific anxiety
- Change in eating habits
- Loss of emotional control
- Loss of sex drive
- Increased arguments
- Behaving "out of character"
- Drop in work performance

As stated earlier, if there is ANY change in normal behavior of a crew member, chances are something is going on with them, whether they admit to it or not. If something did not happen at work, then something is going on in their personal life. Our job as a Company Officer is to recognize the change and intervene with the intent of making sure the employee is able to be productive and safe at work or get them to the needed assistance. Common behaviors of a struggling employee that the Company Officer needs to "watch out" for include:

1. Isolation – disengaging from crew activities
2. Irritability, argumentative, negativity
3. Seems distant, distracted or disengaged
4. Talking less/is quieter
5. Loss of enthusiasm – Loss of interest in work – Lateness, tardiness - fatigued
6. Making light of or using sarcasm regarding serious calls, importance of training/safety, or other crew expectations
7. Change in eating habits
8. Trouble sleeping
9. Any other change from their norm or they behave out of character

While many of us have experienced some of these in our careers, and in fact these can be normal acute responses to working in a high stress environment, they become concerning when they do not subside and begin to impact our ability to do our jobs.

Behavioral issues that warrant a Company Officers response/intervention:

- Isolation – from crew meetings, shift meals, training/shift activities
- Irritability/argumentative/negativity directed at customers or the crew - constant negativity that is causing crew strife
- Distant/distracted/disengaged when it impacts crew performance/safety in the field or they are not paying attending to important information or training
- Talking less/loss of enthusiasm/tardiness when it impacts the off-going crew, your crew readiness, and/or begins to impact crew morale

- Making light of/Sarcasm regarding serious calls, or other serious expectations when it becomes offensive to other crew members
- Drop in work performance
- Decreased personal hygiene
- Any other behavior that impacts the crew's ability to perform at their highest level, safely, and/or creates a hostile work environment

How to Handle (Remember that we address the behavior - NOT the feelings)

Fortunately, if the Company Officer addresses behavioral health concerns when they are first noticed, discusses their concern, encourages self-care, requests available resources, and then supports the employee, all while LEADING BY EXAMPLE (e.g., exercise, coughing up apples to keep them from filling our backpack, High-Low at evening meal, etc.), in many cases the issues will be remedied because Firefighters are resilient and sometimes, they just need to be reminded to continue self-care.

As the Company Officer, you should also be familiar with available resources to point the employee to. You ARE NOT their counselor, but you can remind them of resources of people they can talk to in confidence.

Remember, all verbal counseling sessions should be documented by the Company Officer. The big difference in this category is if you share that documentation with the member having the issue. Most verbal counseling that is done with a permanently assigned member is NOT officially documented on paper that the member signs the document acknowledging that counseling session occurred. I would only do a written record of a verbal counseling with the member signing it if:

- There is a strong feeling the issue was not going away and the problem would eventually escalate beyond my level of authority
- It was for a non-permanent member who I had no previous work history with
- It was for a serious offense
- Any verbal counseling session with a Probationary Firefighter

Review previous chapters for progressive discipline and documentation options. There may also come a time when someone's behavioral health issues warrant immediate action and getting your boss involved. These may include, but are not limited to:

- The smell of alcohol on their breath/person or appear to be under the influence of substances
- They become combative or have anger and/or rage issues
- They give indications of self-harm or harm to others
- Any Title VII HR harassment or hostile work environment issue
- Any behavior that in the Company Officer's opinion warrants the next level of discipline
- You have gone through progressive discipline and behavior has not changed

If behavioral health issues get to the point that others are involved (Battalion Chief, Operations Chief, and most likely the Personnel Department), the employee may now be remanded into a program such as EAP or other counseling and/or a psychological evaluation.

Here is an example:

You have worked with Engineer Ed for the past 10 years. Ed has a great reputation in the organization as knowing the apparatus inside and out and being an amazing mechanical trouble shooter. As a matter of fact, this was true the first 5 years you worked with Ed. The past five however, beginning with the loss of Ed's dad, then a divorce 2 years ago, you have seen a slow decline in Ed's enjoyment and enthusiasm at work. You have noticed Ed disengaging from the crew banter, preferring to exercise alone, and spending more time in the dorm when the rest of the crew is together watching TV. You have chatted with Ed in the past about what you have noticed, but he has denied any problems and until today, this has never impacted his ability to do the job. This morning, Ed showed up at work right at shift change, went into the locker room, and failed to talk with the off-going driver. He is very quiet at shift briefing and sarcastic when other crew members say something to him. You go into the bay while he is checking his apparatus and ask him if everything is alright. He simply states, "I'm fine." You respond with "Well you don't look like you are fine and if you need a break from work, let me know." He responds non-verbally by going back to his equipment check.

Does this warrant a follow-up conversation? I believe so. You call Ed into your office for "corrective feedback."

CO: *"Ed, this morning when I saw you show up for work on the hour and go into the locker room without checking in with the off-going driver, it frustrated me a bit because the off-going driver had to leave to get their kids to school. I am worried that we may have missed any important issues regarding the apparatus. What I need from you is to show up to work early enough every shift to go over the state of the apparatus with the off-going driver."*

Ed: *"This is the first time this has happened. Quit busting my butt over it. Our Firefighter chatted with the off-going driver and the apparatus is fine."*

CO: *"I get that Ed, but what I've also noticed over the past year or so is a change in you that worries me. When I watch you go into the dorm during down time when the rest of the crew is chatting, exercising, or watching a movie, it worries me because that is not like you."*

Ed: *"I come to work and do my job. I've got the same stuff going on in my life that others have, so don't worry about it."*

CO: *"But Ed, I am worried about it because I've noticed the change in you. And showing up to work as the other driver is leaving is beginning to impact our work. If you aren't already talking to someone about what's going on with you, we do have available resources. We have a Peer Support Team that you can talk to or point you to someone that could help. We also have an EAP."*

Ed: *"I'll think about it."*

CO: *"Please do that. I like working with you, but I miss the old Ed. I've got to have all of us game ready when we show up. Let me know how I can support you."*

A member hearing about the issues being noticed by their supervisor and having a formal counseling session, along with the adjustments that are required to get things back in balance, send a clear message that the Company Officer is serious about fixing the issue and that changes must be made on the member's part in order for the matter to start resolving itself.

Any issues that progress past this level of counseling may require the lawful part of the "system" to be involved in the process. Again, this includes your boss, the Personnel Division, and if in place, the Union. This issue has not escalated to that point yet, but after this career counseling with Ed, it would be wise to document the events leading up to the conversation with Ed, as well as giving your Battalion Chief (supervisor) an informal heads up on the matter in case the issue does not resolve.

Example Continued

For the past few months (following the corrective conversation), Ed has been showing up to work a little earlier. He is still a bell ringer, but allowing for the off-going driver to give an apparatus report to him. He also seems to be making an effort to engage with the crew, but he is still irritable. This morning, however, he shows up right on the hour, looks like he slept in his uniform, is unshaven, and his red eyes make you wonder whether he is fit-for-duty.

CO: *"Ed, let's have a chat in my office. When I saw you arrive right on the hour and not getting an apparatus report, it worries me. Plus, you don't look like you are ready to work. Are you okay?"*

Ed: *"I'm fine. I just had a long night."*

CO: *"Ed, I'm really worried about you and wonder If you should even be here. You don't look well. I'm going to call the Battalion Chief and take us out of service until we can get you replaced."*

Ed: *"I just had a long night. I'm okay."*

CO: *"Listen Ed, I am really worried about you and don't think it's safe for you to be here. I'm going to get the Battalion Chief involved. We have resources available here for you and if need be, I will do what I can to help you get back on your feet. Let's get you covered and get you some help."*

At this point, you will need to follow the progressive discipline recommendations laid out in the previous chapters of this book. This includes calling your boss and following their direction. As presented when discussing APIs, Ed will probably need to be remanded into an EAP or counseling because his mental wellness appears to be the main contributing factor causing his behavioral issues. Next, I describe some of the resources a department can use to help get Ed back on track.

Resources Inside of the Organization

Peer Support Team – This is an internal resource of co-workers with special training in CISM. Typically, their responsibility is to check on crews/individuals following a powerful emergency incident that has the potential to create a stress reaction. Their job is to evaluate the crew/individual and get them operational or pulled out of service. They are also a great resource for reminding the crew of tools for resiliency and other self-care options. Many states have laws that protect conversations with a trained peer (unless a mandated report is required), so co-workers feel safe talking to them. They also are a great resource for referrals to the mental health community.

Employee Assistance Program (EAP) – EAPs are usually a voluntary, completely confidential, work-based program that offer free assessments, short-term counseling, referrals, and follow-up services to employees who have personal and/or work-related mental wellness issues. Some Firefighters that are in the system can also be remanded into an EAP to assist in dealing with some of the other issues related to the performance/behavior issue the member is having on the department.

Resources Outside of the Organization

Culturally Competent Clinicians – Currently, very few EAP's specialize in treating PTSI or addiction issues. Members who are having these types of issues must seek out "culturally competent" clinicians who have been identified as those who understand the fire service, the personnel who work in it, and what they are exposed to daily. They also are up to date on best practices for the treatment of trauma. Many Peer Support Team members know who these people are. These clinicians may also be covered by your current health insurance carrier.

There are several programs available for the treatment of first responders suffering from addiction and/or post-traumatic stress. Here are a couple:

IAFF Center of Excellence - https://www.iaffrecoverycenter.com

The IAFF Center of Excellence offers a range of programs for the treatment of substance use disorders, as well as co-occurring behavioral health issues. Treatment is evidence-based, which means our methods have been proven effective through research and scientific inquiry. Our multidisciplinary approach — combining the expertise of doctors, nurses and clinicians from different disciplines — means we treat the whole person, not just the addiction or co-occurring disorder.

The IAFF Center of excellence has also identified "culturally competent" clinicians in each state as a resource for their members.

West Coast Post Trauma Retreat https://www.frsn.org

The West Coast Post Trauma Retreat program is for first responders whose lives have been affected by their work experience. This residential program provides treatment and educational experience designed to help current and retired first responders recognize the signs and symptoms of work-related stress, including PTSI, in themselves and in others and provides treatment and tools for continued recovery.

The core of the program includes intensive treatment in group and individual format, provided by "culturally competent" clinicians, peers, and a chaplain. The retreat also includes a 90-day plan for follow-up treatment and action steps.

Conclusion

Unlike much of the acute symptomology of emergency worker stress, which can be handled in the cab of the apparatus or around the kitchen table (if the culture supports it), when the stress symptomology begins to interfere with the Company Officer's expectations or becomes a performance/safety issue, it is typically because of a delayed/chronic stress response.

For the Company Officer:

- **Establish expectations early**
  - o **See something, say something**
- **Lead by Example**
  - o **Show by example the importance of self-care**
  - o **Exercise, coughing up apples, High-Low, checking in on each other**
- **Know the organization's resources**
  - o **Point the employee towards the proper help early**
- **When needed, follow progressive discipline guidelines**
  - o **The employee still has to be accountable for their actions**
  - o **The Company Officer can guide, but the employee has to take responsibility**
  - o **Know when to get your boss involved**

Delayed/chronic stress symptomology is bigger than the individual or crew to handle on their own. It takes specialized treatment by professionals who are competent in working with first responders. The quicker the individual seeks assistance, the easier it is to get back on their feet.

Work hard. Be nice. – Tim W. Dietz

Chapter 29

Fit for Duty

According to OSHA, the definition of fit for duty is - *an individual is in a physical, mental, and emotional state which enables the employee to perform the essential tasks of his or her work assignment in a manner which does NOT threaten the safety or health of oneself, co-workers, property, or the public at large.*

This book would add to this definition: "being sober and completely free of the effects of any drugs or alcohol while on duty."

The major Fit for Duty events that could present themselves to a Company Officer include:

1. Mental health
2. Physical health
3. Impairment due to drugs or alcohol
4. Insubordination

When looking at all these categories, Company Officers MUST consider, "Would I want this Firefighter in charge of the safety and welfare of one of my family members?"

1. Mental Health – Tim W. Dietz

As a Company Officer, you are ultimately responsible for the safety and operational capabilities of you and your crew. We know when someone is dealing with overwhelming or acute stress that their ability to be cognitive is suppressed, therefore impacting decision making abilities. This is not safe! As the boss, you need to be aware of the Behavioral Health "Watch-Outs" to keep your crew functioning safely. The "Watch-Outs" that would warrant a conversation/check-in include:

1. Bad Calls
2. Employee Behavior Change

1. Bad Calls - As discussed earlier in this book, each individual interprets emergency calls differently based on genetics, previous exposures to trauma, learned coping patterns, how close the call hits personally, etc. Realistically, you may want to check in with your crew after any call that may not been the norm, but certainly after:

- Calls involving kids, SIDS
- Violent death
- Multiple patients
- Disfigured bodies
- Fire fatalities
- Known victims
- Human to human harm (intentional)

- Calls with risk of injury to responders
- Line of Duty deaths
- Dealing with victim's family members at a scene
- Any call emotionally charged
- Or several of these types of calls compressed in a short period of time (3 or 4 shifts)

It is best to create the culture on your shift of an expectation that we talk about things that bother us - things that may be impacting our ability to stay focused. Remember the "coughing up the apple" analogy.

2. Employee Behavior Change - As a rule-of-thumb, if there is ANY change in normal behavior of a crew member, chances are something is going on with them, whether they admit to it or not. If something did not happen at work, then something is going on in their personal life. Our job as a Company Officer is to recognize this and intervene with the intent of making sure the employee is able to be productive and safe at work. The symptomology typically looks like this:

- Employee begins to isolate or disengage from the crew
- Employee becomes more irritable, argumentative
- Employee seems distant, distracted, or disengaged
- Employee talks less or is quieter
- Loss of enthusiasm or loss of interest in work
- Makes humor (sometimes morbid) out of everything (this is a way of deflecting)
- Change in eating habits
- Any other change from their norm

Firefighters tend to be very resilient to stressors. In most cases, a conversation (by you or a member of the Peer Support Team) that acknowledges it was a bad call or that they have a lot on their plate can help normalize their response to the issue. Remind them that they are resilient and that they have tools for self-care (exercise, talk to someone, eat healthy, avoid alcohol as a way to cope, etc.). Remember the available resources you can point them to.

If there is still a concern regarding an employee's ability to be operational at work, what are your resources? Do you have a Peer Support Team that can respond? Their job, in part, is to try to get the person back to cognitive (operational) and if not, to refer to the organization's guidelines/policies about relieving someone of duty. Some organizations allow the Battalion Chief or Peer Support Team member to take the overwhelmed person's unit out of service for up to an hour to let the individual/crew "catch their breath" and have a chat with the Peer Team member without interruption. If a person does need to be relieved of duty, organizations that have behavioral health programs in place tend to use administrative leave with these employees as long as they make it back their next duty day.

To recap, your role in all of this is to make sure you and your crew are operational and safe. If an employee displays signs/symptoms of overwhelming stress or has just returned from a bad call, it is your duty to check-in with them to make sure they are okay. If they are not, know your and your Firefighters' options and resources to remain at work or be relieved of duty.

Work hard. Be nice. – Tim W. Dietz

Physical Health – John Brunacini

The OSHA definition of fit for duty includes the term "physical." We begin here because this is what the Company Officer ultimately has to manage when it comes to physical fitness. Is the employee "physically" fit for duty? The definition of "physically fit for duty" can vary widely from department to department.

When things vary widely in our service from one department to another, a good starting point is having some sort of national standard to base activities on. The major national standards and programs that help guide fire departments in managing their membership's physical fitness are:

1. NFPA 1582 – Standard on Comprehensive Occupational Medical Program for Fire Departments
2. NFPA 1583 – Standard on Health-Related Fitness Programs for Fire Department Members
3. IAFF – Wellness & Fitness Initiative

1. NFPA 1582

NFPA 1582 attempts to standardize medical and fitness protocols into the fire service including the following:

- General physical job performance requirements for a Firefighter
- Types and scope of medical exams
- Annual medical evaluation benchmarks
- Annual fitness evaluation benchmarks
- Evaluation and classification of most known, specific medical problems/disabilities and the proper medical and fit for duty responses (example: 1582 states that if you have one eye or you are deaf, you cannot be a Firefighter in the field)

2. NFPA 1583

NFPA 1583 attempts to standardize medical and fitness protocols into the fire service including:

- Administrative coordination and data collection
- Fitness assessments
- Physical fitness training programs
- Peer fitness training program overview
- Implementation of best practices

3. IAFF – Wellness & Fitness Initiative

IAFF – Wellness & Fitness Initiative attempts to standardize medical and fitness protocols into the fire service including:

- Detailed annual physical exam benchmarks, exam guidelines, and testing methods

- Physical fitness program goals and objectives
- Injury and physical rehabilitation
- Behavioral health
- Administrative and supporting appendix

All 3 of these documents support and complement each other in trying to describe the level of health and fitness required to support firefighting activities along with the medical standards that support both the maintenance of the member and in determining if they are physically fit for duty (able to engage in firefighting activities).

All 3 documents have a consensus of what "physically" fit for duty is. It includes:

- Body Composition (body fat%) - men: less than 20% and women: less than 30%
- Aerobic Capacity – minimum of 42 mL
- Muscular strength and endurance to perform a set number of firefighting tasks under a certain time frame - CPAT
- Flexibility – measured in many ways

The best way to evaluate this level of fitness is through the performance of actual, physical, job-related activities that can occur at the typical fire scene (stretching hose, raising ladders, pulling ceiling, etc.). Because it is so easy to validate the level of fitness based on performing actual job activities, it has been institutionalized and incorporated into the Firefighter hiring and testing processes in the form of the CPAT. The CPAT is done wearing a simulated SCBA (weighted vest) and it consists of a sequence of events requiring the candidate to progress along a predetermined path from event to event in a continuous manner until the last event is completed in a predetermined time frame. This test was developed to allow fire departments to obtain pools of trainable candidates who are physically able to perform essential job tasks at fire scenes.

The CPAT's physical evaluation has become the benchmark for all professional firefighting personnel in the US in setting the **minimum level of fitness required** to actively engage in firefighting. If a Firefighter in the field cannot perform the tasks required in the CPAT, they DO NOT possess the **minimum level of fitness required** to actively engage in firefighting. Previous examples have demonstrated how to process a member having these issues.

To finish the background information needed when addressing a physical fitness or health issue, I will recap the Tier Medical ranking system that was covered in a previous chapter.

- Tier 1 – Low body fat (below 10%) – higher than normal aerobic capacity – superhuman. People in this category were mostly younger than 30 years old and you could see their abs.
- Tier 2 - Medium body fat (around 15%) – high to average aerobic capacity – a normal human in good shape – This was mostly everyone over 30 years old on the job.
- Tier 3 - High body fat (20%+) – low aerobic capacity – the absolute minimum physical condition that a member can be in and still operate in the field. Members in this category must be making progress to get back to being in at least the Tier 2 category.

- Tier 4 – A member's physical condition does not allow them to be a Firefighter in the field. This can be due to a medical issue/condition or from being grossly out of shape.

As presented earlier, Firefighter Neglected was at the beginning of a Tier 3 status. He was 30 years old with high body fat and low aerobic capacity, but he was not a diabetic, he did not have high blood pressure, nor was he taking any medications. The longer he was assigned to the station, the better shape he was in because the Company Officer was using the fire truck as a workout machine. When he finally connected with a Peer Fitness trainer, his progress rapidly increased and he went from a Tier 3 back to a Tier 2 within 90 days.

But what do you do when a Tier 4 walks through the doors at the beginning of the shift? A true Tier 4 person is not physically capable of performing the job to the point that it could also endanger their own health (and their crew's). Company Officers (and the rest of the department) must base their actions when dealing with members having these types of issues on NFPA Standards and the IAFF's Wellness & Fitness Initiative. These provide guidelines on what to base being physically fit for duty on. All a Company Officer can do is recognize that a member could be at a Tier 4 status, temporarily relieve the member from duty, and then send them to the department's physician (or ER) for them to determine if the member is physically fit for duty.

Many times, it will be obvious that a member is not in good health and that they should not be on a fire truck delivering service. They will probably agree with the Company Officer. With this group, you should just act in the best interest of the member and the company, send them to the department's physician (or ER) and then call your Battalion Chief. Here is an example: a middle-aged Firefighter arrives to work, they are ashen grey, they are having difficulty breathing, and they are looking distressed enough that the other crew members treat them like a patient and they have to deliver ALS service to one of their own crew members.

For a member that you know will not agree with the Company Officer and the encounter could possibly create some negative feedback, the Officer should call their Battalion Chief to get their support before taking any action with the member. At the end of the day, the member could come back to the station with a physician's note in hand that states they are physically fit for duty. The doctor wins every time. If this is the case, get the fire truck out and start exercising.

3. Impairment Due to Drugs or Alcohol

Before this book presents on dealing with issues that involve impairment due to drugs or alcohol, I must state that all your AHJ's SOPs must be referred to and followed. This book will present the most common guidelines that many departments use to address these types of issues.

If a Company Officer has enough evidence to believe that a member of the company is under the influence of drugs or alcohol when reporting for duty or during the work shift, they have the responsibility to verify the employee's condition while relieving them of their duties. The Company Officer's Battalion Chief must be immediately notified of the situation and they (or their designee) must respond to the fire station. The member's Union representative should also be contacted if requested by the member.

The probability of liability to the department and to the Company Officer is extreme if an employee who is suspected to be under the influence of drugs or alcohol is allowed to remain working in any capacity or is allowed to drive a private vehicle from the work site. A member who is believed to be impaired must not be allowed to operate any vehicle or other machinery until the condition of the employee has been determined.

If a supervisor observes an employee who appears to be under the influence of alcohol or drugs, they must also seek the opinion of their Battalion Chief (or their designee) before reasonable grounds can exist for any drug or alcohol screening. Reasonable grounds must exist between 2 supervisors before requesting the employee to take a drug screening and/or blood alcohol test.

Evidence of impairment could include the following:

- Smell of alcohol or other drugs emanating from the employee's body
- Overly dilated or pinpoint pupils
- Red and/or swollen eyes
- Slurred speech with the inability to carry on a rational conversation
- Unsteadiness
- Nervous and/or erratic behavior
- Irritable and combative to reason
- Failure to follow or comply with simple commands

Any evidence of impairment should be documented in writing prior to the Battalion Chief arriving at the fire station. If the member indeed appears to be impaired, the Battalion Chief will facilitate getting the member the proper drug or alcohol screening test. Not to sound like a broken record, but Company Officers must understand that they are the "sheriffs" who enforce the rules. They are not the "judges" who get to decide the punishment for violating them. From this point forward, the member is now in the system and the matter will be mostly out of the hands of the Company Officer.

4. Insubordination

The definition of insubordination is - *the defiance of authority; refusal to obey orders*

Insubordination in the workplace happens when a member of the company intentionally refuses to obey a Company Officer's lawful and reasonable order(s) or they display a form of extreme disrespect to the organization and its management. Such behaviors would undermine a Company Officer's level of respect and ability to manage. Therefore, it is a reason for some of the most severe disciplinary action - up to and including termination.

Examples of insubordination include:

- Refusal to obey direct, lawful orders of a supervisor
- Disrespect shown to supervisors and management in the form of vulgar or mocking language
- Directly questioning, insulting, or mocking management's policies and decisions

Being relieved of duty for insubordination does not happen very often (thankfully). I only witnessed this happen once in my career and my Father told me he only had to deal with it a dozen or so times in his 35 plus years of managing 2,000 people on the department.

When clear insubordination does happen, this is a management situation for the Company Officer where their only option is to stabilize the situation and then relieve the member of duty (on the spot!). Send them home and tell them that someone will contact them within the next 24 hours. This is a high risk, high consequence, zero decision making time problem and the Company Officer must act decisively. There is no time to call your boss - just send them home.

Obviously, the Company Officer would need call their Battalion Chief immediately after relieving the member of duty. Hopefully, there was a good reason, based on the insubordination, for relieving the member of duty and it will be easy for the department to support the Company Officer's decision. If it was a spur of the moment, knee jerk reaction of "go home" that was not based on much other than high emotions, the Company Officer had better get ready for a negative reaction from their Battalion Chief and the above Brass. As a matter of fact, if this was the case, it would probably go worse for the Company Officer than it would for the member who was sent home.

Summary

I would like to end *Managing a Fire Company* the way it started - with the 8 expectations of a Company Officer:

1. Someone who respects and values their co-workers and the public they serve
2. Someone who creates a happy, harassment free working environment
3. Someone who will keep their entire crew's focus on delivering excellent customer service throughout the shift
4. Someone that the organization put into a position to understand, follow, and enforce all the department's SOPs, policies, rules, and regulations
5. Someone who acts as the overall safety manager of their crew that will not hesitate to stop unsafe or dumb acts
6. The overall training officer of their crew
7. A supervisor that addresses personnel and service delivery issues as soon as they occur, keeping them on the smallest scale possible
8. Someone who will manage being nice

My hope is that *Managing a Fire Company* has provided some useful information, insight, and/or guidance in fulfilling these expectations.

Best wishes and stay safe!

John Brunacini

John Brunacini
Captain, Retired
Blue Card Co-Founder

John Brunacini lives in Phoenix, AZ with his wife, 2 dogs, and cat. John retired as a Fire Captain from the Phoenix Fire Department in October 2006 after serving 26 years. He served in the positions of Firefighter, Engineer, and spent his last 14 years as a Captain. During his time as a Captain, he worked in the field as the Company Officer on Ladder 201 B-Shift for 10 years, he managed the department's Command Training Center his last few years with the department, and he developed and managed the Phoenix Fire Network. After retiring, John became a co-founder of the Blue Card Incident Commander Training and Certification Program that was released in 2008. At the end of 2020, after 14 years of developing and managing Blue Card, John retired from the company and has since written and published *Managing a Fire Company*. John is currently in the process of developing a corresponding Company Officer training and certification program that is based on and is supported by his new textbook.